READING APPALACHIA
from LEFT *to* RIGHT

READING APPALACHIA
from LEFT *to* RIGHT

Conservatives and the
1974 Kanawha County Textbook
Controversy

Carol Mason

Cornell University Press
ITHACA AND LONDON

First published 2009 by Cornell University Press
First printing, Cornell Paperbacks, 2009

Printed in the United States of America

Design and typesetting: Jack Donner, BookType LLC

Library of Congress Cataloging-in-Publication Data

Mason, Carol, 1964–
  Reading Appalachia from left to right : conservatives and the 1974 Kanawha County textbook controversy / Carol Mason.
      p.   cm.
  Includes bibliographical references and index.
  ISBN 978-0-8014-4728-0 (cloth : alk. paper)
  ISBN 978-0-8014-7581-8 (pbk. : alk. paper)
    1. Textbooks—West Virginia—Kanawha County. 2. Multicultural education—Curricula—West Virginia—Kanawha County. 3. Language arts—Curricula—West Virginia—Kanawha County. 4. Culture conflict—West Virginia—Kanawha County. 5. Ethnic conflict—West Virginia—Kanawha County. 6. Community and school—West Virginia—Kanawha County. I. Title.
  LB3047.5.W4M37 2009
  379.1'560975437—dc22

                                    2008055509

Cornell University Press strives to use environmentally responsible suppliers and materials to the fullest extent possible in the publishing of its books. Such materials include vegetable-based, low-VOC inks and acid-free papers that are recycled, totally chlorine-free, or partly composed of nonwood fibers. For further information, visit our website at www.cornellpress.cornell.edu.

Cloth printing   10 9 8 7 6 5 4 3 2 1
Paperback printing   10 9 8 7 6 5 4 3 2 1

For Mom

Contents

List of Illustrations

READING APPALACHIA
from LEFT *to* RIGHT.

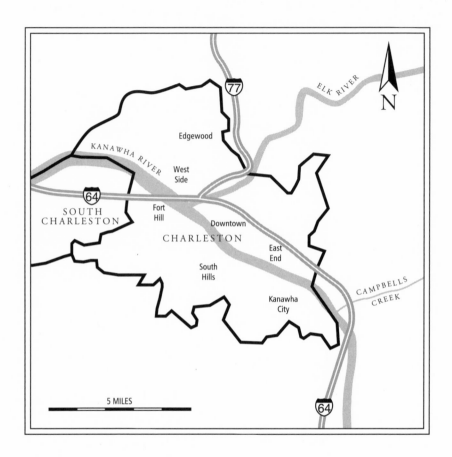

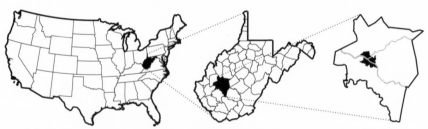

FIGURE I. The city of Charleston, West Virginia, in Kanawha County. As the county seat and state capital with two interstates, two rivers, a railroad system, an airport, and three television stations, Charleston was not a culturally or geographically isolated place in 1974, although the curvature and steepness of the mountains that rise up around the city may make it seem so. Artwork by Dan Carter.

Reading Appalachia

With two rivers, the Elk and the Kanawha, merging in the middle of it, Kanawha County was probably always a place of meeting and exchange. Before the Civil War, a significant salt industry thrived on the riverbanks. After the Civil War, coal became a prominent industry, followed by chemical refineries. Kanawha County in the late 1960s and early 1970s covered 907 square miles, including the city of Charleston, which has been the state capital since 1885. In 1975, Charleston's population included 67,348 residents, 10 percent of whom were African American. "Less than 1 percent of the population" of the entire county in 1970 was "nonwhite" and "only 2.9 percent" were "first or second generation foreign-born."[1] Other significant population bases in the county include those to the west of Charleston, such as South Charleston (an incorporated city), Dunbar, Cross Lanes (the largest unincorporated town in the state), Nitro, and St. Albans. To the southeast of Charleston are considerably smaller communities including Marmet, Belle, Cedar Grove, East Bank, Chesapeake, and Montgomery. Kanawha County was experiencing a surprising growth in industry and population at the time when America's most violent curriculum dispute erupted. The 1974 Kanawha County textbook controversy took place largely in the city of Charleston, which was, relatively speaking, an urban hub of commerce, industry, and government.

As the county seat and state capital with two interstates, two rivers, a railroad system, an airport, and three television stations, Charleston was not a culturally or geographically isolated place in 1974, although the curvature and steepness of the mountains that rise up around the city may make it seem so (see figure 1). Affluent areas within the city included Edgewood and South Hills—which overlooks the downtown area and was often vilified as the bastion of elites known as "hillers." Less affluent areas within the city included the East End, where the board of education office and the state capitol building are located. Just outside the city limits was a more rural community known as Campbells Creek, where some textbook protesters set up a headquarters. Working-class residents of Campbells Creek were often derisively referred to as "creekers." Although the labels "hillers" and "creekers" hardly originated with the textbook controversy, they helped fuel the perception that it was primarily a class conflict between privileged urban professionals and downtrodden rural coal miners. Contrary to popular assumption, however, "less than 5 percent of the county work force [was] engaged in mining. This small fraction [was] considerably less than the 16 percent of the labor force employed in the chemical industry," which was central to the city of Charleston at the time.[2]

Made up of coal, natural gas, and brine-based chemical works including international corporations such as Union Carbide, DuPont, and Monsanto, the Kanawha Valley's industrial economy at the time of the textbook dispute seemed to be faring better than expected in a recession. In January 1975, the *New York Times* reported that the area was

> making a good recovery from the 1969 closing of a mammoth FMC Corporation ordnance plant in South Charleston. A new American Motors Corporation automobile stamping operation and other steel fabricators have moved into the abandoned FMC factory space. Scores of mines lie just outside the city, and coal is expected to have a banner year now that the United Mine Workers strike is ended. The long decline in Appalachian population may have ended, too. According to the Appalachian Regional Commission, there is a "return flow" population trend. One out of four jobs in the crippled Midwest automobile industry has been filled in recent years by Appalachian whites who fled hard times in the mountains.[3]

Whether they were returning from Detroit or had never left the valley, Kanawha County residents in the early 1970s were optimistic about opportunities in the "sprawling industrial complex." Rates of unemployment and per capita income for the entire state were closer to the national average than they had been in previous decades.[4] "By almost any standard of measurement, West Virginia had drawn perceptibly closer to national norms" by the 1970s.[5] Although fairly abundant, however, jobs in the Kanawha Valley were not guaranteed to secure prosperity for anyone but the corporate owners. Like the coal mining companies, chemical manufacturers were mostly absentee corporations who exploited workers and the environment. It was in this beautiful and toxic valley that the textbook controversy took place.

A Controversy Unfolds

In April 1974 the Kanawha County Board of Education gathered for a routine meeting in Charleston. On the agenda was a report from a textbook selection committee that had worked ten months to decide which new language arts curriculum to recommend for adoption for all levels, through grade twelve. The curriculum they chose included more than three hundred titles from mainstream publishers. The major series of the books were D.C. Heath and Company's *Communicating* (grades 1–6) and *Dynamics of Language* (7–12), Scott, Foresman & Company's *America Reads* (7–12) and *Galaxy* (7–12), and Silver Burdett company's *Contemporary English* (7–12). Additional books were recommended as supplemental texts, including McDougal, Littell & Company's *Language of Man* (7–12) and *Man* (7–12), and Houghton Mifflin Company's *Interaction* (K-12).[6] In dutiful fashion, the selection committee described the books they chose and their procedures for ensuring that the books met a state-sanctioned mandate to include multiethnic and multiracial literature in the new curriculum. Everyone seemed surprised when the only female board member, Alice Moore, objected to the selection committee's report by raising questions about the books, even though she admitted she had not yet read them. With a flurry of accusations about the committee's purpose, its relationship to national "anti-American" trends, and particular concerns over lessons in dialect that she and others referred to as "ghetto" language, Alice Moore sparked the controversy.

She succeeded in delaying but not stopping the purchase of the curriculum, which proponents saw as tools to teach reading and writing as artful communication in relevant multiethnic social contexts. Book supporters did not mind that this new language arts curriculum eschewed phonics, replacing them with "reading for meaning" and "look-say" methods. But opponents of the curriculum were skeptical of the methods and contents; they said the books advocated unprincipled relativism, promoted antagonistic behavior, contained obscene material, put down Jesus Christ, and upheld communism. Throughout the spring and summer, thousands of protesters mobilized, objecting to the books as well as to the board's selection process. At a board of education hearing on June 27, 1974, more than a thousand citizens showed up to debate the new textbooks. After listening to them for nearly three hours, the school board voted 3–2 to adopt the books.

Testimony from the protesters varied in terms of emotionalism and argument, with some articulating points regarding the duty of elected officials to serve the people's will, and others raising precise questions about the appropriateness of the content. Internal documents demonstrate that pro-textbook board members considered closely some of the specific complaints against the new curriculum. For example, school board staff itemized each complaint featured on a flier urging protesters to "take the textbooks to court" and examined each against what the books themselves said, circulating the results in a memo. In response to the charge that the "elementary books undermine faith in God and make Bible stories seem like myths!!" school board staff reported:

> Myths are defined as ancient stories created in order to explain the world in which people lived. Myths often became part of the religion of the people. Some of the characters were usually gods, and the stories would tell how men were first made or explain why there were seasons or perhaps even tell why the rabbit had a short tail (p. 12, Level 5). Beginning with level 3, each book has two or three myths including "Story of First Woodpecker," Greek, Japanese, Indian, and African examples. No Bible story is included. Never is a Bible story called a myth. Examples do not undermine faith in God. Rather, all peoples have religious beliefs.

This was one fairly extensive explanation of what school board staff considered to be the actuality behind eighteen claims on the flyer. The memo of these explanations was twenty-three pages long, a substantial response to one flyer distributed by protesters. School board members who disagreed with the protesters on particular points apparently did not do so out of careless disregard of their specific complaints about the content of the books.

More general complaints about the lack of representation in the textbook selection procedure were another matter, however. At least one board member, Harry Stansbury, was concerned enough by charges about an elite conspiracy of educators that he researched the backgrounds of each of the teachers who served on the original textbook selection committee. What he learned was that all five teachers were raised and educated in West Virginia; two were not born in West Virginia but had been residents since at least high school. The selection committee members, all women, had bachelor's degrees and some graduate credentials from such familiar local institutions as Marshall University in Huntington; West Virginia State College in Institute; Concord College in Athens; Morris Harvey College in Charleston; and West Virginia University in Morgantown. Therefore, to Stansbury, protesters' claims of infiltrating elites seemed far fetched. But the question of parental involvement in book selection was a salient point that the board would not fully consider until forced to do so later. Alice Moore and protest leaders felt ignored by the board's June decision to purchase the curriculum and kept mobilizing residents of Kanawha County throughout the summer.

When the academic year began in the fall, organized protests increased.[7] In late August, parents agreed to boycott the schools and some businesses, most notably Heck's, Inc., a department store linked to one of the school board members, Russell Isaacs, who had voted for the books. During the first week of September, according to the local newspapers, "nearly twenty-five percent of the county's 45,000 students did not report to the first class day of the school year"; about "2,000 people attended an anti-textbook rally at Campbells Creek"; "3,500 coal miners walked off jobs in a wildcat strike not due to start until November" to show support for the opposition; and "protesters shut down the city bus system, leaving 11,000 customers without transportation." One minister, Charles Quigley, publicly prayed for God to strike down the three board members who supported the books; it was viewed as a death threat. Calls for the resignations of various school officials proliferated. Facing these profound demonstrations of dissent, the school board closed the schools for three days, removed the controversial books from the classrooms, and called for a group of citizens and parents to review the books. In the process of filing a suit to prevent use of the textbooks, Ezra Graley, another minister, was arrested for contempt of court. By the end of September, he and the other leading protest ministers, Marvin Horan and Avis Hill, ended a rally in disagreement as to whether or not continue the boycotts.

In October and November, tensions were so high that members of both sides of the controversy issued threats and committed acts of violence. Gunshots were fired by book opponents and proponents at picket sites and schools. Arson and bombs briefly closed down Wet Branch, Midway, Chandler, and Loudendale elementary schools. School buildings were vandalized, sometimes with Klan and Nazi insignia. Fifteen sticks of dynamite caused significant damage to the board of education office building.

Ministers broke an injunction against more than five picketers at businesses and schools, resulting in fines and incarceration. A federal grand jury indicted several men for conspiring to blow up more schools and television and radio towers.

Parents continued boycotts amid continuing protests and the arrest of school board members for "contributing to the delinquency of minors." Rallies and marches opposing the "filthy" and "ungodly" books grew. A march organized in favor of academic freedom attracted about one thousand supporters of the books and of the school board. Two days later, four times as many protesters walked three miles from the civic center to the state capitol building in a formidable show of resistance. Some students—supported by liberal parents, clergy, and teachers—staged counterprotests and claimed their right to read. Private Christian schools were set up as alternatives to the public school system in Kanawha County. Meanwhile, the review committee approved by the board of education could not reach a consensus: a majority recommended accepting "all but 35 of the 325 books," while a minority recommended banning 180 of the books. With the committee's input, the school board took a vote on November 9, 1974. The ruling was in favor of returning almost all of the controversial books to the classroom, with the exception that "the 35 most controversial books were . . . placed in school libraries to be read only by students with parental permission."[8] Consequently, every kid came home one day with a permission slip to be signed or not. Every parent had some say in the matter of the child's education.

In December, a West Virginia teachers' association invited the National Education Association to Charleston to investigate the chaos. At approximately the same time, the Ku Klux Klan made its first public appearance of support for the textbook protests when a grand dragon (state leader of the Klan) arrived from Ohio to discuss the issue on a Huntington radio station. By this point, news teams from national and international broadcasters had visited the area; Kanawha County became the subject of discussions on the CBS news magazine *60 Minutes* and the biggest talk show of the time, *Donahue*. In January 1975 national Ku Klux Klan leaders made a media splash with a rally on the West Virginia capitol steps and legal hearings regarding the October bombings of schools began. Some residents of the upper Kanawha Valley proposed seceding from the county, effectively dividing it in two.[9] But by and large, the direct action of marches, rallies, and vandalism waned.

Perhaps the protests subsided in January because attention to the Klan and the bombings were tainting the Kanawha Valley as a place of extremists. Or perhaps protesters felt they had won a substantial victory in forcing the board to create a review committee, in getting the most objectionable books out, and in compelling some school board officials to resign. Or maybe it was just the drizzly winter that kept the masses from gathering. When spring came, the coal strikes were over, the big rallies were gone, and the books were in the classrooms.

Ethnicity, Appalachia, America

Reading Appalachia from Left to Right takes seriously the protesters' claim that the selected texts had the power to interfere with students' sense of community—their sense of belonging to family, to Appalachia, and to America. According to the protesters, the multiethnic language arts curriculum represented a battle for "our children's minds" and "control over our children," who were being subjected to an "alien" philosophy espoused by the books. Clearly the protesters felt threatened and were figuratively circling the wagons against enemy attack, drawing a boundary within which "we" reside as a community and upon which "they" encroached. In so doing, the protesters articulated a community bound by what they considered to be proper linguistic, literary, and moral standards. Also, some illiterate parents who wanted their children to have what they did not, the benefits of literacy, objected to the new books because they lowered standards in education. These types of objections pointed to a fundamental truth about the power of textbooks and the process of education, which is that our sense of ourselves as "a people" is instilled in us by institutions such as schools, where we learn to relate to one another through verbal and written skills. Schools teach us a common language and conventions of communication that give a community its sense of identity, a sense of belonging, of being one of "the people," or *ethnos*, to use the Greek term. Or, "let us simply say that schooling is the principal institution which produces ethnicity as linguistic community."[10]

To introduce new methods of schooling is to alter that production of ethnicity, that production of understanding ourselves according to conventions of communication and norms of language usage. For an example of such norms, consider how West Virginians sometimes insist on the name "mountaineers" rather than "hillbillies" to show pride in Appalachian heritage. Of course, some embrace the term "hillbilly," reclaiming it from its use as a term of derision. In either case, language creates that sense of ourselves as a people, as an ethnicity. The protest of a new language arts curriculum was, intentionally or not, tantamount to protesting a new linguistic community and an altered sense of ethnic identity. The result, if not the intention, of the protest was that it brought into question and defined anew what it meant to be a concerned parent, a responsible citizen of Kanawha County, a loyal American, or, as one protester put it, a "true son of Appalachia."

Validating the protest of the books in this way—as a legitimate concern over the power of education and textbooks to create a sense of community, a production of ethnicity—will not resolve the ambivalence of that term, *ethnicity*, whose definition is the source of great consternation. On one hand, ethnicity is used as a category to denote people of color in particular. It therefore often serves as a racial distinction, distinguishing between whites and nonwhites. On the other hand, ethnicity is also often seen as synonymous with culture: a shared sense of geography, traits, tradition, and practices that characterize a group of people. In this capacity, ethnicity is a universalizing term, suggesting that all people have an ethnicity, regardless of race. Together, these paradoxical paradigms of understanding ethnicity suggest that it is fluidly defined rather than naturally given, a process rather than a fact.[11]

In examining the textbook controversy as a yearlong process of drawing boundaries and making claims about who a "true" Appalachian was or who a "concerned parent" was or who "our children" were and could be under the influence of a new language arts curriculum, *Reading Appalachia from Left to Right* examines the *ongoing* linguistic production of ethnicity in the Kanawha Valley. The fact that all the protesters were white, according to all consulted records, is a significant aspect of this production, especially since the books they objected to showcased writings by people of color.[12] But it would be simplistic and one-dimensional to claim that people protested the books *because* they were white or "not quite white" in the way that "hillbillies," "rednecks," "white trash," or Appalachian "hicks" are said to be.[13] It is unfair to suggest that the protest of multiracial literature confirmed some essential ethnic character that secures West Virginians' identity as feuding hillbillies, white trash, and the like.

The emphasis on ethnicity in *Reading Appalachia from Left to Right* is not, however, an attempt to dodge questions of racial stratification or racism in the Kanawha Valley.[14] On the contrary, it is an attempt to illuminate them in relation to, and as part of, the institution of education and the power of language that concerned protesters. Writing off the protest as the result of a reactionary bunch of racists would ignore the very legitimate claim that the protest, and other curriculum disputes, made: that new schooling *can* yield an altered sense of community with new social identities and different social relations. In fact, a general history of education reveals that American schooling developed because of this basic belief. Consider this sketch of pertinent changes since the nineteenth century, which contextualizes some key assumptions underlying the Kanawha County textbook protest.

Progressive education, "a subject of endless confusion and controversy," emerged in the 1920s as a response to the industrial nineteenth century's rote memorization and moral didacticism that reflected the mechanistic regimentation of factory assembly lines. Such discipline was replaced by more "child-centered" approaches that included "individual projects, exhibits, and field trips." Economic collapse and the Great Depression furthered interest in this type of education, situating the school as a place for relief from poverty and for envisioning a social order capable of providing sustenance and, later, able to ward off fascism. Throughout the 1930s, school emerged as a welfare institution and "many teachers without necessarily intending to came to accept an activist role for the state."[15]

After World War II and its restoration of prosperity to the United States, critics of progressive education said it was not only an outmoded idea but one too close ideologically to the new national enemy, communism. A return to "basics" was called for by three groups: "academicians who opposed the power of professional educationists; intellectuals who had philosophical objections to the instrumentalist thrust of progressive education; and popular writers who merged these themes with criticism that the schools were too collectivist." However, federally sponsored innovations in education again emerged in the late 1950s. The U.S. response to the 1957 launching of *Sputnik*, the Soviet satellite that initiated the space race and heightened the cold war between the two countries, was to launch new science and math curricula; history and social sciences were next in line for revamping. Last and least, "the teaching of English and modern foreign languages underwent serious reevaluation in the late 1950s and the 1960s, but neither enjoyed the coordination (and for English, the funding) common to similar efforts in the natural sciences."[16] Thus, the call for curricular innovations coincided with anticommunist efforts to identify "subversives," which culminated in the red-hunting hysteria known as McCarthyism (after Senator Joseph McCarthy of Wisconsin). Schools thus became a "crucible in Cold War America": teachers were made to sign loyalty oaths or were fired, and the anticommunist scrutiny of new learning materials schizophrenically emerged at the very moment when the government was sponsoring and encouraging curricular reform.

By the early 1970s the extremism of McCarthy had run its official course, however; the blacklisting and termination of presumed "reds" were no longer pursued. But the watchdog mentality and recycled objections to progressive education from the 1940s remained forcefully intact.

In addition to this brief general history of education, scholarship on curriculum disputes demonstrates that, throughout the nineteenth and twentieth centuries, textbooks have been the contested terrain upon which the "national story" has been written and rewritten according to various perspectives. Some of this scholarship recognizes the role of populist rhetoric among textbook protesters, taking into account key tropes from era to era. This scholarly approach to curriculum disputes examines educational texts as *reflections* of cultural conflicts in society, and protesters as historical agents producing such conflicts.[17] Other research recognizes schoolbooks as textual producers of nationalism and the nation-state itself.[18] Recognizing that textbooks produce readers as national subjects, rather than merely reflect the cultural conflicts already existing, is a working assumption of *Reading Appalachia from Left to Right* and corresponds with the fundamentally true claim that a curriculum has power to change relationships and cultural identities. The protesters had good reason to question how a new language arts curriculum would affect future generations and current social relations between parents and children, parents and teachers, the formally educated "elite" and the "masses" whose education was not obtained primarily in schools.

That is not to say, however, that all the protesters were equally high-minded or unified by one philosophical approach in opposing the controversial books. On the contrary, to speak of the protesters in toto belies the different groups, the particular factions within groups, and the various arguments against the books (and against the school board) that existed. Those who felt the books' purpose was to "niggarize the nation" joined with Klan leader Ed Miller to protest the curriculum in pointed hoods on the steps of the West Virginia capitol building or at the foot of a burning cross at Witcher Creek.[19] Those who wished to thwart the one-world Jewish-socialist government that the books were supposedly advocating appreciated the articles in the *Liberty Bell* magazine, which was published by the local John Birch Society bookstore owner, George Dietz. For those "business and professional people" who considered the books to be full of obscene, anti-free-market, socialist (but not necessarily Jewish) propaganda, they tapped their foot to "Elmer's Tune," a local column written by chemical company owner Elmer Fike.

Then there were the bulk of the protesters, the "concerned parents" who saw the books as an attack on "our" children and "our" way of life. Ministers Ezra Graley, Charles Quigley, Avis Hill, and Marvin Horan were inspirational organizers who fueled the apocalyptic sense that "our children's souls" were at stake and that we would answer for our actions for or against the books on Judgment Day. Alice Moore appeared as the quintessential concerned mother even though her rhetoric and reasons for opposing the curriculum varied, beginning with what were perceived as race-based arguments that later gave way to warnings about the deleterious effects of "humanistic" education. She denounced the Klan and worked instead with Elmer Fike and the ministers, as well as others—nationally known Christian advocates such as Charles Secrest from the Christian Crusade, Robert Dornan of Citizens for Decency, Texas textbook monitors Mel and Norma Gabler, James McKenna from the nascent Heritage Foundation, and Connie Marshner from the Heritage Foundation and the Foundation for a Free Congress.

Without acknowledging this variety of protesters, scholars and journalists represented the controversy as one homogenous thing or another. In addition to caricatured accounts of degenerate hillbilly racists, there were two other key explanations (see figure 2). One excoriated Alice Moore as a narcissistic instigator who loved media attention and creating a fuss all around her. This explanation feminized the protest, portraying it as the frivolous or tragic result of a meddling woman, and infantilized the protesters as Moore's unruly, uneducated children. The other prominent explanation, far more learned, was no less gendered. Depicting the protesters as working-class heroes, some accounts conjured up the image of the gritty coal miner, that masculine icon of noble resistance to economic exploitation and modern corruptions. In all three prominent explanations for the controversy, the protesters were either romanticized or demonized.

These dichotomous representations reflect America's general ambivalence toward Appalachia. There was no separating the actuality of Kanawha County protesters from the Appalachian stereotypes that preceded them. Inseparable still, the myths and the realities of Appalachia need to be analyzed together to account for why the Kanawha County protesters could signify on one hand all that is good and right with America and, on the other, all that is bad and wrong. Appalachia has long

FIGURE 2. The media depicted textbook protesters as degenerate racists and throwbacks to Puritan piety. James Dent, Charleston Newspapers. Reproduced with permission.

functioned as a cultural and geographic imaginary where modern ways are supposed to be resisted and transgressed. Understanding more about Appalachia's personification, the hillbilly, illuminates why the protesters were seen either as heroes or savages. Constructed through historical, literary, sociological, and popular discourses, the hillbilly has always defied categories, transgressing racial, sexual, and gender boundaries.

Beginning with William Byrd's 1728 portrait of white settlers in North Carolina, which "introduced many of the standard tropes" and reflected "the ambiguity that would thereafter always characterize hillbilly imagery," Appalachians have been portrayed as people who do not conform to gender roles considered to constitute a supposed natural order.[20] Byrd described Appalachian women as too physical, often taking on the manual labor that their male counterparts appear too lazy to do.[21] In the nineteenth century, writers portrayed Appalachian women as transgressors of gender roles by lampooning the essentialist notions of purity and femininity that comprised the Cult of True Womanhood in the urban centers of the eastern United States.[22] Similarly, stories of Appalachian men—most notably and quintessentially Davy Crockett—also represented a challenge to bourgeois gender roles, "invert[ing] absolutely the values and admonitions of the male moral reformers" of the time.[23] By the time the word "hillbilly" first appeared in print in 1899,[24] Appalachian men and women were well established as transgressors of modern, middle-class gender roles.

Moreover, as sexual beings, hillbillies such as Crockett defied categories produced by the sexologists, physicians, and moral reformers of the nineteenth century. Tall tales of Crockett's polymorphous perversity included episodes with animals, men, and women that suggested a kind of "liminality," according to Carroll Smith-Rosenberg. She defines liminality as "the stage of being between categories and the power inherent in that process."[25] Like an adolescent who is neither child nor adult, "the hillbilly" is a liminal figure in American culture and letters, exuding a sexuality that can be construed as comically or dangerously crossing the bounds of proper sexuality.[26]

Especially in this capacity to offend middle-class sensibilities, "hillbilly" in the twentieth century emerged as a derogatory term for poor whites. As the poster population for the midcentury War on Poverty, images of Appalachian whites in particular were used to upset the bourgeois myth of American classlessness.[27] But manufacturing paternalistic empathy for Appalachians also produced a byproduct of fear and hatred of "rednecks" and "white trash."[28] As a stereotype of impoverished living, "hillbilly" is akin to "white trash," a term that "calls our attention to the way that discourses of class and racial difference tend to bleed into one another, especially in the way that they pathologize and lay waste to their 'others.'"[29] Depicting Appalachians as trash or as hillbillies thus inextricably conjoins matters of poverty with matters of race. Moreover, "stereotypes of white trash and 'hillbillies' are replete with references to dangerous and excessive sexuality [such as] rape (both heterosexual and homosexual), incest, and sexual abuse," even though "such abuse occurs in all segments of the population."[30] In this way, the hillbilly serves as a foil for middle-class social mores, defining modern norms against the perceived abnormality of a liminal subject whose sexuality, gender, class, and race are distinctly "other."

As a white "other," the hillbilly has a particular racial status defined by premodern "nobility" or "backwardness":

> Despite their poverty, ignorance, primitiveness, and isolation, "hillbillies" were "one hundred percent" Protestant Americans of supposedly pure Anglo-Saxon or at least Scotch-Irish lineage, which countless commentators of the late-nineteenth—and early-twentieth centuries, greatly concerned by waves of Southern and Eastern European immigrants, took pains to prove. Thus, middle-class white Americans could see these people as a fascinating and exotic "other" akin to Native Americans or Blacks, while at the same time sympathize with them as poorer and less modern versions of themselves.[31]

This racialization implied in any representation of the hillbilly can be maligned or championed. In this way the hillbilly's ambiguous liminality is matched by America's ambivalence toward those labeled hillbillies. Female Appalachians, for example, are idealized or demonized not only in terms of racial purity or inbreeding but also as all-natural "hillbilly gals" or unnatural "mannish misfits."[32] (One need only think of the media manipulation of two West Virginia privates stationed in Iraq, Jessica Lynch and Lynndie England, to see that such idealization and demonization of Appalachian women are alive and well in the twenty-first century.)[33]

As representatives of mountain living and country life, hillbillies can thus reflect either (1) heroism, bravery, and loyalty to traditional ways or (2) a deviance, sadism, and primitivism that is said to fly in the face of modern progress (see figure 3). In other words, the hillbilly "served the dual and seemingly contradictory purposes of allowing the 'mainstream,' or generally non-rural, middle-class white, American audience to imagine a romanticized past, while simultaneously enabling the same audience to recommit itself to modernity by caricaturing the negative aspects of premodern, uncivilized society."[34] And of course, since modernity and "civilization" are frequently presumed to be connected with Western and white achievements, the dual function of the hillbilly is as much a matter of race as it is a marker of primitivism and poverty—and as much a matter of race as of gender and sexual transgression. With such a history as this, the hillbilly helps explain America's ambivalence toward Appalachia and its residents.

Overview

Recognizing how such an ambivalence played out in representing the textbook controversy is the next step in the examination of its various effects in Kanawha County and beyond. "Soul on Appalachian Ice," an introduction, provides voices in dialogue about the disputed textbooks and states the argument of *Reading Appalachia from Left to Right*. Chapter 1, "A Modern American Conflict," then examines the ways in which media and scholarship portrayed the controversy of 1974. Observers of the protest perpetuated the tendency to view events in Appalachia as symbolic of America, and to view Appalachians ambiguously as courageous resisters

FIGURE 3. Supposedly allergic to new ideas, hillbillies represent antimodern intolerance. But textbook opponents were innovative and represented new alliances, tactics, and discourses. *Charleston Gazette*, November 18, 1974. Reproduced with permission.

of modernity's corruptions or as backward hillbillies incapable of social change. Scholars and journalists who claimed the Kanawha County textbook controversy was essentially "class warfare" too heavily relied on the icon of the white male coal miner as the representative subject of all things Appalachian. This approach ignored the important role that women and womanhood played in the protest and relegated issues of race to the margins of the textbook controversy.

Chapter 2, "True Sons of Appalachia," argues that white supremacist organizations were not as peripheral as they seemed to be. While the media mocked the Klansmen who opposed the books, the local John Birch Society bookstore owner, George Dietz, escaped scrutiny. Dietz's publishing house, which produced the libertarian *Liberty Bell* and the pro-Hitler *White Power Report*, also supplied protesters with hundreds of thousands of leaflets. The increasingly anti-Semitic discourses and the political alliances forged during the textbook protest indicate how the Right, including white supremacists, moved away from using the anticommunist John Birch Society and segregationist George Wallace as models. What eventuated by the end of the 1970s was more inclusive, national organizing among white supremacists that brought together pantheistic neo-Nazism with the Christianity-based Ku Klux Klan. This alliance was already operating during the textbook controversy and the avowed white supremacists in West Virginia were at the forefront of articulating the discursive shift to a more "Aryan" collectivity by deploying ideas about Appalachia.

Chapter 3, "Sweet Alice and Secular Humanism," examines the role that Alice Moore played, a role that reflected earlier and contemporary female conservatives and was reprised in later campaigns by New Right leaders. In terms of shaping discursive strategy as well as the actual tactics played out in the public sphere, Alice Moore was a model for Connie Marshner and countless other "concerned mothers" who, as idealized white women, contributed significantly to conservative politics.

Chapter 4, "Reproducing the Souls of White Folk," is a theoretical examination about what happened on the local level. Locally, the result of the textbook controversy was a production of ethnicity. This was not necessarily in the sense that white citizens rose up to denounce writings by people of color and the desegregated world they represented. Rather, the textbook conflict was a process that reified protesters' authority as white Christians without acknowledging that race was a factor. Expressing concern over "our" children's "eternal souls" was not only a spiritual issue. It was a concern about maintaining and promoting "Appalachian heritage" *as* a white, Christian culture in an increasingly multicultural world. It was a way to express that concern so that it did not seem overtly political or racial, but only natural—as natural as a mother's love.

Chapter 4 therefore applies feminist readings of political theory and studies of whiteness to the 1974 Kanawha County textbook controversy for the purpose of examining how gender was integral to the late twentieth-century rise of American cultural conservatism. Specifically, Rey Chow's insights on the racialization of "soul" help illuminate the emergence of a spiritualized narrative of white ethnic struggle in which "concerned mothers" save "our children." Kanawha County was a discursive crossroads at which two narratives of soul intersected: one depicting ethnicity as alienated labor and the other depicting ethnicity as dominion over victimhood. The second narrative of soul was the one through which the historically progressive working class of Kanawha County became aligned with conservatives and, sometimes, avowed white supremacists—the narrative by which the "souls of white folk" were reproduced for generations to come.

Chapter 5, "The Right Soul," returns from the heady theories of ethnicity to a concrete example of pastor Avis Hill, whose personal story of becoming involved in politics also serves as a cautionary tale about seeing him and other evangelicals as simply dupes of right-wing organizers. It would be easy to claim that the Right began in the 1970s to "strip Appalachian soul" as some thought leftist volunteers did in the 1960s. But Hill's story reminds us that such a conclusion is too simple, even as we recognize how seductive the language of "soul" might be, and realize that the ongoing production of ethnicity in Kanawha County reflected and perpetuated a rightward turn in the culture of American protest.

As is evident by now, the analysis of *Reading Appalachia from Left to Right* relies on some particular terms, specialized language, and many quotations. It is important, therefore, to note that the appearance of quotation marks throughout *Reading Appalachia from Left to Right* indicates words and phrases from documentary sources and is not intended to signify sarcasm or derision. It is also important to recognize that vocabulary such as "Right," "fundamentalist," "conservative," "whiteness," and the like have been chosen with care and on principle. Borrowed from a multitude of disciplines, academic conversations, and specific scholars, definitions for such keywords appear in the appendix that follows an epilogue, which provides final insights into the pleasures and dangers of reading Appalachia and writing this book.

FIGURE 4. Opponents and proponents, such as textbook selection committee chair Nell Wood, publicly debated the virtues and vices of the language arts curriculum. Chet Hawes, *Charleston Daily Mail*, October 3, 1974. Reproduced with permission.

Soul on Appalachian Ice

"This is not a minister's battle," Donald Dobbs insisted, speaking into a microphone. Five members of the Kanawha County Board of Education and a crowd of fellow West Virginians listened on a rainy June evening in 1974. Among them was Alice Moore, the only woman on the board of education and the one who first raised objections to the multiethnic language arts curriculum—more than three hundred titles encompassing instruction for students enrolled in kindergarten through high school—that had been adopted for use throughout the West Virginia county. Although he was flattered to be asked to represent other clergy, he said he was speaking for himself, speaking out against the new textbooks as a concerned father. Fifteen other citizens also signed up to publicly debate the vices and virtues of the books. Despite the sound system's inability to reach the far recesses of the auditorium, people were there to be heard. More than a thousand were in attendance for the school board hearing that lasted nearly three hours. Audio recordings of the event captured the nuance of voices and the crowd's reaction.[1]

One of the first speakers, Dobbs took his allotted five minutes to make a "twofold" objection to the content of the books and their implications. Like Alice Moore, Dobbs said the books were lowering standards by teaching students poor grammar in the form of dialectology. Like Moore, he also pointed out "moral objections" to the curriculum, noting its inclusion of Eldridge Cleaver, the black nationalist author of the 1968 bestselling prison memoir, *Soul on Ice*.[2] Although listed only as supplemental reading for advanced placement, college-bound high school students, *Soul on Ice*—or, more precisely, its notorious analysis of rape as an insurrectionary act—was cited often as the smoking gun, the evidence that corruption and "moral degradation" were what the curriculum had to offer. Deviating from the standard led to "works by such men as Eldridge Cleaver," Dobbs explained, a man who does not "adequately represent the Negro or the white in the morals he presents." Fighting these books, which were adopted to fulfill a state mandate for implementing multiethnic language instruction, was not a minister's battle; it was "a people's battle, a battle which every concerned American should be interested in," Dobbs declared. The crowd applauded his remarks vigorously.

Alice Moore then took the opportunity to question Dobbs. Although the hearing was ostensibly for the entire board to respond to and weigh the concerns of the public, mostly it was Moore who interacted with the speakers. What did Dobbs think about how the books told students to pretend they are God and think about how they would change the world? "I don't know the reason that a teacher would tell a student to pretend he was God but it somehow, to me, lowers the standard of God, for us to be able to bring it down to our level," Dobbs responded as Moore simultaneously finished his sentence. "Down to the human standard," she agreed. And what did Dobbs think about leading a child to consider Bible stories as myths? Dobbs then discussed how one of the books asked students to compare the story of Androcles and the Lion with the story of Daniel in the Lion's Den, which he believed "is a true story because I believe in the miracles of the word of God and I don't think many people would want to tear down those things and consider them as myths and yet they're compared in the same light." Moore affirmed this interpretation of the textbook: "Right. They're told to compare the two stories for the similarities of them and they discuss the reality which would force the child to see that the story of Daniel in the Lion's Den couldn't be true because a lion doesn't act that way. That's the point that they make."

Following Dobbs in the lineup of citizen speakers was pastor Ronald English, who identified "the substantive issue being raised on this particular battlefront" as "our collective commitment to racial balance and racial harmony," not, he added, "in terms of bodies being integrated but in terms of awareness and lifestyles." Referencing local history, he acknowledged that the integration of schools in Charleston had been achieved commendably and calmly in response to the ruling of *Brown v. Board of Education* twenty years earlier. This multiethnic curriculum was the logical extension of that desegregation, he suggested, and rejecting it was tantamount to "not-so-subtle discrimination in the city of Charleston."

Moore responded to this charge by directing her first question to the issue of "derogatory" representations of God and Christianity that she saw in the books. English replied that what she may see as derogatory toward religion might not be what he sees. Moore then addressed forthrightly the charge of discrimination, which resulted in an interesting exchange.

"Again, with regard to representing minorities," Alice Moore made clear, "I certainly have no objection to any minority being represented in a textbook. I've never suggested any objection to this. But, is it your feeling that in order to represent minorities, specifically blacks, that we should represent them with the Eldridge Cleavers and the George Jacksons and people of this type?" Ronald English replied: "When you say 'people of this type' [it] assumes that 'that type' is not representative or that there is some kind of defect in that type, and that was what I was just speaking to." Talking over him in a flush of incredulity that he would not find militant black nationalists morally defective, Moore asked, "You don't think that?" and laughed a little. English steadily responded, "No, I do not," and continued despite a collective gasp from the audience: "I think they have a message from the other side of the American experience that ought be told. I would say also that the NAACP has endorsed the multicultural approach as well as some of the kind of texts that I have seen written in the supplementary materials."

In response to this appeal to the authority of the NAACP, Moore referenced local history herself:

> Well, I'll mention one other thing then. Booker T. Washington is from this area and is a highly admired man in this area. I found one reference to Booker T. Washington in this series of books under objection, and this one reference is derogatory—a poem that is derogatory to Booker T. Washington. Now, I haven't found anything else that holds him up. I haven't found anything else that represents black people in any way other than the people like Eldridge Cleaver and George Jackson and the people of this type. I really haven't. Have you?

She laughed a little again. In response, English concluded on a dual note of resignation and assertion: "Well, you seem to refer to those persons as defective and that's why I'm not sure that I can raise any level of awareness. But I will say that those persons are in a line of protest that I think is a part of the American experience from Tom Paine to Martin Luther King Jr." Moore thanked him and moved on to the next speaker.

Alice Moore's concern that the books presented African American views only from a militant perspective ("the Eldridge Cleavers and George Jacksons and people of this type") was addressed about an hour or so later when it was English teacher Sophia Nelson's turn at the microphone: "I can assure you there are black writers other than Cleaver. There are respectable black writers. Perhaps you just don't recognize their names since they haven't been in [the curriculum] before. But there are quite a number of them. You might look for Langston Hughes, Countee Cullen, Claude McKay, Gwendolyn Brooks." She went on to say that she "would not like to have white America tell us black people which black person we must have represented" in the books. As for Booker T. Washington, Nelson partly aligned herself with Moore: "You may like Booker T. Washington a great deal more than some other people do. I like Booker T. Washington a great deal more than some of these other people. But I would not insist that there be several selections in the book by Washington because he was born in western Virginia." The crowd rustled with restlessness, agitation, or distraction.

As for lessons in dialectology, Nelson argued that "this is not a lowering of standards" by explaining how studying dialects instilled a respect and knowledge of Appalachian culture. She shared stories of teaching English at the historically black West Virginia State College. "I had a student, oh, about forty years old, who in reading Chaucer found that the best thing she learned was that her grandmother was not so ignorant as she had always thought. She had considered her grandmother ignorant because" she used phrases such as "when that." Examining dialects helped "West Virginians not only to use what is called the standard dialect but also to respect themselves and the speech of their parents, their grandparents, to learn that they need not be ashamed of being Appalachians and sounding like Appalachians, to know the difference between regional dialect and incorrect language." According to Nelson, this pedagogical approach was better than "talking down to" students or "pretending that we cannot understand them if they say 'I seen it' because we want them to learn to say 'I saw it.'" Nelson made a final effort to dispel the presiding assumption that "there is something new in having nonstandard dialects" in the language arts curriculum by reading from Eugene O'Neill's play *The Emperor Jones*. Read in sonorous tones, O'Neill's words attested to the literary value of dialect, the aesthetic effect of nonstandard English, and its inclusion in classic American literature.

Responding to this dramatic assertion that new curriculum was not an introduction of wildly different content or methods, Moore distinguished between reading dialects and speaking them, implying that the books were more about indoctrination into, rather than an illustration of, different types of speech. Despite Nelson's anecdotal evidence that studying dialects bridged the generation gap, Moore maintained that dialectology lowered standards of learning and living, teaching students to disrespect the authority of God, home, and country. The books were a breach with the past, according to Moore. Something suspiciously and treacherously new was afoot in the Kanawha Valley.

As these public interactions indicate, the 1974 Kanawha County textbook controversy often entailed claims of what the battle was not. It was not a minister's battle, it was not a racist reaction, and it was not about what came before. As the controversy moved on into the summer and erupted at the beginning of the academic year in the fall, becoming the most violent curriculum dispute in American history, both proponents and opponents of the books felt they were part of something unprecedented. Protest culture was an old tradition in West Virginia and had a particularly rich history in the Cabin Creek and Paint Creek areas of Kanawha County.[3] Historians of the area at the time recognized the textbook controversy as resembling the past but also as being something significantly different:

> About the only way you can explain this current protest is to talk of it in terms of community spirit, the same kind of community spirit that existed in the days when the socialist movement was rampant on Cabin Creek . . . . In those days, the communities along Cabin Creek were more numerous. There was community control of nearly everything. Each community had its own constable to handle crime. Each had its own school system, its own fraternal organizations and large numbers of churches. The people were prosperous. Times were good. People were confident in the course they had set for themselves. With the coal industry booming the way it is today, conditions are much the same on Cabin Creek as they were in the early days of this century. Community spirit, a feeling of oneness, is alive on Cabin Creek again. This time, however, the community spirit is reactionary instead of socialist.[4]

Despite this shift to a reactionary posture and regardless of a formidable history of organized, strategic rebellion against economic exploitation, onlookers to the textbook controversy attributed the ensuing boycotts, blockades, strikes, gunshots, and bombings to empty stereotypes of angry Appalachians or the cartoon image of feuding hillbillies. This was not a throwback to old fights, real or imagined.

As these local voices attest, implicit and deep questions were newly emerging. How does language serve as a marker of belonging? How does it create the borders that determine who is in and who is outside a community? What is the power of a school board, a classroom, or a text? As ministers, teachers, board members, and parents discussed the proposed language arts curriculum that June evening, they were weighing who is authentically Appalachian and who is not, who should speak for whom, whose concerns and perspectives are honored and whose are not, whose needs or difficulties are recognized and whose are not, and what it means to be a good American and parent. In these and subsequent exchanges, a local community was testing and re-creating its borders and boundaries in ways that reestablished some social distinctions and reconfigured others.

For example, even though Alice Moore did not outright object to the inclusion of minority writers, the process of debating the books nevertheless created divisions along racial lines. The tensions evident in the dialogues between Moore and Nelson or English were only the beginning. When the Ku Klux Klan publicly appeared halfway through the school year in support of banning the textbooks and lending legal aid to a man convicted of bombing an elementary school, those tensions escalated. In this way, protesting the books redrew the established lines of racial difference in Kanawha County. But it also created alliances that crossed social boundaries in very important and innovative ways.

Alice Moore's involvement, for instance, was itself a transgression of sorts. She had won her place on the school board by waging a campaign based on challenging sex education in the schools. "Put a Mother on the Board" was her winning slogan. Her maternity and her fundamentalism compensated for the fact that she was a relative newcomer to the Kanawha Valley, arriving just a few years before her 1970 bid for the school board. Transgressing the double taboo that evangelicals and women should not bother with politics, Moore was at the forefront of two waves of mobilization sweeping the nation in the 1970s and endured vociferous ridicule and attack from the media for presuming the right to speak out, get involved, and organize as a female fundamentalist.

. No less ridiculed and attacked were working-class evangelical ministers such as Donald Dobbs, Marvin Horan, and Avis Hill who felt compelled to enter the public arena for the first time in their lives. Usually self-ordained and committed to proselytizing and organizing church activities, protesting ministers from the Kanawha Valley were inspired by the textbook controversy to break with tradition and become involved in local politics in a variety of ways. Those prone to the apocalypticism that was gaining prominence through publications such as Hal Lindsey's 1970 *Late Great Planet Earth* and broadcasts of Christian media felt an urgency that led toward direct action, including protests and marches. Those influenced by the right-wing organizers who came to the area agitating for "militant populism" were compelled to link the textbook controversy with anti-busing campaigns in northern cities. The violence that erupted likely was a combined result of apocalyptic urgency, agitation by militant populists and white supremacists, and the legacy of the coal wars, about which people remembered only "the violence of the early days of the union movement":

> Only a very few old-timers ever mention the socialist movement, perhaps because it is confused with the Communist movement of today, and has been for nearly a quarter of a century. Few people remember socialism on Cabin Creek. But they all know the role violence played on the creek in those early days. The tradition of violence has been handed down. The tradition of socialism hasn't.[5]

The state's protest culture, which historically had been geared toward progressive labor changes in the coal and chemical industries, thus became rerouted toward conserving dominant "values" in schools and other institutions. What was at stake was the "souls of our children" and "the soul of the nation," white working-class protesters said, and they made heretofore unlikely alliances with middle-class entrepreneurs, factory owners, and organized white supremacists to oppose the curriculum.

If Eldridge Cleaver's title, *Soul on Ice*, refers to the classic narrative of ethnic struggle to free one's people from the numbing alienation of modern American capitalism, then the Kanawha County textbook controversy might be referred to as soul on Appalachian ice, suggesting another narrative of ethnic struggle that emerged after the 1960s, a story of struggling to claim legitimacy as white protesters, indeed as white *protest*ants.[6] On one hand, then, in *Reading Appalachia from Left to Right* I seek to rescue the controversy from those who ruthlessly or blithely belittled it as a hillbilly feud, acknowledging again what some had readily articulated at the time:

> The dissatisfaction of the Appalachian protestor is no less than the dis–satisfaction of the civil rights militant. The Appalachian protestor is no less proud and protective of his culture and way of life than are members of ethnic minorities. The Appalachian protestor may at times give way to extreme statements and violent actions, as have members of other groups asserting their rights. While condemning the violence, the bigotry, and the foolish remarks, we must give the Appalachian protestor's basic beliefs and feelings the same respect we now seem willing to give those of other protest groups.[7]

The protesters were not backward fundamentalists, backwoods rednecks, or down-home dupes.

Even so, in *Reading Appalachia from Left to Right* I seek to go beyond a simple, defensive reassertion of the dignity of the protesters, tempering it with the irony that many of the books' opponents, Alice Moore included, sought to eliminate any voices of protest from the curriculum, especially if, as we have already seen, they were connected to "Black Power" but also if they smacked of feminist or antiwar sentiment, all of which were on the nightly news and in the daily headlines. Those issues that made proponents of the books applaud their relevancy were the very ones that convinced protesters the books were anti-American and anti-Christian. Thus the controversy has often been said to be an initial face-off between liberals and conservatives, a first skirmish in the culture wars, the beginnings of the religious Right, and one of several origins of New Right organizing.[8] *Reading Appalachia from Left to Right* adds depth and richness to these basic claims, illuminating the dispute's historical significance with details drawn from archives, oral histories, personal interviews, and the contested texts themselves. The research shows that Kanawha County was a discursive crossroads where Old Right ideas gave way to New Right alliances, tactics, and narratives that shaped curriculum disputes and cultural conservatism for decades to come.

Reading Appalachia from Left to Right entails more than a descriptive history. What emerged from the research was a compelling question of how a defense of the protesters was also, inadvertently or not, a production of Appalachia as a white ethnicity. Why and how was it important to national and international audiences that this dispute was happening in Appalachia? What did Appalachia signify to those who argued against the books on behalf of maintaining Appalachian heritage? How did "Appalachia" continue to signify whiteness, despite voices such as Ronald English's,

Sophia Nelson's, and that of the Charleston NAACP? Highlighting the eruption of this sometimes implicitly, sometimes explicitly white struggle into the political discourses for which the 1960s are so well known, this book examines the 1974 textbook controversy to theorize ethnic struggle that produces whiteness as an essential property of protest in the rightward shift to cultural conservatism and, to a much lesser but still significant extent, to the resurgence of organized white supremacism in the Kanawha Valley and nationwide throughout the 1970s. *Reading Appalachia from Left to Right* thus invites an exploration of the effects, not the origins, of the textbook controversy, including that production of whiteness, the impact of women activists in the rise of the Right, and the reclamation of spiritual rhetoric—those invocations of "soul"—from progressive forces that shaped the civil rights, peace, and feminist movements after the Second World War.

FIGURE 5. By 1974, the media were accustomed to framing Appalachian "class warfare" as matters of entertainment and pathos. Photojournalists echoed documentary styles from the Great Depression and the War on Poverty. William Tiernan, *Charleston Daily Mail*, September 3, 1974. Reproduced with permission.

CHAPTER ONE

A Modern American Conflict

Who is this Kanawha County protester whose image was widely distributed (see figure 5)? Staring down the camera with a look of defiance, she fit the bill of a news media that, by 1974, was accustomed to serving images of Appalachia not as information but as entertainment and affectation. Reproducing the photograph in the *New York Times* with no caption, editors must have assumed it spoke for itself. But what assumptions were readers to make?

Was it that the protester is pathetic because she does not know that grammatically she should have written "the difference *between* communism and freedom"? In seeing the word "hillbillies" were readers to assume that she was ironically using the derided mountaineer identity as a point of positive identification and political solidarity? Or, as with so many previous images of women and children said to document the War on Poverty of the Lyndon Johnson administration, were readers to associate this woman with the downtrodden working class whose plight deserved sympathy and perhaps charity? Going back farther to representations of the early twentieth-century Paint Creek coal wars, in which West Virginians used the trope of children for their cause, was this image chosen because it showed the issue was a mothers' concern? The newspapers let the photo stand on its own, failing to report the protester's name or to quote her. So readers did not learn, for example, which constitutional rights she felt were being denied her. She was not taken seriously. She was simply the bouffant-framed face of Appalachian resistance, circa 1974.

As a representation of the textbook controversy, this image helped build on the established Appalachian iconography of angry working-class protesters. The protesters were often portrayed as a unified collectivity, a single-minded social movement that was seen as either entirely righteous or entirely reactionary. Media and scholarship deployed blatant stereotypes or employed latent sociological assumptions that dichotomously represented West Virginians as uncivilized, innately violent, racist, and antimodern—or as noble working-class heroes resisting modernity's corruptions.

In this way, such representations avoided nuanced analysis and perpetuated the discursive tendency to see mountaineer Appalachians ambivalently. Like the "hillbilly" discussed in the prologue, the protesters in Kanawha County "served the dual and seemingly contradictory purposes of allowing the 'mainstream,' or generally nonrural, middle-class white, American audience to imagine a romanticized past, while simultaneously enabling that same audience to recommit itself to modernity by caricaturing the negative aspects of premodern, uncivilized society."[1] Kanawha County protesters, who were romanticized or demonized as hillbillies, symbolized America's ambivalence toward the social changes of the 1960s.

In this chapter I explore the three leading explanations for the controversy: class warfare waged by alienated workers and mothers; antimodern fundamentalism based on biblical literalism; and inherent racism due to cultural isolation and backwardness. In thus representing the Kanawha County textbook controversy, even the most sophisticated scholars and knowledgeable journalists succumbed to the tendency either to idealize the protesters as righteous resisters against modern corruptions or to demonize them as antimodern reactionaries. It is important to recognize this dichotomous representation because it precludes a more intersectional approach to the controversy, in which race, class, and gender are all taken into account, and because it obscures the historical relevance of the controversy.

Class Warfare in Kanawha County

In the context of reporting on the Kanawha County textbook controversy, "class warfare" became a euphemism for feuding, trigger-happy Appalachians, whether writers viewed the violent aspects of the conflict sympathetically as a legitimate protest against prolonged economic exploitation, or disdainfully, as stereotypical behavior of mountain people. Newspapers as far removed from Appalachia as the *South China Morning Post* spread the word about Kanawha County's "Class Warfare over U.S.

Textbooks," as one article called it. This article noted the poverty of West Virginians and ended with the threat of imminent violence.[2] The idea of class warfare is worth investigating on two points: one, it assumes that working-class loyalty was the single motivation of protesters and an over-riding explanation for the protest; and two, "warfare" suggests that protesters were predisposed to resort to violence.

Participants on both sides of the conflict recognized that resentment of class privilege and resistance to class control were important factors of the controversy, but not its raison d'être. Residents of Campbells Creek, for instance, had sophisticated reasons for opposing the new curriculum. Linda Wright, a high school student living in Campbells Creek at the time, remembers protesting the books because she, like her mother, had no faith that the teachers employed at her school could effectively teach the new books, some of which featured open-ended questions about social dilemmas with moral consequences.[3] The younger, better trained, better paid, more committed teachers at the larger, affluent schools located on "the hill" would naturally do a better job, Wright suggested. But in Campbells Creek, there was no trust in the teachers. Wright discussed them to explain why trust was lacking.

In this small community, the supposed personal and criminal histories of the teachers were well known because they had taught several genera-tions of students. "I had some really bad teachers," Wright said, sharing a litany of offenses and pathologies for which they were known. She remem-bered that one was taken away in handcuffs because of a nervous breakdown; one was a convicted shoplifter; another was an alcoholic who came to class drunk; and another held "pot parties" for students. Many were teachers who had taught Wright's parents, had been around well past their prime, or had lost jobs in the better schools. One teacher told Wright, "I'm here because nobody else would keep me."

Wright resented how objections to the books were met with an impa-tient command to trust the teachers as professional educators because she knew the disparity between those "good teachers" in South Hills schools that regularly produced National Merit Scholars and college-bound gradu-ates and those teachers she had encountered:

> That's what they kept saying during this whole textbook sadness: trust me, trust me. Trust us. We've been educated. We know how to teach this material. And then you get these questions at the end [of selected readings in the contested textbooks] going, well, should you take your

grandparents out on an iceberg and leave them to die? Or, when is it
okay to steal? And we're going, OK, you know, you don't want that
second-grade teacher that got arrested for shoplifting teaching that kind
of thing.[4]

Instead of demanding an unlikely redistribution of resources that might
alleviate the perceived personnel problems in the less affluent schools,
Wright and her mother argued that the books' open-ended questions
about moral dilemmas were inappropriate.

Their objections were met not only with a command to trust the professionals but also with hostility and demeaning condescension. An account
from *The Nation* corroborates Wright's memories of the situation: "When
the teachers and consultants first presented their selections to the board,
much of their defense consisted of totaling up their years of college education and urging the parents to trust that they knew best what to teach
children. To blue-collar parents, this was insufficient assurance. It smacked
of middle-class 'talking down to the laboring class of people,' as one
mother expressed it."[5] Wright experienced explicit acts of condescension.
She remembered a woman who gave her a book with the admonition to
"read this and you'll understand why you're the way you are." It was a
book on snake handlers. Some arrogant supporters of the books never
thought twice about putting all Appalachians in the same category, in this
case associating Linda Wright with an obscure ritual of holding poisonous
snakes in church, a religious practice whose constitutionality had been
defended by a Court of Appeals in Tennessee just a year earlier, in 1973.[6]

Wright singled out the Reverend James Lewis as one defender of the
textbooks who was insensitive to class issues and dismissive of "fundamentalists"—a word frequently delivered with derision during the
controversy. As the controversy died down, Lewis reflected on his role in
the class dynamics of the controversy: "One of the things that has both-
ered me, though, is that middle-class, middle-age[d], supposedly liberal
people like us have been mindlessly and routinely discriminating against
the working class and the poor people right here. We've contributed to
their political disfranchisement. Charleston doesn't have a black-white
problem; it has a creeker-hiller problem, and we're part of that problem."[7]
Apparently Lewis gained self-consciousness about his approach to the
"creekers" involved in the protests. According to participants on both
sides of the textbook debate, then, class antagonism between the affluent
residents of Charleston and the less wealthy inhabitants of Campbells

Creek was formidable. Because the conflict reflected the most common images of Appalachia as a culture of poverty, the idea of the textbook controversy as class warfare prevailed.

But seeing the conflict this way obscured the simple fact that school board member Alice Moore and businessman Elmer Fike, the two leading instigators of the conflict, were not motivated by class consciousness. Alice Moore appeared to be relatively affluent. On one hand, many locals saw her as a lady with an aristocratically southern accent who used her femininity to push political objectives. On the other hand, accounts portrayed her as downtrodden and fed up, an ill-informed provocateur without formal education or a populist heroine of the people. Moore insisted that the protest was "not a class or economic issue, but the media has made up their mind that it is, so they only present that side, showing only poor, uneducated protesters. Why don't they show the rich, educated type?"[8] Elmer Fike, a wealthy industrialist, also campaigned against the books. His leadership in the protest fanned the flames between liberals and conservatives and raised the question of whether working-class consciousness was a motivating factor.

Fike, a chemical engineer who worked for Monsanto Company before starting his own chemical company, was president of the Business and Professional People's Alliance for Better Textbooks.[9] He regularly wrote "Elmer's Tune," a column that appeared in three West Virginia newspapers, and eighteen of his columns were about the textbook controversy. He went on record as saying that the "textbook publishers in 1974 were too interested in giving attention to minorities and 'disenfranchised groups.'" Famously antiunion, he believed that the "textbooks were anti-business and socialist in nature," thereby a threat to the free-enterprise system in America. He also argued that the textbooks presented what he called "'peace-niks' and other groups such as environmental protection advocates who were harmful to the traditional business atmosphere in Kanawha County and America."[10] As an articulate, politically active, wealthy businessman prone to exploiting the environment, Fike did not fit the stereotype of an Appalachian working-class warrior.

But Fike's participation did not prevent some sociologists from arguing that the uprising was fundamentally an "episode of working-class opposition" from a region historically associated with such activism. In the pages of *Social Forces*, Dwight Billings and Robert Goldman argued with Ann Page and Donald Clelland, stating that, despite Fike's inclusion, the textbook protests emerged from "a heightened sense of occupational consciousness" that had developed over many years. To support their claim, Billings and Goldman dubiously stated that "the hotbed of opposition was the Paint Creek and Cabin Creek sections of the county—sites of some of America's most violent labor conflicts when the United Mine Workers struggled to organize these mining communities before World War I."[11] In fact, it was Campbells Creek, not Cabin Creek, where the Reverend Marvin Horan set up a headquarters in which working-class protesters planned rallies, also held in Campbells Creek before moving on to Charleston.[12] Sociologically and geographically, differentiating between Campbells Creek and Cabin Creek may be splitting hairs, and Billings and Goldman were not the first to suggest that Cabin Creek miners were the vanguard of the textbook protesters.[13] Moreover, Billings and Goldman were correct to complain that the mere presence of middle-class protesters should not disqualify a movement as working-class opposition. But their objections relied on the idea that class consciousness was the force mobilizing parents who followed Marvin Horan and other preachers from the rural areas to protest. They conceded that acknowledging the role of class consciousness does not answer the question of "why this tradition of [working-class] dissent was expressed [during the Kanawha County textbook controversy] as a defense of fundamentalist religion and of what would otherwise appear to be conservative values."[14]

Although class allegiances were strong and articulated willingly throughout the protests, other factors complicate representing the conflict as class warfare. Billings and Goldman's interlocutors Page and Clelland "found little in the statements of the anti-textbook faction to support these explanations" that class consciousness fully explained the conflict. In an effort to situate the events historically, Billings and Goldman relied too much on their academic knowledge of the past and not enough on local knowledge and "contemporary facts—what the textbook protesters themselves say and do."[15]

For example, when asked about Fike's influence, what his role was and who his followers were, Marvin Horan replied, "His followers are our followers, we work together, our movement is not divided. He is a businessman, so his activity is on a higher level than ours." Responding to the follow-up question of what "higher level" meant, Horan said, "Well, they are businessmen. They own the factory, and we work for him. We also have lawyers in this, that takes care of our business that we don't have the education to do. However, they respect our position and we respect theirs, and we work hand in hand."[16] Horan's portrayal of Fike indicates a general acceptance of the socioeconomic hierarchy in the Kanawha Valley. Horan was not employed by Fike Chemicals; in saying "we work for him," Horan raised the question of the relationship between the working-class protesters and the middle-class protesters. Were Horan and the other ministers pawns in a campaign orchestrated by Moore and Fike, or someone else—such as the lawyers he mentions, who were associated with the conservative Heritage Foundation based in Washington, D.C.? Were they paid for arousing their neighbors in a way that the middle class could not? These questions will be explored later; the point here is that Horan's statement recognizes a class system without challenging it.

Despite Horan's deference to Fike and other businessmen and lawyers whose work was "at a higher level," journalist Calvin Trillin depicted him as the epitome of the working-class warrior pitted against the upper classes. Like many news stories, Trillin's *New Yorker* essay focused on Horan and the coal mining strike, which followed a boycott of the schools and put economic pressure on the board of education to remove the controversial books from classrooms. The trouble is that Trillin lumps all the protesters together and presumes they are all working class, and hence are either miners or politically aligned with them. Despite knowing that Horan was a truck driver, Trillin uses him to authenticate his thesis that the textbook controversy was essentially class warfare *because* it involved a miner's strike. Trillin argued that the protesters had "at their disposal the one weapon they have always used in class warfare; their use of it transformed the school boycott into an industrial strike." He goes on to quote Horan, who told the school superintendent, "The common man don't know what to do except what he's done, and that's to go home and sit down. It's his strong back that keeps the system going, and when he don't like something he just goes on home and sits down."[17] Trillin presented a plausible list of possible reasons why the miners agreed to strike in relation to the textbook controversy, careful to make the valid point that participation in the strike did not necessarily signal miners' objection to the books, but only solidarity with co-workers. Despite these nuances of the conflict, Trillin concludes that "maybe the mass actions of men as resentful as West Virginia coal miners are not susceptible to analysis."[18]

Trillin made a lot of false assumptions in order to portray the textbook controversy as class warfare. He misidentified all the protesters as working class, assumed that all working-class people were aligned with coal miners, presented a truck-driving preacher as the voice of the miners who called for a strike, then concluded that the strike was based on resentment, not rationality or strategy, and was therefore, perhaps, actually beyond analysis. In contradistinction to Trillin, *The Nation* analyst Curtis Seltzer was aware that "one pitfall in such journalistic analysis [of protesters] is that it tends to oversimplify how representative the actors were. This is especially true with respect to coal miners."[19] Seltzer delved into possible reasons why the miners decided to strike, presenting a more detailed account of the miner's protest that launched the book controversy into the international limelight. In particular, the strike was seen more as an opportunity to deplete the coal stock, which would result in better contract terms, which were to be negotiated the following month.[20] Seltzer avoided the mistake of others of using the miners' involvement to oversimplify the textbook battle as class warfare.

Clearly, journalists used the phrase "class warfare" because it added an air of sensationalism that sells newspapers and magazines. Part of that sensational appeal was that it tapped into established stereotypes of Appalachian—if not simply American—culture as essentially violent. The early frontier lawlessness of the United States never seemed to abate in Appalachia, according to the stereotype, because that region never left those frontier days. Presumed to be socially, culturally, and politically retarded, Appalachians are seen as "our contemporary ancestors" or "yesterday's people" prone to yesterday's warring ways.[21] Even those sympathetic with the protesters' cause were not beyond perpetuating this preconception. Again, Calvin Trillin supplied an example when he wrote that "there is an assumption that any dispute involving mountain people—particularly mountain people who are miners—will end in violence."[22] Trillin's passive voice suggested that this assumption was not only his but also was operating in the Kanawha Valley itself. The prejudgment of Appalachians as inevitably if not ineluctably violent is not simply reported but reproduced for all *New Yorker* readers. Trillin was writing well before some of the violence (bombs, assaults, Mace attacks, rifle shots) of the controversy happened.

The notion that the controversy was essentially or originally "class warfare" should be highly suspect, given that (1) Fike's and Moore's motivations and arguments blatantly denied that the protest had a working-class orientation; (2) the relationship between the miners' strike and the textbook protest was more opportunistic than principled; and (3) the man most touted as working-class hero, Marvin Horan, claimed he worked *for* Fike and the "businessmen," not against them, in protesting the books. The majority of citizens disgruntled with the books was compelled to engage in legal, nonviolent means of protest and deplored any violence as tainting their cause, so describing the controversy as warfare was at best a misnomer.

Alienated Mothers

Another supposed source of the textbook controversy was related to the presumed cause of class warfare: alienated parents, specifically mothers. This claim is connected to the idea of alienated workers and is an extrapolation of the myth that Alice Moore was merely a "concerned mother" who by happenstance gained knowledge of some unorthodox new textbooks. Contrary to scholars who lump the Kanawha County conflict in with other curriculum disputes, and contrary to right-wing advocates of parents' rights with regard to such disputes, we should reject the idea that this struggle was sparked by maternal instincts that were spontaneously translated into civic duty.

In *Textbooks on Trial*, a book exalting the famous anti-textbook crusaders Mel and Norma Gabler of Texas, Moore is portrayed as a woman with no previous knowledge of textbook disputes; she was "a latecomer to curriculum protests," inspired to get involved "when sex education came to Kanawha County."[23] *Textbooks on Trial* portrays Moore as an established Kanawha County citizen who was pushed into politics by the popular demand of her peers, launching a bid for election on the school board in 1970. Many other accounts, however, see Moore as a self-proclaimed "politician" who moved to the area a few years before running for the school board, a woman with ulterior motives and connections to national groups.

In particular, Moore was widely thought to be a plant from the John Birch Society, which in 1974 was ten years away from its heyday in the early 1960s. At that earlier time, the John Birch Society facilitated the mobilization of Citizens' Councils that "slowed, but ultimately could not prevent, the [racial] integration of schools" mandated by the 1954 decision in *Brown v. Board of Education*.[24] The late Emmett Shafer, who was principal of one of the elementary schools that was bombed in 1974, said Alice Moore became a board member with the backing of the John Birch Society and for the express purpose of challenging the status quo according to the group's ideology.[25] During a radio debate, an unidentified caller asked Moore point-blank whether she was *ever* associated with the John Birch Society. Moore denied it: "Absolutely not."[26] But if she was not officially an associate *of* the John Birch Society, she certainly associated *with* members of the group. She told one interviewer that she "knew the local leader of the John Birch Society, but that he was not involved in her election," referring to her 1970 election to the board of education.[27] According to her opponent in that political race, Moore spread "lies inspired by Birchers."[28] Rev. James Lewis attributed Moore's success to her "great ability to speak rapidly without drawing a breath, overwhelm[ing] her opponents with a steady barrage of Birch propaganda."[29]

Research has not revealed evidence of Moore's direct ties or official affiliation with the John Birch Society, although her rhetoric undeniably reflects its antieducation publications. Moore said that while she was never a member of the John Birch Society, she remembered her father bringing home some of its publications. So despite membership status, it is likely that Alice Moore was familiar with the rationales and rhetoric of the John Birch Society. But pinning the Birch label on Moore is not as interesting as considering why there was suspicion of the John Birch Society in the Kanawha Valley, and why there was so little suspicion of her association with other groups.[30] Few contemporary reports on Moore recognized that she was associated with the group that initiated the national concern over sex education in the 1970s, the Christian Crusade based in Tulsa, Oklahoma.

Moore was visited by the Christian Crusade's Reverend Charles Secrest, a protégé of the Reverend Billy James Hargis, an anticommunist evangelical minister of national stature. Secrest wrote fund-raising letters based on what he learned in Kanawha County.[31] Moore also traveled to Tulsa to speak with a Christian Crusade audience, delivering an hourlong lecture that was recorded; tapes were advertised for sale at five dollars apiece. The Texas textbook monitors, the Gablers, publicized this connection in their nationally distributed material, reprinting an article written by Secrest in *Christian Crusade Weekly*.[32] This nexus of connection is as rich as the presumed link with the John Birch Society, but it was overlooked.

Without acknowledging Moore's association with the Christian Crusade, anti-textbook accounts succeeded in portraying her in populist terms, as a lone concerned mother who was fighting a corrupt and negligent system on behalf of all the alienated parents of Kanawha County. Although few would argue that West Virginia state or local bureaucracies were known for their political integrity, the idea that the textbook selection was an example of school board tyranny was based on an accusation about the selection process that simply was not true. Moore complained that "the people" had no say in the selection of the new curriculum.

But, in fact, concerned parents were given ample opportunity to examine the proposed books, which were on display in public libraries for four weeks before the board was scheduled to meet about the books.[33] Alice Moore complained about the number of books on display. She intimated that displaying the controversial books along with others was a ploy to confuse parents and to camouflage the "dirty books" by placing them in a field of better ones. But more telling was her insistence that the books needed to be "in my hands" and in the hands of "the people." "I can't run downtown," she said during a meeting. In an interview later, she articulated this same disdain of inconvenience, admitting that she "did not take advantage of an opportunity to go up to the board to see them because of a lack of time."[34] Moore's frivolous complaints gave way to a vaguer critique of a careless, anonymous school board running roughshod over unsuspecting parents, epitomized by Alice Moore herself. The idea that the protests began because of alienated parents hinges on this presentation of Moore, which obscures her ideological and political links to national evangelical leaders.

As we will see in chapter 3, Moore both reflected a tradition of conservative women activists and shaped new strategies for conservative women to model. Like feminists, Moore endured sexist dismissals of her political involvement. Despite her political connections to the Christian Crusade, it was the male, working-class evangelical preachers who bore the brunt of representing the fundamentalist element of the controversy. In accordance with the stereotypes of Appalachia, fundamentalists were not like Moore; they were poor, inarticulate, and resentful—to recall Trillin's impression—beyond analysis. Moore and other affluent, well-organized, strategic evangelicals of the county and of the nation were shadowed by the bright light put on the likes of Marvin Horan. When it came to considering Christian fundamentalism as a cause of the protest, the elite evangelicals escaped scrutiny.

Antimodern Fundamentalists

With God on Our Side, a 1996 Public Broadcasting System film documenting the rise of the religious Right in the United States since World War II, helped perpetuate the notion that the Kanawha County textbook controversy was an organic, grassroots uprising of Christian fundamentalists. Ignoring outside influences and specific local concerns, the film presents Kanawha County as representative of the nation after the 1960s and Watergate. The White House scandal and Nixon's resignation solidified a deep distrust of the federal government. This antigovernment sentiment was electrified locally as evangelical ministers portrayed the board of education as bureaucrats disconnected with "the people."

Recordings of meetings held by the board of education reveal eloquent expressions of such antigovernment distrust. One woman compared the protesters' situation with the Watergate situation to illustrate the hypocrisy of the double standard of prevailing "law and order." She said that the federal officers convicted in the Watergate conspiracy were pardoned and given eighty thousand dollars, but protesters who picketed the board of education were "fined a thousand dollars and thrown in jail."[35] Other concerns at the time included the fact that West Virginia had the highest state death rate for casualties in Vietnam, and that the state government routinely put the business interests of coal companies before the interests of working people. Fresh in people's minds was the 1972 Buffalo Creek disaster, in which a deluge of mining sludge killed 125 people and destroyed five hundred homes because safety standards were overlooked for the sake of profit.[36] Although *With God on Our Side* ignored such local events, it accurately situated the concern over new books in the context of anger at the government, which was seen as passively tolerating if not actively fostering the so-called anti-Christian values that had become popular since World War II.

In particular, *With God on Our Side* portrayed the Kanawha County textbook controversy as the first grassroots uprising of white, evangelical Christians who were threatened by the social changes of the 1960s. Changes wrought or reflected by the civil rights movement, the women's liberation movement, the Stonewall rebellion and gay liberation, the legalization of the Pill and abortion, the banning of school prayer, the distribution of sex education—even the landing on the moon—all were taken as signs of a nation severing its ties to God. *With God on Our Side* characterizes the textbook controversy as an inevitable clash of cultural values.

The events in Kanawha County were portrayed as a precursor to what are now called the culture wars. Scholars and reporters alike perpetuated this idea even before the term "culture wars" was familiar. In 1974, a *Commonweal* reporter described the controversy as a "full-scale eruption of frustrations against a worldly culture imposed in an area literally a world apart from the rest of the country."[37] Journalist Ben A. Franklin also portrayed the "Appalachian creekers" as "literally, a world apart" in his regular updates for the *New York Times*.[38] And Marshall University professor William Denman, writing for the *1976 Free Speech Yearbook*, reveals where this idea of the unevolved Appalachian fundamentalist comes from:

> There is little doubt, from a reading of the sociological literature on the nature of the Appalachian mountaineer, that a sizeable majority of the white, essentially Scotch-Irish residents of the Appalachian mountains have, well into the century, maintained a strong set of values. This value structure, incorporating a firm belief in God, with Jesus Christ as Savior, along with a resolute faith in the Bible as the expressed Word of God, permeates Appalachian culture not only in the rural but in the urban areas as well. This fundamentalist religious faith, coupled with traditional social and political mores, give the Appalachian a value system that is, in many ways, increasingly out of harmony with the changing value structures of a sizeable portion of the rest of contemporary America. The heart of the textbook controversy in Kanawha County, West Virginia, is a clash of values.[39]

Thanks to the prevailing sociological literature of the time, if not to the images perpetuated via popular culture and documentaries about the War on Poverty, it was very easy to portray the textbook protesters as unwilling or incapable of tolerating social change, much less of fomenting it themselves.

One problem with this conventional understanding of the fundamentalist roots of the textbook controversy is that it overlooks the issues of language and literature. The controversial books, after all, were language arts books. Scholars who have attended to this crucial aspect, however, have examined the language issue simply as a more precise expression of naturally inevitable cultural dissonance. Even with a focus on language, scholars saw a conflict of antimodern and modern tenets, a conflict between backward, biblical literalists and more enlightened, progressive educators. The problem was organic, according to these scholars, growing from the fact that those uneducated mountain folk were stubbornly sticking to an archaic notion of language that the books, as products of years of research in linguistics and education, had rendered obsolete.

Why did some of the protesters call for a return to basal readers featuring phonics, a method associated with learning letters and words by rote memorization? Why did they reject the "look-say" method, which promotes an appreciation of figurative language and contextualized "reading for meaning"? Scholars suggested that these preferences were due to the protesters' general religious beliefs, those supposedly backward, traditional ideas that precluded new knowledge. James Moffett's book on the controversy, for example, carefully delineated the specific objections to the look-say method of teaching reading. Despite the fact that discussions of phonics *versus* look-say methods of reading appeared in right-wing and church-related publications, Moffett's interviews with protesters pursued a line of questioning that led him to an overly narrow focus on the religious aspects of the dispute. Moffett provided a compelling analysis of how this successor of phonics-based education alarmed people who, because of their religion, prefer literal readings and the discipline of learning by rote. According to Moffett, textbook protesters championed the phonics method because it diverted the child's attention away from the content of the reading matter and directed it to "particles of language too small to have any meaning." He explained that "what phonics really amounts to for those who are sure they have a corner on God's mind but are very unsure of being able to hold their children's minds is *another way to censor books* (unconsciously, of course) *by nipping literacy itself in the bud*."[40] This reasoning is based on the assumption that the protesters wanted to censor the books because they rejected new knowledge.

Moffett ultimately concluded that the protesters were resisting new ideas, held in a condition of "not-wanting-to-know."[41] He referred to this resistance as "agnosis," which is the opposite of "gnosis," a "direct and full knowledge." "To their credit," Moffett concluded, "the underlying concern of the book objectors was religious. But what stands in the way of gnosis, the goal of all religions, is agnosis, which is the blocking of consciousness, as anesthesia is the blocking of the senses and amnesia is the blocking of memory."[42] Moffett's interesting ethnographic research and often insightful analysis ultimately reinscribed the textbook controversy as essentially the result of a fundamentalist aversion to change in social consciousness, a rejection of modern ideas.

Because of this supposedly indigenous, fundamentalist predisposition to rejecting new knowledge, hence social change, the "clash of cultural values" was seen as unsurprising and nearly inevitable. Scholar George Hillocks Jr. wrote, "When the values of the curriculum makers and the textbook editors are nearly the same as those of the parents whose children attend such schools, a monolithic curriculum, despite its other problems, will at least not be viewed as an imposition of values. But when the values of the two groups do not match, and the Kanawha County protest is a case in point, the curriculum is almost bound to be regarded as unsatisfactory, or worse, by parents."[43] Even though Hillocks's work is grounded in the fields of language instruction and education policy, his sense of the practically inevitable "ideological conflict" relies on the same assumptions as other scholarship and reportage on the textbook controversy. The assumption is that the protesters' fundamentalist values are organic, localized, and practically part of the natural setting of West Virginia, where everything supposedly is retarded. The textbook controversy was actually called the second Scopes trial, in which fundamentalist values that are antithetical to change locked horns with modern sensibilities. For many, the textbook controversy was not only bound to happen because of the conflict in values but also because West Virginians retained the antimodern values that the rest of the country saw as discredited by the Scopes trial of 1924, when the teaching of evolution was upheld against fundamentalist dissent. The Kanawha County protesters were seen as ridiculous throwbacks to the early twentieth century.

Quite to the contrary, the particular parameters in which protesters waged their complaints were new. With their emphasis on opposition to relativism, situational ethics, and secular humanism, the leading protesters were not espousing the Protestant fundamentalism of the 1920s. The protests reflected an emphasis not on the Christian duty to defend creationism as biblical truth but on the more conspiratorial fear of an alien and actively anti-Christian culture. This millennialist fear of anti-Christian forces was inspired by a new wave of evangelicalism that had not yet been nationally acknowledged in 1974, but was being embraced in communities nationwide. Only two years later, *Time* magazine heralded 1976 as "the year of the evangelical." The harbinger of this new manifestation of evangelical millennialism was a 1970 book by Hal Lindsey, *The Late Great Planet Earth*, the preface of which contains an appeal to students who felt their education had been failing them. The book was all over the Kanawha Valley by 1974.

Despite his claim that the ideological conflict was nearly inevitable because of staid cultural values, Hillocks's own account of the protesters attests to the influence of new formulations of fundamentalism that were circulating in the Kanawha Valley:

> For the fundamentalist this staunch, unflinching belief in the Bible as the revealed word, and therefore as the most important source of truth, has several ramifications. Two of these set fundamentalism apart from mainline Protestant churches: a belief in biblical prophecy, especially

those pertaining to the return of Christ and the millennium; and a
belief in Satan as the powerful, highly intelligent enemy of man. When I
interviewed various pastors in Kanawha County and inquired about beliefs
in the millennium, I was almost invariably referred to a book called *The
Late Great Planet Earth*, by Hal Lindsey.[44]

Likewise, when asked whether he were aware of this book, Rev. James
Lewis recounted a tale of a desperate young Charlestonian who had sought
his counsel during the textbook controversy. After having read *The Late
Great Planet Earth*, the man had been filled with dreadful expectation of
the last days of humanity and God's wrath.[45] Lewis's and Hillocks's
accounts suggest that the book was not only a popular reference for
Kanawha County pastors but also was a profound touchstone for individuals in their congregations.

Moreover, these accounts contradict the prevailing idea that the fundamentalist values of the protesters were homegrown and indigenous to the
Kanawha County mountaineers. Intentionally or not, *The Late Great
Planet Earth* was part of the Right's antidote to the Left's Port Huron
Statement, providing a conservative spiritual answer to students'—and
parents'—disenchantment with government and the Establishment. The
book sold more than ten million copies in its first seven years and was *the*
best-selling nonfiction book in the United States in the 1970s. It was
enormously influential, arguing that the 1948 reestablishment of the state
of Israel was the beginning of the fulfillment of biblical prophecy regarding
the Second Coming of Jesus Christ and his promised reign on earth for a
thousand years, a millennium. With this new understanding, fundamentalists began to see events as signs of the End Times.

Political events acquired new religious meaning to those who understood that the Judgment Day was imminent in a way that it had not been
before 1948. For instance, Rev. Marvin Horan's warning to a crowd of
protesters, "If we don't protect our children, we'll have to account for it
on the Day of Judgment," carried a new urgency in the context of a new
fundamentalism articulated in *The Late Great Planet Earth*.[46] People did
not have to read the book to be influenced by its ideas, which validated old
ones and established a new urgency. Testifying in a federal grand jury
investigation in January 1975, textbook protester Delbert Rose explained
that Horan's biblical injunctions and apocalyptic speeches inspired Rose to
bomb a school in October 1974: "Several hours prior to Rose's bombing
of Midway school, he said Mr. Horan read Bible passages at the anti-text-

book headquarters. According to Rose, one of the passages read was, 'There is a time to live and a time to die . . . that one must fight fire with fire . . . a time to kill and a time to be killed . . . a time to live and a time for hate . . . a time for war and a time for peace.'" Rose was convicted and spent two years in a federal penitentiary in Kentucky.[47]

The textbook controversy, therefore, was not an antimodern throwback to the 1920s, a never-evolved fundamentalism of "yesterday's people" living in the deep recesses of mountain folkways cut off from the rest of American society. On the contrary, it reflected and advanced the very contemporary formulation of postmodern millennialism and post–civil rights conservatism. Forging this conservatism necessarily entailed restructuring arguments against racial integration and equality.

Race-Based Resentment

Much evidence suggests that the textbook controversy was caused by white people's fear and resentment toward people of color, specifically African Americans whose political work in the 1950s and '60s reformed, if not revolutionized, race relations in the United States. In particular, one policy geared toward equitable representation of racial minorities was accepted by the Kanawha County Board of Education in 1970. In accordance with a mandate from the federal Department of Health, Education, and Welfare (HEW), the board of education set out to select a curriculum expressly inclusive of writings by authors of color and other "multi-ethnic" literature.

In June 1973, the textbook selection committee appointed by the Kanawha County school board sent out letters inviting publishers to submit sample books for review. Many companies offered versions of what had become the industry standard: books that taught the skills of reading and writing as communication in "multi-ethnic" social contexts. Formal hearings, including fifty-three presentations of different curricula and group readings of sample texts, occurred from November 1973 to January 1974. Debates within the committee ensued. The committee made a special effort to abide by the selective criteria approved previously, examining very closely the books for multiethnic and multicultural content, careful to reject those books that had only cosmetically or superficially updated their content to satisfy the new standard. For example, the committee rejected one line of books because the publisher's sole effort to present people of color was to alter illustrations of children, coloring their faces but not changing their features to resemble any ethnic or racial difference. In March 1974, after nine months of intensive work, the selection committee made its recommendation to the board of education to adopt particular sets of books.[48] The painstakingly chosen language arts textbooks fit the bill issued by HEW.

For Alice Moore, HEW was part of the problem. "HEW definitely had something to do with this, they have an influence on textbook publishers," Moore said. "HEW and the federal government promote this stuff."[49] Was "this stuff" that was so reprehensible to Alice Moore the inclusion of literature by writers of color? That depends on *when* she was asked.

Moore's race-based claims about the books became less prevalent over time. In fact, one teacher who served on the book selection committee had the impression that discrediting the books because of their multiracial content was a strategy that was dropped deliberately. According to Nell Wood, when representatives from the NAACP and other black community leaders were invited to listen and observe the early school board meetings dealing with the textbooks, Alice Moore changed her tune. "It was in June [of 1974] that the emphasis switched from racism to Christianity," Wood claimed in an interview, noting that at first Moore had "attacked the books for black authors [and] use of dialect." Asked whether this was a subtle or obvious switch away from blatant racism, Wood replied, "It was obvious. It was obvious to anyone who wasn't blind and deaf."[50]

Recordings of the school board meetings lend credence to Wood's claim. At the public hearings organized in June 1974, one proponent of the books said, "I recognize that in the earlier criticisms of these books great emphasis was placed on too much that was not white and middle class. I can understand how people who are white and middle class might be a little startled because it is so unusual to have black writers."[51] Audiotapes of earlier meetings clarify why Wood perceived discussions of "the use of dialect" as a matter of racism as much as rejecting African American authors. On April 11, 1974, Moore framed her objection to "dialectology" with a diatribe of suspicion about the National Council of Teachers of English. Moore said she didn't "agree with anything they say. If they're playing a big part in this adoption, I don't think I want" to go through with the adoption of the textbooks. Like her distrust of HEW, this suspicion of a teachers' group "behind" the book selection indicates the conspiratorial worldview Moore embraced. More to the point, her objection to studying dialects seemed to be based on a fear of exposing Appalachian kids to black vernacular and coercing them to practice it.

Moore objected to a particular lesson that asked students to rewrite a paragraph using a "New England dialect" featured in a reading sample that contained "dat" instead of "that." She complained that "English is being watered down" and suggested, again, that this crusading purpose of the "NAET" was part of a sinister "trend." She was surprised when she was informed that lessons in dialectology had appeared in the "old books." Then her interlocutor tried to calm Moore by noting that only two books, one aimed at eighth graders and the other written for eleventh-grade students, contained units on dialectology. Moore objected that "it doesn't take a unit," suggesting an infectious nature of the dialects themselves. She saw the teaching of dialect as antithetical to endorsing "standard American speech," which she did not attempt to define. She announced with authority that the "NAACP opposes this approach," ostensibly because it encouraged the use of black vernacular—or "ghetto dialect," as she called it on another occasion—which presumably precluded the advancement of people of color. Moore said, "The outcome of the course would be that middle-class students would learn to speak in ghetto dialect."[52]

Contrary to Moore's claim, the local chapter of the NAACP was not aligned with her opposition to the books. From the beginning, the NAACP saw the textbook protest as a racist effort. In addition to attending subsequent school board meetings, no doubt in response to Moore's speaking on their behalf, members of the NAACP took action against the protesters on three occasions. In the fall of 1974, boycotts and hostile rallies forced the board to extract the books from classrooms and to agree to convene a formal citizens' review committee. The NAACP issued a statement whose first item acknowledged the "introduction of multi-cultural and multi-ethnic textbook materials" as the cause of the controversy. It went on to denounce "uncontrolled mob violence" and the governor's unwillingness to discharge state troopers to dispel it. Most emphatically, the NAACP called for the board of education to "seat at least 3–5 representatives from the Black community on the Textbook Review Committee of eighteen (18) in order to insure a broad-based racial composition."[53]

The Beta Beta Omega chapter of the sorority Alpha Kappa Alpha wrote a letter to the school board to "urgently and respectfully request that black representation will be included on the citizens' advisory committee to review the textbooks. We praise the Textbook Committee for their courage in selecting textbooks which portray the 'inter-cultural character of our pluralistic society.'"[54] Also on the occasion of convening a citizens' review committee, the Official Black Caucus of the West Virginia Education

Association sent a letter requesting that "Blacks be represented on your Review Committee" because of the state-mandated "multi-ethnic, multi-cultural materials included in these texts."[55] Clearly the black community saw the cause of the controversy as resistance to multiracial material in the books and sought to mitigate such resistance in the newly founded citizens' review committee.

The NAACP was compelled two other times to voice opposition to the protesters. It held a press conference in January 1974 when the Ku Klux Klan held public rallies. The West Virginia Human Rights Commission also ran a cover story in its newsletter indicting the Klan's cross burning and recruitment. In March 1975, NAACP members returned to the school board to criticize its handling of the textbook controversy. They expressed surprise "at the audacity and nerve of some white people" to represent them. Moore was, of course, singled out as an inappropriate spokesperson for black opinion. "We don't need Alice Moore, Elmer Fike or Rev. Horan (Rev. Marvin Horan) to decide who should represent us," said a member of the Business and Professional Men's Club. The president of the NAACP reminded the board that "we have said from the onset that the objectives [of the protest movement] are racist."[56]

Early in the controversy and often thereafter, the phrase "get the nigger books out" circulated as graffiti and utterance. According to one report, placards exclaiming "get those nigger books out of our school" were "held up in Campbells Creek and put in the storefronts," although residents of Campbells Creek deny this and Alice Moore downplayed it by recognizing that "it would take one person to put them up in all the storefronts."[57] But according to school board member Harry Stansbury, there were "plenty of anti-Black posters that the protesters were carrying in some of their parades, like 'Get those Nigger Books out.'"[58] Ronald English, a black Baptist pastor, saw this phrase as the basis of the controversy: "The way it came down, as far as the community response was, a lot of times the books were called nigger books."[59] The way it came down was undeniable racism.

Although Moore stopped focusing on black vernacular language in the books, racist overtones remained. For example, protesters' objection to Eldridge Cleaver's *Soul on Ice* being listed as optional supplemental readings for advanced placement, college-bound students was couched in the old southern myth of the black rapist. Cleaver's discussion of raping white women as an act of insurrection was difficult for the staunchest advocates of the books to defend. Moore repeatedly denounced Cleaver as a revolutionary rapist, as someone who *advocated* raping white women, a claim we will explore in chapter 4. According to audio and visual recordings, her voice had a shocked, urgent, and tremulous pitch when she made this objection, breaking from her usually cool, slow southern cadence. Elmer Fike promoted the same objection with the idea that if it were necessary to include authors of color, it would be better to include supposedly respectable authors. In an interview, teacher Doris Colomb reported that

> every time I saw [Elmer Fike]he would be bringing me another book that had some writings by a Negro writer. And he said if we are going to have writings by blacks, why can't we have this and this and this and this? These are good writings by Negro writers. Why do we have to have Eldridge Cleaver, and so on and so forth. I realized that what Elmer Fike was saying was that the black experience is OK as long as it is the same as mine. If it is different, then forget it.[60]

Colomb's insight notwithstanding, Fike's objection to Eldridge Cleaver also served as playing male voice-of-reason to Moore's female hysteria over the need for protection from black rapists. In this regard, white women (as supposed victims of Eldridge Cleaver's revolutionary militancy) and "our children" (as supposed victims of Eldridge Cleaver's revolutionary words) were one and the same body needing protection from those "filthy books" that supposedly showcased militant black writers.

This overtly stated fear of black revolutionaries paralleled a corollary fear of social integration among the races, which was less blatantly expressed. One Kanawha County teacher who defended the adoption of the books discussed how she realized fear of racial integration was key to the protests:

> I think it was a second-level book in the *Communicating* series had a version of "Jack and the Bean Stalk" that people objected to. We all leafed through it and couldn't figure out why they were having such a fit over "Jack and the Bean Stalk." Well, openly, they were saying, "You're teaching children to steal, and you're teaching them to kill." You know, it didn't make sense. Anyway, when this board member came in, we asked him. We were in the room next door here. And I'll never forget. He took the book, and he put it down on the table. "It's not what's in the book— it's the *cover*." Well, we hadn't even *thought* of that. It was a collage of several different figures on the cover, and in the foreground there are two

children, and the little girl is carrying a big bouquet of daisies, and the
little boy is leaning over like this [bending forward], smelling them. And
he took his finger and went like this, clockwise, and he said, "*That's* what
they're objecting to, in my area," and he circled that little boy and girl.
The little boy is black, and the little girl is white."[61]

This cover illustration (see figure 6), according to Nell Wood, was the
trigger of the race-based objections with which Alice Moore initiated the
controversy. Wood remembered, "Several times I had this book pointed
out to me. And in fact, at one of the meetings one of the protesters said,
'This is what it's all about.' . . . Here's a little girl with a bouquet and a

FIGURE 6. A particular textbook deemed controversial for its cover
as well as its contents. D.C. Heath and Company, 1973.

little black boy smelling the bouquet. And my contention is that this began racism in March (of 1974)."[62] From Wood's point of view, protesters were objecting to the coupling of a black boy and a white girl, with the bouquet of daisies representing a romantic gesture or a sexual symbol. In such a reading, the image is an even more insidious version of the idea that black men should rape white women. Alice Moore's portrayal of the rape of white women as a black revolutionary practice and the teaching of dialectology as an indoctrination in black vernacular was seemingly underscored by the symbolic imagery of a black boy smelling a white girl's white flowers.

This interpretation of the events need not invalidate Campbells Creek resident Linda Wright's aforementioned testimony of class resentment as a formidable force among protesters. She and others saw the new method of presenting moral dilemmas to students as inappropriate since teachers in the less affluent schools were reportedly struggling with moral ambiguities of their own. But Wright herself attests to how this class resentment coincided with, or reinforced, racial indignation in Campbells Creek, which was less than five miles away from Witcher Creek, the site of a Klan cross burning in February 1975. In an interview, Wright discussed how her neighbors were excited when the Klan got involved; its presence stoked the anger of residents, especially the men.

On November 10, 1974, after an anti-textbook rally, word got around that a "car full of blacks came across the turnpike and they were mouthing that they were going to come into Campbells Creek and burn one of the churches." The "rumor had swept Campbells Creek, spread by word of mouth and by citizens band radios." As many as a hundred white men gathered at the various churches with shotguns and walked the streets until police came to break up the mob. Wright's mother told her to hide under the bed.[63]

About the Witcher Creek cross burning itself, Wright said that it did not amount to much, since no African Americans lived there. Had they held a cross burning in Rand, a black community not far from Campbells Creek, the Klansmen "probably would have got mugged," she said with an embarrassed laugh; "they would have been run out of Rand." Like many journalistic accounts, Wright dismissed the Klan as ineffectual, just "all talk and no do." This was a reasonable assessment given the fact that Klan membership was at an all-time low nationally. But it also raises the question of how "racism" or "racist" was defined locally.

Wright's account demonstrates the existence of mob rule used to police the neighborhood as well as a lynching mentality serious enough to bring out legitimate law enforcement. It also demonstrates Wright's reluctance to see the action of her neighbors as racist rather than as simply a matter of defensive vigilantism. Likewise, Alice Moore opposed accusations of racism even while circulating the most inflammatory myth of the black rapist, which was a virtual call for lynching in the late nineteenth and early twentieth century. This was the case in Charleston in 1921, for example, when a lynching atmosphere developed as a Leroy Williams faced dubious rape charges from a white woman.[64] Clearly some textbook protesters remembered this atmosphere: in September 1974 a group calling itself the Vigilante Committee for Decency in Our Schools, Kanawha Valley Region circulated a letter pointing out that "as recently as 50 years ago" members of the school board "would have been lynched for less than their present activities."[65] The letter did not "advocate anyone doing this, since these creeps are not worth going to jail for," but it nevertheless attested to the memory and mentality of lynching in Kanawha County. Alice Moore made no such statements about lynching and kept her distance from organized white supremacists, denouncing them outright. Discursively, however, her frequent protests of Eldridge Cleaver as someone "who wanted to rape white women" struck the same chord that Klansmen did when they warned anti-textbook crowds about "niggers that rape our daughters."[66]

The question of what constitutes racism arose in the midst of such similar messages by Moore and white supremacists. In Moore's defense, one citizen, Jerry Wellman, wrote a letter that expressed why objections to African American authors and to the books generally should not be considered racist. As he explained, "racism or racist is an excessive and irrational belief in or advocacy of the superiority of a given group, people, or nation, usually one's own, on the basis of racial difference having no scientific validity." Therefore, he was "appalled" at "Mrs. Moore being called a racist during the last board meeting."[67] Following Wellman's logic, Moore and other protesters were not racist because their beliefs were not irrational, excessive, or unscientific. On the contrary, as his letter explained, they were civilized, unlike the "authors of the material in question [who] have made no contribution to civilization." Wellman's letter concluded with an appeal to "keep instructional material consistent with American Principles" that are rational and scientific in nature. He explained at length:

> Eugenics is the science of improving the physical and mental qualities of human beings, through control of the factors influencing heredity, as by

controlled selection of parents. Eugenic is of, relating to, or serving in the production of physically and mentally improved off-spring or breeds, especially among human beings. Born with good physical and mental qualities. Euthenics is the science of improving the physical and mental qualities of human beings, through control of environmental factors. Books in both sciences should be put in the public school libraries and especially Eugenics and Race.[68]

Spelled out blatantly here is an implicit logic that fuels the fear of social integration among the races, as represented by the book cover featuring a black boy and white girl, by the portrayal of black revolutionaries as rapists, and by the objection to dialectology as a means to promote black vernacular. What was at stake was a "control of environmental factors," to use Wellman's phrase, which affect the "off-spring" of the protesters.

Another blatant articulation of this underlying logic to the protests is found in an article from *The Citizen*, a publication of the Citizens Councils of America, the group that led the fight to preserve racial segregation of public schools in the 1950s. The February 1975 article, "Pro-Integration Textbooks Opposed," argued that the

> barely-mentioned but major motivation of the [Kanawha County] protesters stems from their resentment of the use of the textbooks to teach racial integration. It is based on the parents' wise discernment that here, in the pages of their children's school books, are false doctrines which will encourage their white sons and daughters to merge their racial identities with those of blacks in every phase of social life. It is founded on the conviction that the destruction of time-honored social and cultural values will lead to marriage between whites and Negroes and, ultimately, to the fulfillment of the social revolutionists' goal of racial suicide and/or mongrelization. This little-known reason for the parents' anger is their resentment of court-ordered racial integration . . . resentment which has reached the boiling point.[69]

Alice Moore and other protesters never publicly announced their conviction in this way, but their objections and complaints about the books certainly resonated with overt racial resentment.

Should we therefore conclude, as *The Citizen* article did, that "court-ordered racial integration of schools" (the 1954 Supreme Court ruling in *Brown v. Board of Education*) is the source of the textbook controversy?

Some of the protesters' participation in antibusing campaigns suggests so. In particular, the evangelical minister Avis Hill traveled to Boston, Louisville, Detroit, and McKeesport to protest busing black students to predominantly white high schools to achieve racial integration. Others who had a political awakening with regard to the textbooks joined with antibusing forces, lending credence to the claim that racial integration of schools was intolerable to protesters.

But to conclude that a firmly rooted desire for racial segregation was the single source of the textbook controversy is to ignore the advice of historians such as David Roediger, who "warns us against claims that any significant drama in U.S. history is 'really about race' or that any single dynamic is isolated from the social processes within which it unfolds."[70] Especially in the case of Avis Hill, who was like millions of American evangelicals who would become politicized throughout the 1970s and 1980s as part of the religious Right, we see the fallacy of concluding that the textbook protesters were essentially motivated by anti–African American resentment and that the protests were "really about race" and nothing else.

Historical Relevance

Undeniably, racial hostility played a role in the textbook controversy. But to understand that role and its significance or insignificance, it is necessary to recognize that the various articulations of Christian politics, conservative women's activism, and white resentment expressed during the textbook controversy expanded well beyond Kanawha County and West Virginia. The Kanawha County textbook controversy was rife not only with the predictable stereotypes, but with a less acknowledged but nonetheless profound ambivalence that continues to characterize the relationship between America and Appalachia.

Each of the three presumed explanations relies on and reveals an underlying ambivalence about the hillbilly, an "image/identity [that] has always been a site of contending attitudes toward modernity."[71] The tendency to conflate the textbook controversy with debates about modern American life were obvious in the case of depicting protesters primarily as fundamentalists, who were presumed to be, by definition, antimodern. In a slightly more convoluted way, the idea of alienated workers and mothers was also a comment on modernity. Claiming class warfare as the impetus for protesting books implicitly acknowledged West Virginians' exploitation and colonization by capitalist coal, chemical, and lumber companies.[72] In reports of the protests, "class warfare" functioned either romantically to convey an opposition to modernity's supposed progress or derisively to denote a reluctance to accept modern ways. The proposed language arts curriculum was, in this way, a metonymic stand-in for the whole of modernity, and the so-called class warfare waged against it was variously applauded or maligned as symbolic American resistance.

Blaming racist intolerance of literature written by people of color was less obviously, but no less effectively, a comment on American modernity. Claiming the protests were the product of hillbilly bigots or racist rednecks was tantamount to accusing West Virginians of being uncivilized and not modern enough. This ambivalent attitude toward the hillbilly was prevalent among media and scholarly accounts of the textbook controversy.

Moreover, this ambivalence enabled the dichotomous representation of the conflict. Calvin Trillin's overt suggestion that the textbook controversy and its participants were "not susceptible to analysis" was often an implicit assumption in the work of scholars such as Hillocks, Moffett, and Goldman and Billings, when they presumed that the conflict was a predictable, organic uprising due to differences between the traditional fundamentalist working class and the more modern middle class or the progressive educated elite. Especially with its ties to New Right and Christian conservatives—those strategists who designed the "culture war" approach to politics that would come to characterize the Reagan era and beyond—it is no small thing that a conflict so complicated and nuanced as the Kanawha County textbook controversy was portrayed in such a dualistic way so that West Virginia protesters were represented either as the violent, uncivilized Other or as the courageous resister fighting against unbridled corruption.

Alice Moore, Elmer Fike, Avis Hill, and others were not culturally isolated, antimodern traditionalists clinging to the past. Rather, they signaled the rise of various kinds of conservatism and right-wing action. Whether or not we agree politically with their protest more than thirty years ago, we have the opportunity now to provide a more nuanced analysis that acknowledges how protesters were, in fact, taking on new roles and expressing innovative and sophisticated rationales with which subsequent groups of alienated parents, Christian fundamentalists, and white supremacists would make new demands and wage new battles for years to come.

FIGURE 7. At a February 15, 1975, Witcher Creek cross-burning in support of the local textbook protest, Klansmen gave Nazi salutes, indicating an emerging right-wing alliance. *West Virginia Human Rights Commission Newsletter*, August 1975.

CHAPTER TWO

True Sons of Appalachia

The Kanawha County textbook controversy, like other curriculum disputes that preceded and followed it, was an opportunity for people to articulate their individual and collective position in relation to national identity. As education historians Jonathan Zimmerman and Joseph Moreau have shown in their histories of U.S. curriculum disputes, protesters of textbooks throughout the nineteenth and twentieth centuries often deployed populist demands for inclusion in or control over "the national story," that is, in the narrative of how America developed as a nation, as variously delineated in textbooks.[1] Some protesters in Kanawha County were saying what was said decades before and would be repeated in textbook battles for years to come: experts were treading on the rights of parents to control education according to local customs and conventions. In this way, the Kanawha County textbook controversy was hardly unique in its deployment of populist statements about elitists conspiring to exclude them from deciding local education policy. But some essays, such as those published by local print shop owner George Dietz, stated their position on the textbooks on the basis not only of conspiracist fears but also of an essential white identity.

As Dietz's *Liberty Bell* magazine showed, the Kanawha County textbook controversy was unlike other curriculum disputes because it involved discussions that explicitly forged identities in relation not only to nation but to region and race as well, often conflating the three. "A Message to All True Sons of Appalachia" was one of those discussions that argued that White Anglo-Saxon Protestants in particular were under attack, an explicitly racialized argument that went beyond the conspiracist populism that characterizes so many other curriculum disputes. In addition to the "All

True Sons" essay, *The Liberty Bell* published others, offering readers an unusual mix of populist and explicitly racialist commentaries on the textbook controversy.

George Dietz's magazine was, therefore, important even in its relative obscurity because it showcased in one forum competing voices from the Right, namely those from the anticommunist John Birch Society, which was losing membership and influence, and those from a more revolutionary and ultraright faction, which would grow stronger. With Dietz's help throughout the 1970s and 1980s, racialist discourse gained influence as part of a global resurgence in white supremacist organizing. The Kanawha County textbook controversy was a turning point for Dietz because it marked his relinquishing the John Birch Society's anticommunist rhetoric and his promotion of an explicit anti-Semitic discourse instead. Like members of the Ku Klux Klan who operated in the Kanawha Valley during the textbook controversy, Dietz emerged from the conflict publicly espousing the Jew as the enemy. In this chapter I examine three agitators on the ultraright—Ed Miller, George Dietz, and William Pierce—who saw the textbook controversy in Kanawha County as an opportunity to recruit and build hope for a white nation resisting supposed Jewish control.

In focusing this chapter on what anyone would have to agree were fringe operators during the textbook protests, I do not mean to suggest that these white supremacists were the true instigators or the real ideologues generating the conflict, the behind-the-scenes masterminds who orchestrated the entire ordeal. They are not representative of the majority of the protesters. Their overt, virulent racism did not reflect the general climate of the Kanawha Valley, where multiracial alliances thrived during the 1970s and earlier.

The prominent slave economy of the antebellum Kanawha salt industry notwithstanding,[2] the history of labor relations in West Virginia is full of examples of how workers of various ethnicities and races worked together to secure rights and fair wages. Especially in the mining business, according to sociologist Dwight Billings, "racist rhetoric on the part of coal operators did not deter white miners from uniting with black workers in their common struggle to build a union movement in those sections of Appalachia (especially southern West Virginia) where significant numbers of black miners were imported as 'scab' laborers."[3] At the beginning of industrialized coal, "blacks and whites entered in the industry on more or less equal footing in Appalachia, and neither group questioned the other's right to make a living in the mines."[4] But after World War I "Afro-Americans found it increasingly difficult to retain the small foothold they had acquired in supervisory and skilled positions" with southern West Virginia coal companies.[5] The local history of labor relations in Charleston around the time of the textbook controversy follows suit. Despite the lingering institutional stratification that perpetuated inequalities in housing, medical care, and other social conditions for people of color,[6] an alliance of black and white sanitation workers executed a successful citywide strike just before the curriculum dispute.[7] So it is inaccurate to conclude or suggest that the overtly hateful, blatantly racist, and even revolutionary politics of Miller, Dietz, and Pierce were widely representative of the citizens of Campbells Creek, Charleston, Kanawha County, or West Virginia.

But this does not mean that the avowed white supremacists involved in the textbook controversy were totally negligible or merely incidental. Why look at what a bunch of fringe "extremists" said about the textbook controversy and beyond it? There are several reasons. They provide a useful contrast. With so many accusations about racists and militant revolutionaries flying around the Kanawha Valley at the time, examining the writings and actions of self-identified white supremacists draws a bright line between those with intentionally bigoted, truly revolutionary motivations and the bulk of the protesters or defenders of the books. In addition to looking at these white supremacists for a significant contrast, we can also examine them as a useful context in which to think through a couple of interesting questions about what was happening during the textbook controversy and as a result of it.

First, a question that may appeal to the historian of political ideology or social movements: How was organized white supremacism affected by the conflict in Kanawha County? At this point in history, the Ku Klux Klan had long lost its middle-class base, which had made it popular in the 1910s and 1920s, and neo-Nazis were still regrouping after the 1967 shooting of American Nazi Party founder George Lincoln Rockwell. The textbook controversy brought together neo-Nazis and Klansmen. At this point in history, such an alliance was unusual because Klansmen considered themselves staunchly American and Christian.[8] They were therefore reluctant to buddy up with neo-Nazis, who championed Germany's Adolf Hitler, America's enemy in World War II, and were not particularly devoted to Jesus Christ, also known as Jesus of Nazareth, a Jew. The white supremacists who were involved in and wrote about the 1974 textbook controversy were shaping a resurgence in white supremacist organizing nationwide. Miller's story illustrates how the Ku Klux Klan in the early 1970s was fragmented but eventually overcame its factionalism in a so-called nazification of its ideology, image, and tactics. Dietz's story similarly emphasizes the move away from segregation and red-baiting and toward anti-Semitism that came to characterize a well-connected Aryan Nations. And Pierce's story offers a parallel to Dietz's, in that he dropped his alliance with prosegregation politician George Wallace for the same reason and around the same time that Dietz renounced his John Birch Society affiliation. In the summer of 1975, at the close of the textbook controversy in Kanawha County, both Dietz and Pierce rededicated their respective publications and organizations to values that most accurately can be described as National Socialist if not Nazi.

Second, examining these white supremacists helps explore the question of how the textbook controversy perpetuated "Appalachia" as a signifier of not just whiteness but white superiority. As Miller, Dietz, and Pierce opposed the textbooks, they not only appealed to an existing Appalachian heritage but also re-created it in white supremacist terms. In effect, they sought to reconstruct Appalachians' identities via cultural narratives that were explicitly deployed to politicize subjects. In the cases of Dietz and Pierce, their publications and organizations not only turned to more explicitly anti-Semitic discourse but also shared a move from critiquing media and literature to creating media and literature. On one hand, Dietz and Pierce shared with the bulk of protesters the idea that the adoption of the books was an affront to local control of education, as well as the widely articulated idea that the language arts curriculum itself was a means of indoctrination or brainwashing. On the other hand, Dietz and Pierce apparently disagreed with the various leaders of the protests—Alice Moore, Marvin Horan, Avis Hill, Elmer Fike, and others—as to who it was that was attempting to indoctrinate and brainwash "our children" with the new books. Moreover, while evangelical protesters decided that the proper responses to the new curriculum were, variously, to open Christian schools, boycott the public schools, or dynamite them closed, Pierce and Dietz focused on making available alternative texts and media both during and after the controversy. It is not surprising that many of these texts employed the tropes of nineteenth-century racism as well as the tropes of Appalachia that were forged in the same historical moment. Adapting these tropes for the latter part of the twentieth century, Dietz and Pierce deployed "Appalachia" anew and formulated a particular sense of white supremacy that would influence hundreds of thousands.

Miller, who did not become a recognized leader among the ultraright but worked with the most notorious Klansmen of his time, was like so many other book protesters in the single, important regard that he was asking the same questions about who were or should be the "true" spokespersons for residents of Kanawha County—what constituted "us" as West Virginians, Appalachians, and Americans.

Not Born-Again Christian

For those who would like to see the textbook controversy as a matter of entrenched fundamentalism and racism that is supposedly endemic to the hills of West Virginia, the Klansmen who protested the books appeared to be case in point. According to one political cartoon published in the Charleston *Gazette*, they were degenerate racists emerging from the sewer to support the antimodern ideas of their supposedly puritanical counterparts (see figure 2). But just as the evangelicals involved in the protests were not merely throwbacks to yesteryear's religious fundamentalism, the Klansmen who protested the textbooks were striving for a contemporary formulation of their white supremacism. In particular, they sought to distinguish themselves from the evangelical protesters to get away from the antimodern, Bible-thumping label. The story of Ed Miller and his mentors illustrates how Klansmen at the time were struggling to cohere, to create a unifying story of white identity in contradistinction to born-again Christians and in the aftermath of civil rights victories that ended the fight to maintain racial segregation. The Klan's public involvement in the Kanawha County textbook controversy began in the last months of 1974, gained a lot of press in the spring of 1975, and fizzled out, like the rest of the textbook protests, during the fall of 1975. Ed Miller's journey through these months provides a good primer of key players and organizations in Klan history of the time.

In November 1974 Ed Miller, a forty-one-year-old Charlestonian and former coal miner with a square jaw, high cheekbones, and trim body, founded an anti-textbook group called the Non-Christian American Parents, noting that they believe in God but are not "born again."[9] Miller then disbanded the group and gained bigger media attention by becoming the area organizer, or kleagle, of the National Knights of the Ku Klux Klan.[10] Although plans to revitalize a West Virginia Klan were promoted as early as 1946 by none other than U.S. Senator Robert C. Byrd, who later denounced his Klan affiliation as a matter of misguided youthfulness, in 1974 there was no organized Klan in operation in the state. So Miller's new title was bestowed upon him by Dale Reusch, the grand dragon—or state leader—of the Ohio Ku Klux Klan. To some, Reusch was a Jackie Gleason/ Ralph Cramden look-alike with his protruding belly, fleshy face, and hefty six-foot-plus frame.[11] In December 1974 kleagle Miller accompanied grand dragon Reusch to Huntington, West Virginia, about an hour west of Charleston, where radio station WGNT interviewed the men about the textbooks.

The chain of Klan command at the time meant that Reusch had been appointed grand dragon by James Venable, a seventy-year-old lawyer and imperial wizard of the National Knights of the Ku Klux Klan based in Stone Mountain, Georgia. In December 1974 or January 1975 Kanawha County's new kleagle, Ed Miller, traveled to Stone Mountain to meet Venable, who agreed to speak at an anti-textbook rally on the West Virginia capitol steps on January 18, 1975. Among umbrellas and American and Confederate flags, pointy-hooded Klansmen made inflammatory speeches, pleas to support Marvin Horan—the protest leader indicted of conspiracy to bomb schools—and invitations to join the Klan in the winter drizzle.[12] In the days following this spectacle, Grand Dragon Reusch dominated the news as the Klansman in charge in Kanawha County.

Reusch announced three initiatives: an investigation that he hoped would lead to a vote by the people about the textbooks, the opening of an office designed to provide legal services to protesters, and a cross-burning ceremony at Witcher Creek, about fifteen miles from Charleston and approximately five miles from Marvin Horan's anti-textbook headquarters and the site of the bomb making in Campbells Creek. Ed Miller also promoted the impending cross-burning with the excitement of a fresh convert brimming with newfound knowledge and a link to the past: "There at the mouth of the [Witcher Creek] hollow, where the backwater is, there used to be an open field and years ago, as many as 3,500 or 4,000 klansmen used to meet there. Come rain, shine, snow or what, all good Americans will show up. It'll be a regular Klan meeting. Jesus said the cross is the light of the world and we'll light the cross up."[13] On February 15, they did just that. About a month later, however, the glory that Miller and his new mentor, Reusch, shared in the blaze of that cross became overshadowed by infighting.

What exactly transpired that led Reusch to denounce Miller and strip him of his kleaglehood in March 1975 is difficult to determine. A significant disagreement occurred during a Saturday meeting, a few days after which Miller's car was shot with bullets while parked near his home. Miller immediately made another trip to Stone Mountain, returning with news that he was now the king kleagle of the West Virginia Klan because the imperial board of the National Knights of the Ku Klux Klan said so. This pronouncement was countered by Reusch, who said he, too, had been the target of a drive-by shooting and that probably there was a federal agent infiltrator attempting a divide-and-conquer tactic. Nevertheless, Reusch was steadfast in his accusation that it was Miller who had been creating dissention among fellow Klansmen. To resolve the dispute, Reusch invited five grand dragons from surrounding states to try Miller at the end of the month. On March 29, 1975, another cross-burning ceremony at Witcher Creek featured a tribunal that ultimately upheld Reusch's authority and ousted Miller.

A few months later, those same grand dragons banded together to separate from Venable's National Knights of the Ku Klux Klan and become a new group called the Invisible Empire, Knights of the Ku Klux Klan; Reusch was named their new imperial wizard.[14] The fuming, grandfatherly James Venable from Stone Mountain remained imperial wizard of the National Knights of the Ku Klux Klan, and it is anybody's guess whether the split with his state leaders, those five grand dragons, was initiated by him or by them. The younger dragons suggested Venable was becoming senile, and Venable countered that he had banished them for "runnin' over states creatin' trouble and getting' in undesirable members, takin' in anybody who had fifteen dollars."[15] Venable was not the only Klansman who considered Reusch a lousy representative of the Klan.

By April a third major Klan organization came to Kanawha County to investigate bad publicity generated by Reusch's involvement in the textbook controversy. It was the United Klans of America, whose invisible wizard was Robert Shelton. Shelton denounced Reusch and took the rejected Charlestonian, Ed Miller, under his wing. A professional Klansman, Shelton was a good twenty years younger than Venable and about ten years older—and far more seasoned—than Reusch. Powerful enough in political circles to help "put John Patterson in the Alabama governor's mansion in 1958, a feat he repeated four years later" for the segregationist George Wallace, Shelton had no kind words for Reusch, whose aspirations included a bid for U.S. presidency as well as imperial wizard of the Klan.[16] Shelton sneered, "I wouldn't vote for him for dogcatcher."[17] Shortly after Shelton arrived in Kanawha County, Reusch was arrested for possession of fireworks and a single stick of dynamite, which Reusch claimed was planted in the trunk of his car. This did not stop him from organizing another Witcher Creek rally in late May to raise funds again for Marvin Horan's legal fees, or from attempting twice in August 1975 to diversify the protest to include busing and abortion with events that drew fewer than two hundred people each.

These flailing efforts were no more effective than those of Ed Miller, who attempted his own protests throughout the fall of 1975. In September 1975, Miller appeared with four other robed men as members of United Klans of America to protest the board of education on the lawn of its Elizabeth Street office the morning after a cross had been found burning there.[18] In December Miller filed a dubious complaint with Charleston police about a "children's sex education" book on display in the downtown Diamond Department Store.[19] Less contrived was his heartfelt letter to the *Charleston Gazette* editor, a swan song intending to "let the public know a few of my opinions about some of the past."[20] Clearly situating his textbook protest activities as part of the recent past, Miller's letter praised Marvin Horan, the man convicted of conspiracy to bomb, for having "more religious love for me than" other preachers involved in the protests. By the time his letter was published in January 1976, the textbook controversy was over and the showy activity of various factions of the Ku Klux Klan was sputtering out as well.

Miller's interactions first with Reusch, then Venable, and finally Shelton speak to the kind of infighting among Klansmen that was characteristic of the Klan nationwide at that time. In addition, Miller's story attests to a generational shift that was occurring not only in leadership but also in ideology. Interviews with Miller's mentors reveal how each man, representative of three different generations of Klansmen, was dealing with the so-called Jewish question that was becoming so prominent in the wake of the civil rights movement. A revival of anti-Semitic conspiracism was sweeping right-wing America in the 1970s, and Miller's mentors lent insight into how the Klan was moving away from scapegoating blacks and toward scapegoating Jews.

For all his virulently racist ideas of blacks as mentally inferior and predatorily hypersexual, grand dragon Dale Reusch was convinced that Jews were the ones who were secretly in power. An exchange recorded by journalist Patsy Sims during a spring 1976 visit to Charleston, when Reusch had abandoned hope for the presidency and filed for West Virginia's vice presidential primary, comically demonstrates how adamant his feelings were about Jews. In a hotel room late at night after a cross-burning rally, Reusch and Toronto grand dragon Jack Prins educated Sims about how even President Lyndon B. Johnson had been subject to Jewish rule. According to Reusch, Johnson "triggered the House UnAmerican Activities Committee investigation of the klan in the sixties."

"Yeah, he started the investigation," Reusch said, and then leaned over to confide: "His wife is Jewish."

The word "Jew" excited Prins. "Lady Bird is translated 'Fogle,' and 'Fogle' is a real Jewish name."

"I didn't know 'Fogle' was her name," I said.

"'Lady Bird,'" Prins corrected me.

"But 'Lady Bird' is only a nickname."

Prins was adamant, his Dutch accent growing heavier. "'Lady Bird' was reeeally 'Fogle.' I don't know where we got the information she was Jewish. . . ."

Reusch came to his rescue. "National States Rights Party. They exposed it. An' Eisenhower, they call him the *Swedish* Jew. Not a German Jew. *Swedish* Jew.

"That's worse," Prins moaned. "They gave me the name, the way he changed his name." He strained but couldn't remember.

The two men became engrossed in a game of one-upmanship. "Roosevelt was a Jew," Reusch said. "It was *Rosenfelt!*" To which Prins added, "Yes, and his wife was a member of about thirty Communist front parties."

"They're the ones that allowed the Communists in the Pentagon," Reusch said. "Dexter White, Alger Hiss . . ."

Prins interrupted, "Dexter White, his name is 'Weiss.' He's a Jew."

"All Jews!" Reusch exclaimed.

"All changed their names!" Prins railed.

Reusch slouched back in his chair and echoed the scratchy recording played at the rally. "We're not anti-Jew, we're pro-Christian." And then he unwound the klan's version of racial evolution: "The Jews own the nigger. The nigger is the tool that destroys the society that we live in. So who owns the nigger but the Jew."[21]

Although Sims's account suggests the men are ridiculous to consider Lady Bird Johnson and Roosevelt to be secret Jews, these ideas were not only circulated by, according to Reusch, the National States Rights Party during the 1970s; they are derived from early twentieth-century right-wing writers whose work clearly had a lasting effect.

It was, for example, Nesta H. Webster who, according to scholars Chip Berlet and Matthew Lyons, "synthesized conspiracy theories concerning Jewish elites and the Illuminati Freemasons in *World Revolution: The Plot against Civilization* (1921) and *Secret Societies and Subversive Movements* (1924). While much of her work stressed non-Jewish elites, anti-Semitic stereotyping runs throughout it. Webster helped write the original *London Morning Post* series that introduced *The Protocols of the Elders of Zion*," the famous bogus blueprint of how Jews purportedly intended to conquer the world, "to a wide British audience. In the 1930s and early 1940s Elizabeth Dilling and many other rightists applied many of Nesta Webster's themes to Roosevelt and the New Deal, portraying communism as Jewish and Roosevelt as an agent of the conspiracy, or, in some versions, as a secret Jew himself."[22] Although conspiracies about Jews thus persisted throughout the twentieth century and Klansmen targeted Jews long before the night that Prins and Reusch rattled on to Patsy Sims, the post-World War II rendition of such conspiracies was changing the Klan.

Robert Shelton said as much in his interview with Sims. "I'm more understandin' now about the various conspiracies," Shelton told the journalist. "In the beginnin', the basic issue was the separation of the two races, black and white. Now that's just a mere knot on the wall compared to the many problems we're confronted with."[23] He proceeded to joke about Jews with Sims. Elsewhere Shelton is quoted as saying, "I don't hate niggers. But I hate the Jews. The nigger's a child, but the Jews are dangerous people. . . . All they want is control and domination of the Gentiles through a conspiracy with the niggers."[24] Nevertheless, Shelton's age and experience kept him from a Hitlerian stance. In fact, he admonished David Duke, the young, handsome new Klansman from Louisiana who gained so much attention in the early 1970s, for being affiliated with the American Nazi Party: "His entire movement is nothin' in the world but the National Socialist White People's Party, or the Nazi Party."[25] So even though Shelton was partial to believing the conspiracy theories about Jews, he was not inclined toward neo-Nazism. No doubt his experience in the "air force during the last half of the forties" kept him from embracing that brand of racist anti-Semitism.[26] "Of course," he explained a distinction, "I do think of myself as a racist. . . . But they have smeared the word 'racist' to associate it with somethin' like the Gestapo or Hitlerism or Nazism."[27]

The elderly James Venable also applied a historical perspective to describe how the Klan's battles in the 1970s were being perceived differently from those of bygone times. "The klan of eighteen hundred and sixty-six had only about three things they could fight: the carpetbaggers, the scalawags, and the nigger element. 'Course, we had Catholics. They've always been against us. But they were minor things. The klan of nineteen hundred and fifteen, we had many, many things to fight, but we got a thousand now today to fight, where they only had a hundred." Immediately, then, Venable turned to Jews. "The redness of his nose and cheeks spread as he lambasted the Jewish control of the banks and news media, the ADL (Anti-Defamation League) and kosherized food."[28]

All three generations of leaders were witness to the shift in Klan focus and belief that the "international Jew" was, even more than blacks or communism, the white man's enemy. Under their tutelage, Charlestonian Ed Miller struggled to revive Klan membership in West Virginia and to determine its ideological and tactical priorities. So Klan activity in West Virginia during the textbook controversy was representative of the Klan nationwide. Throughout the country, Klan groups collectively had not yet determined whether they were a political organization, a vigilante force, or a Christian, antigovernment paramilitary group. According to the FBI, Klan membership was at an all-time low of about fifteen hundred nationwide in 1974.[29]

By the end of the decade, however, Klan groups were revived with a new look and a new purpose; it was the so-called fifth-era Klan. In 1979 a massacre of demonstrators protesting the Klan in Greensboro, North Carolina, reflected the resurgence of Klan vigilantism and its new articulation as a Christian Patriot group dressed in fatigues and street clothes rather than white-hooded regalia. Also in 1979, groups of Klansmen joined other white supremacists, including neo-Nazis, gathering as the Aryan Nations. An especially influential 1992 speech about "leaderless resistance" resulted in a paramilitarized Klan that believed the real enemy of the white race was not blacks but Jews. This switch to seeing a Jewish conspiracy as the gravest danger to white supremacy is known as the "nazification of the klan."[30] Rather than focusing on blacks or Catholics as well as immigrants and Jews, which they saw as enemies in the late nineteenth century and early half of the twentieth century, the Ku Klux Klan began to focus on the Jews' supposed clandestine control of U.S. federal forces, what became known in the 1970s as the Zionist Occupied Government, or ZOG. This "fifth-era Klan" was not your great-grandfather's KKK.

Or, as the man who first constructed Klan history into five different eras explained to Charleston *Gazette* readers during the textbook controversy, they should recognize the "Klan Changing" its approach, ideology, and impact.[31] Robert E. Miles, former grand dragon of the Michigan Ku Klux Klan and future host of Aryan Nations meetings on his Cohoctah, Michigan, farm, wrote to the editor of the *Gazette* in April 1975 while he was serving the third year of a nine-year sentence for "his role in planning the bombing of empty school buses that were to be used in a busing program in Pontiac [Michigan] during 1971. He was also convicted of an attack on a Willow Run, Michigan school principal, who was tarred and feathered."[32] The Kanawha County textbook controversy garnered his attention. From his cell in Marion Federal Prison in Illinois, Miles wrote to explain to Charleston *Gazette* readers that "central government was really the foe all along, not blacks, who are tools and excuses for greater grabs at power by governmentalists."[33] While grateful "for all the fantastic and free publicity" generated by the press's attention to Klan involvement in the textbook controversy, Miles chastised the *Gazette* editor for reducing the Klan's recent efforts to a cover-up of old racist ways. "Camouflage, editor, or a new look? Does only the left change and the center but never the klan? Or is it that the shadows on the wall have reality and promise of fulfillment that makes it so odious to you? Is it that their hour of power is what you see and hear in the night winds about you?" Hokey in its spooky poeticism, Miles's message was nevertheless accurate in reporting a revitalization of the ultraright in which Klansmen such as Ed Miller adopted more paramilitary tactics and an anti-Semitic ideology that would allow for larger alliances among different factions of white supremacists and the militia movement of the 1980s and 1990s.

Prefiguring such larger alliances, Klan activity during the textbook controversy certainly demonstrated a significant commingling if not full-scale collaboration of the Klan and neo-Nazis. The evidence most strikingly available is the photograph of the February 15, 1975, rally at Witcher Creek (see figure 7). In addition to the burning cross, a classic symbol from the earliest days of the Klan, several Nazi-style salutes of one upraised, angled hand are clearly evident. The United Mine Workers of America was wary of this nazified Klan activity in and around Kanawha County, claiming that the organization was anti-American for its flirtation with the fascism in the 1930s. The union supported anti-Klan rallies in Harlan, Kentucky, and Charleston, West Virginia, scheduled for the fall of 1975.[34] But time dulled the historical memory of World War II in young minds, and neo-Nazi propaganda machines in West Virginia began unapologetically to distribute their literature worldwide. For newly invigorated white supremacist organizations and individuals emerging in the mid-1970s, scapegoating Jews became the way to answer hard questions about government corruption, both real and imagined.

Understanding the Klan's involvement in the textbook controversy as an important precursor to the national nazification of the Klan brings us to a much overlooked, internationally influential immigrant from Germany. George P. Dietz (1928–2007) arrived in the United States at the age of twenty-nine in 1957, became an American citizen in 1962 while living in New Jersey, then relocated in 1971 to Roane County, West Virginia (adjacent to Kanawha County), where he worked as a real estate broker, chaired the pro–George Wallace "American Party in West Virginia," and set up a print shop.[35] Sympathetic to the anti-textbook cause, George Dietz sought, like Ed Miller, to organize in terms other than Christian fundamentalism. He lampooned the idea of born again Christianity by printing "I have been born again!" around a swastika on self-adhesive stickers, thereby suggesting a rebirth on a grander scale of societal proportions, instead of on the level of mere individuals claiming their new life in Christ.[36] Like Ed Miller's story, George Dietz's trajectory shows how the ultraright considered the textbook controversy not just as a means of community control—not a matter of reactionary defense against a tyrannical bogeyman—but as a means of articulating anew whose claim to local authenticity, hence authority, was viable, drawing boundaries around what it meant to be a "true" Appalachian and a "true" American.

From American Opinion to White Power

Dietz operated an American Opinion bookstore, a clearinghouse for John Birch Society material, in Reedy, West Virginia, about an hour away from Charleston. In addition to stocking publications from John Birch Society headquarters in Belmont, Massachusetts, Dietz published his own magazine, *The Liberty Bell*. His "photo offset printing" business, Raybar, Inc., also produced a steady stream of advertisements and flyers (more than two hundred thousand by one estimate) that protesters of the textbooks used early in the controversy to garner mass opposition to the school board.[37] The leafleting campaign extended throughout the summer of 1974. By the beginning of the fall school season, preachers such as Marvin Horan, Avis Hill, Charles Quigley, and Ezra Graley, who submitted appeals to readers

in a November 1974 issue of the *Liberty Bell*, were armed with inflammatory information printed by Dietz.

The *Liberty Bell* showcased stock arguments from the John Birch Society
regarding the general failure of American education, attributing it to a
communist conspiracy to turn children against parents and society by
indoctrinating them with militant multiracial literature, situational ethics,
and psychological conditioning. These accusations fed a class-based, populist sentiment that the school board was tyrannically institutionalizing a
curriculum without parental approval. Therefore, while thousands of parents rallied against what they saw as lack of representation and input, those
who were also *Liberty Bell* readers were privy to the inside information
that, purportedly, the motivation behind the "tyranny" was "to convert
the great American republic into a helpless branch of their One World-
Socialist society."[38] Essays and commentary linked the local textbook
controversy to a supposed national crisis of education, repeating themes
about impending policies that would give "learning technicians" the go-
ahead to drug students and psychologically manipulate them into acts of
depravity and anarchy.[39] To learn more, *Liberty Bell* readers could buy John
Birch Society literature with titles such as *Forced Bussing: Government
Control of Our Children*, *New Education: The Radicals Are After Your
Children*, *Public Schools: They're Destroying Our Children*, and *The NEA:
Dictatorship of the Educariat*.[40] These booklets and other publications
(books such as *Toward Soviet America*, *The Child Seducers*, *The Romance of
Education*, and a special "Parents Save Your Children" packet) were avail-
able at George Dietz's American Opinion Bookstore on Main Street in
Reedy. Or, with postage paid, Dietz would send the materials.[41]

Another theme in *Liberty Bell* essays regarding the textbook controversy
was to discredit the "look-say" and "whole language" methods of reading
instruction and to champion the phonetic approach instead. In "The Great
Reading Ripoff," *Liberty Bell* readers learned that the latter method is
especially well suited to the study of the English language because "more
than 80% of the words can be read strictly by the sounds of the letters
(phonetics), and even in the exceptions (through, enough, etc.) part of the
words are [sic] phonetic. The exceptions require extra exertion for the
student of English. It is nothing compared to what is required from the
student of Chinese, in which each symbol is unique" because, according to
the *Liberty Bell*, they are visual representations, not based on sounds.
Instead of phonetics, now the "primary aim is to have the children learn
by sight a number of selected words, before the children have learned the

letters and the sounds."[42] The result of emphasizing visual learning in the "look-say" method and combining it with phonetics is "an ever increasing army of illiterates." The "two methods, as unlike as oil and water, are mixed into an illogical system which makes the learning of English more difficult than Chinese."[43] Thus the *Liberty Bell* alerted its readers that the "education establishment" in the United States is deemphasizing phonetics as a "cover-up" to create an "army of illiterates" who will do their bidding just as, it is implied, those godless commie kids did in Red China.

As with the education dictatorship rhetoric, this anti-"look-say" line of argument did not originate with parents who protested the particular books adopted for Kanawha County. In addition to repeating a critique published by the John Birch Society in 1972, it parroted the already established critiques forged by Max Rafferty (*What They Are Doing to Your Children*, 1964), Rudolph Flesh (*Why Johnny Can't Read*, 1955), Samuel Blumenfeld (*The New Illiterates*), and their anticommunist followers.[44]

For locals looking for a quick cure for this "look-say" ill, the *Liberty Bell* suggested buying *McGuffey's Readers*. Ironically, however, the nineteenth-century *McGuffey's Readers* advocated a dual method of reading instruction that presented what protesters saw as an "oil and water" combination. It incorporated learning words both by sound and by sight. For example, in its "suggestions to teachers" preceding the preface to *McGuffey's First Eclectic Reader*, revised edition and copyrighted 1879, the book was recommended for "teaching reading by any of the methods in common use; but it is especially adapted to the Phonic Method, the Word Method, or a combination of the two." The Phonic Method is described as teaching the sounds of each letter, letter by letter, before learning whole words. The Word Method is described as teaching "the pupil to identify at sight the words placed at the head of the reading exercises, and to read these exercises without hesitation." Finally, the suggestions to teachers advocate they use "word method and phonic method combined" "by first teaching the words in each lesson *as words*; then, the elementary sounds, the names of the letters, and spelling."[45] Hardly an "illogical system," what the *Liberty Bell* was sure was a nefarious innovation of communist teachers was essentially right there in the *McGuffey's Readers* since at least 1879. That, of course, did not stop George Dietz from advertising the books for sale to individuals, families, or the alternative Christian schools that were opening in response to the textbook controversy.

One essay, which did not appear to have a tie-in to materials for sale at Dietz's bookstore, stood out as not only defiant in the face of supposed modern conspiracies to thwart America but also vibrantly proud of the white, Christian, Appalachian heritage that supposedly created America. "A Message to All True Sons of Appalachia" attacked the pro-textbook clergy as persecutors of the "blood line of the children of Appalachia, the sons and daughters of the 'Covenanteers' of the Highlands of Scotland. . . , disparaged by our enemies as WASPS (White Anglo-Saxon Protestants)."[46] The piece uniquely discussed the textbook controversy in terms that are not regurgitated Birch conspiracies but, instead, laid out a whole history of battling against "tyrants," creating a coherent narrative that begins with the "godly Germans" and "our Scotch-Irish fathers" being "persecuted and harassed" because they have throughout history refused to worship any other God but Christ.[47]

Providing a timeline of historical examples of those who have withstood "persecutions for righteousness sake," the essay was framed by references to Richard Cameron of Scottish lore, who in the 1680s resisted persecution only to be killed and mutilated as an incentive for his jailed father to recant his faith, which he refused to do. Tracing a history from that moment of defiance for Christ to revolutionary America, including Samuel Doak's religious rally at Sycamore Shoals in Tennessee and the mountaineers' assault on British commander Patrick Ferguson at King's Mountain, South Carolina, in 1780, "A Message to all True Sons of Appalachia" situates the Kanawha County protesters as the last in a long Scots-Irish and German line of "glorious people that suffered for the cause of Christ." Defeating Lord George "Cornwallis' man Ferguson" in 1780 and refusing to "swear allegiance to King George" were responses to "the same threat, to a lesser degree for the present, made by the same powers of darkness against the parents of school children in West Virginia!"[48]

The clincher in this argument was the fact that the pro-textbook preacher under consideration, James Lewis, was an Episcopal priest who came to Charleston in the summer of 1974, just before the textbook controversy heated up in the fall. Not only should "we as the sons of the hills resent" Lewis because of his outsider status, but he was affiliated with a church that, according to "A Message to All True Sons," was responsible for mountaineers being cheated out of their land. It was the Episcopal Church that enforced the 1792 Virginia legislation designed to "rob the children of God" by allowing surveyors to buy the "virgin and valuable hills of south western Virginia, including what is now south western West Virginia and Eastern Kentucky, under which lies untold and immeasurable riches in coal and other minerals as well as its virgin timber." The trick was

that potential buyers had to have an official survey, which required certifi-
cation by authorities at "William & Mary College—an Episcopal
institution." Consequentially, these "Scotch-Irish, Germanic children" of
God were robbed of the "new and free land" that God had given them
because of their "unwavering faith" in Christ:[49]

> No authorized surveyor would waste his time making surveys for the
> pittances available from our Scotch-Irish and German fathers who had
> suffered to gain the land, but their services were completely at the
> disposal of Anti-Christ vultures who then hogged the land in blocks of
> six figures and more. Even such patriots as Daniel Boone and Simon
> Kenton were cheated out of their lands. Now the children of Appalachia
> are forced to dig coal for out of state corporate landlords from under
> land which was literally stolen—all legally and lawfully, you see—from
> their fathers in the first place. By and through the present satanic, Anti-
> Christ banking system our lands have been stolen, our freedom is all
> but gone, and now satanic vultures are attempting to steal the souls of
> our children by corrupting them in our public, government-financed and
> controlled schools.[50]

As in the more common John Birch Society explanations for the textbook
controversy, conspiracism is plenty evident here. For example, the charge
of a "satanic banking system" has a long history in right-wing anticommunism and, as evident in testimony by Ed Miller's Klansmen mentors, is
often associated with the so-called "international Jew." But aside from
such conspiracism, this essay is unique in its situating the conflict explicitly
in terms of region and ethnicity.

Given this view of the textbook controversy, readers of the *Liberty Bell*
could determine whom to trust and whom not to trust, based on their
authenticity as heirs to the "Scotch-Irish" or "Germanic" bloodline, what
constituted the "true sons of Appalachia." It was thus made clear that
someone such as the evangelical preacher Quigley was trustworthy because
"the fact that his name is Charles CAMERON Quigley tells from what
people he sprang." An Episcopal priest such as James Lewis was worthy of
nothing but disdain: "We don't want and don't need Lewis' of any color
around here!"[51] This particular racialization of the actors in the conflict
was a different articulation from John Birch Society rhetoric. Unlike the
John Birch Society, which, historically speaking, "helped to transform
earlier, more blatant, biological forms of ethnocentric White racism and

Christian nationalist antisemitism into less obvious cultural forms," the *Liberty Bell* promoted a racism based on biology, heredity, and blood.[52] "A Message to All True Sons of Appalachia" was infused with the biologically determinist idea that "blood will tell."[53]

And so the pages of the *Liberty Bell* indicated an interesting tension between at least two kinds of right-wing visions of the textbook controversy: one in which racial politics—be they school integration by busing or multiracial textbooks—were a matter of competing cultures; and one in which they were a matter of biological difference. It would not be long after the publication of "A Message to All True Sons" that Dietz would reveal the kind of right-wing politics to which he and *The Liberty Bell* were more devoted.

As the textbook controversy progressed and ultimately died down through the spring and summer of 1975, the *Liberty Bell* denounced Robert Welch, president of the John Birch Society, and relinquished its brand of anticommunism in favor of an overt, biologically based anti-Semitic politics. By August 1975, Dietz officially broke with the John Birch Society because, according to him, it did not share his view that Jews were the puppeteers of the communist threat. Reports from the John Birch Society president painted a different picture, suggesting that the organization had thrown Dietz out for his "un-American" views—reports that Dietz called "reverberations of a belch by Robert Welch."[54] Ever the businessman, Dietz wrote a letter to John Birch Society headquarters in Belmont, Massachusetts, requesting a refund of the remainder of the dues he paid for membership for himself, his wife, and his two children.[55] In response, the Society's director of field activities wrote back, making clear "that an American Opinion franchise no longer exists" in Reedy, that Society material was copyrighted, and that Dietz was no longer authorized to use the organization's name or profit from the reprinting and sale of its publications. Given the fact that Dietz had only joined the John Birch Society in May 1974, when the textbook controversy was just starting to heat up, the John Birch Society officials had cause to wonder whether profiteering was a motivation for his membership. It is unlikely that ideological consistency was the impetus. Born in Kassel, Germany, in 1928, Dietz was a member of the Hitler Youth during the Third Reich.[56] Archival materials offer little to suggest he ever wavered from his upbringing.

The aftermath of the textbook controversy saw George Dietz launch bolder Nazi programs locally, nationally, and internationally. "I met you at the Charleston Textbook Rally in November 1974," a correspondent wrote to Dietz, who published the letter in his overtly neo-Nazi monthly periodical, *White Power Report*. "I have received your publications since then," the fan noted, signing off with "Heil Hitler!"[57] By 1977, Dietz was showing *Triumph of the Will*, Leni Riefenstahl's unforgettable and visually stunning, though morally repulsive, Nazi film to select audiences in Reedy.[58] In May 1977, Simon Wiesenthal announced that Dietz was linked to the "Patriotic Legal Fund" of Marietta, Georgia, which collected "money from some 80 neo-Nazi and neo-Fascist groups in the U.S. and Canada to help former Nazi butchers avoid detection and prosecution."[59] Dietz's publishing efforts now included printing "60 publications in five languages that are used in propaganda campaigns in the U.S., South America, Europe and South Africa," not to mention Germany, where Nazi literature had been outlawed.[60] In 1978, on the occasion of the death of his father, Heinreich Dietz, pictured in his Nazi uniform in an issue of *White Power Report*, George Dietz traveled to Germany.[61] At this point, the Anti-Defamation League of B'nai B'rith considered Dietz the world's leading producer of neo-Nazi materials.

In addition to periodicals, Dietz encouraged readers to build a personal library appropriate for "patriots." Liberty Bell Publications' mail order service included U.S. Army training manuals (including *Booby Traps*, *Chemistry of Powder and Explosives*, *Explosives and Demolitions*, and *Unconventional Warfare Devices*), writings by leading National Socialists and anti-Semites (including, of course, works by Adolf Hitler as well as by Henry Ford, Revilo P. Oliver, Francis Parker Yockey, and George Lincoln Rockwell), classics of Western white literature (works by Friedrich Nietzsche, Ezra Pound) and pantheistic legends (*Gods and Myths of Northern Europe*), and all manner of racist and anti-Semitic materials (such as *Proud to Be a Racist*, *The Hoax of the Twentieth Century*, and the classic hoax publication *Protocols of the Learned Elders of Zion*, in French as well as in English.) Historic speeches, German marches, and battle songs were available on cassette tapes. Dietz did not stop there; he moved on to a new medium.

Ten years after the *Liberty Bell* was first published, George Dietz reported to its subscribers that he had been "working, for the past two weeks, until 4–5 o'clock in the morning, trying to learn 'computerese' so that so that Yours Truly may talk to that monster in ITS language and on ITS terms."[62] One advantage to learning computer skills was security: "From now on, there will be in our offices no more written records, or any of the bulky address plates we have been using in the past, which are prone to 'inspection' by 'undesirables,' and everything will be safely stored on 'disposable' disks.'"[63] Another advantage was expanding communication among white supremacists, an upgrading perhaps of "The Liberty Net," a ham radio network that "as far back as the early '70s, before computer technology was developed," brought right-wing thinkers into conversation with one another three nights a week.[64] With computer skills mastered, Dietz initiated the first white supremacist electronic bulletin board system (or BBS), called Liberty Bell Network, on an Apple IIe, launching a new era of white supremacist organizing in cyberspace in 1983.[65] Not surprisingly, some of the first postings on the BBS were electronic versions of *Liberty Bell* articles.[66]

Shortly thereafter, Dietz "helped Louis Beam to establish the Aryan Liberty Network with computers in Texas, North Carolina, Illinois, Michigan and Idaho."[67] Known for his influential discussions of independent paramilitary cells and their capacity for "leaderless resistance," Beam no doubt saw computer communication networks as instrumental for the type of decentralized action he was promoting in response to government crackdowns on right-wing organizing.[68] Be that as it may, Dietz saw the new bulletin board system as a way to thwart the Jews. Reportedly, Dietz exclaimed with delight to his colleague, "Boy, are the Yids going to scream when they learn about this!"[69] A selling point for the early network was that it was the "only computer bulletin board system and uncontrolled information medium in the United States of America dedicated to the dissemination of historical facts—not fiction!"[70] Dietz was a firm believer that the media was controlled by the Jews, hence full of lies. Anti-Semitic propaganda to that effect was long established and could be found among protesters in Kanawha County.

For example, a two-sided tract asking "Who Rules America?" distributed at anti-textbook meetings claimed that "Jewish control of the American mass media is the single most important fact of life, not just in America, but in the whole world today. . . . Until this Jewish control of American public opinion is broken, continued misfortune, confusion, and decadence shall be our lot, and there can be no national liberation or regeneration." Although the exact same tract had been published by Dietz's *Liberty Bell* press, this particular tract was attributed to another white supremacist organization, the National Alliance. Identical in content and style except for the bottom of the page where readers were referred where to go for more information, the "Who Rules America?" tract demonstrates an ideological coherence between Dietz's publishing house and that of the

National Alliance, which was founded in 1974 by William Pierce. It is unclear who first wrote the tract, Dietz or Pierce. Certainly the two publishers shared materials as well as ideas. Actual collaboration among members of Dietz's and Pierce's groups is less a certainty. And Pierce's personal involvement or interest in the textbook controversy appears to have been marginal.

Nevertheless, Pierce's story is important. Like Dietz's, it provides an ideological and historical context for ultraright activities at the time of the textbook controversy. It also testifies to how John Birch Society-style complaints about multiracial books and the tyranny of the "educariat" coexisted with, and could be sharpened by, the more overtly racist and anti-Semitic views of Dietz and Pierce. Both men wanted to foment a white revolution, realized that creating—not simply critiquing—media was the first step in doing so, and chose West Virginia as the place to do it. These men saw Appalachia as a white haven and their work perpetuated that idea. According to writings by Dietz and Pierce, what was good about Appalachia—the presumed racial purity and cultural isolation of its people—was what all of America should be.

National Alliance, West Virginia

During the textbook controversy, William Pierce was living in Arlington, Virginia, having migrated from the West. With a PhD from the University of Colorado, he had taught physics at Oregon State University during the civil rights movement, which compelled him to ponder questions of race relations. This inquiry led to his giving up an academic career and joining George Lincoln Rockwell's American Nazi Party, which later became the National Socialist White People's Party and published the *National Socialist World*, for which Pierce served as editor. Now in the eastern United States, Pierce was hired by Liberty Lobby founder Willis Carto in 1970 and became leader of the National Youth Alliance, an organization founded as a means to garner collegiate support for Alabama governor and pro-segregationist presidential candidate George Wallace. By 1974, the year Alice Moore made her objections about the books in Kanawha County, Pierce had left the Liberty Lobby and dropped the "youth" from National Youth Alliance. The new National Alliance went into action by publishing *Attack! Revolutionary Voice of National Alliance*.[71] In a 1975 issue, Pierce compared "the busing riots in Boston" with the "textbook boycott in Kanawha County, West Virginia" in terms of resisting the

Jewish transformation of "America's educational system into an indoctrination system."[72]

As with Dietz's *Liberty Bell*, Pierce's *Attack!* took issue with the U.S. education system in ways that would appeal to right-wing thinkers such as the John Birch Society and the anticommunist followers of Max Rafferty. But Pierce's and Dietz's efforts were distinguished from John Birch Society materials in three important ways. First, unlike the John Birch Society, Pierce and Dietz emphasized the supposed Jewish control of the government—hence public schools—and the media. Second, they desired to create new media, including "educational" materials in various genres. Third, they desired revolution, which implicitly entailed violent insurrection. These differences from the John Birch Society were apparent in *Attack!* as much as in some *Liberty Bell* articles.

For example, a 1975 *Attack!* article titled "Gov't Pushes Porn in Sex-Ed Classes" began with a sentiment shared by Birch publications and, in fact, by Alice Moore, who said basically the same thing: "The Federal government, with funds channeled through the Department of Health, Education, and Welfare, is financing textbooks, films, and other educational materials for use in the nation's public schools which are designed to undermine traditional American values and beliefs."[73] But by the end of the article, readers of *Attack!* have learned that it was a Soviet Jew, Sol Gordon, who was authoring sex ed comics with a federal grant. "Despite his Scottish-sounding surname," *Attack!* warned readers, "Dr. Gordon's antecedents are in Grodno, U.S.S.R., rather than the British Isles."[74] Gordon was likewise singled out in a *Liberty Bell* comment on the Kanawha County textbook controversy: "I do know that one Jew, Sol Gordon, is the center of a storm of protest due to his filthy textbooks and lectures."[75] HEW may have been the "tyrannical" bureaucracy behind sex education, but Jews were behind HEW. Or at least that was what *Attack!*—as much as *Liberty Bell*—would have readers believe.

Attack! similarly addressed low test scores, which were presumed to show the destructiveness of a liberal "educational 'Establishment'" that "instinctively abhors all authority, structure, form, order, discipline."[76] But Pierce was not content with arguing that a basic "shifted emphasis" in American schools had occurred, attributing it to communists and liberals. He implied that such a shift was toward "race mixing," which was tantamount to "Education for Death" of the white race by Jewish design.[77] To offset this "race mixing" curriculum, *Attack!* promoted appropriate literature for the race with regular book reviews, and in January 1975 began publishing serially Pierce's own fiction, a fantastic chronicle of resistance against the Jews called *The Turner Diaries*.

The Turner Diaries attests to Pierce's dual intentions to create new fiction, rather than to simply protest literature such as the new language arts curriculum in Kanawha County, and to narrate his readers as white racialists who could accept if not produce a violent insurrection. In addition to providing Earl Turner's hopefully inspirational story of why and how to take arms against the Jewish-controlled government, early issues of *Attack!* included "instructions on the construction of bombs and Molotov cocktails, and advice about how to carry out the assassination of 'anti-White' politicians."[78] In effect, *Attack!* and *The Turner Diaries* were two key reasons why it has been said that "William Pierce doesn't build bombs. He builds bombers."[79] Most famously, Pierce's fiction inspired a young man to become a bomber in 1995. Timothy McVeigh's bombing of the Alfred P. Murrah Federal Building in Oklahoma City is widely regarded as being modeled after a truck bomb described in *The Turner Diaries*. Were men who detonated bombs at schools in Kanawha County likewise inspired by Pierce and his National Alliance staff and materials?

According to Jerry Dale, former sheriff of Pocahontas County and a law enforcement informant on National Alliance practices, Pierce had a strategy of saturating any place where dissent against the government appeared, flooding the area with publications and agitators in hopes of recruitment at least and insurrection if plausible. As an intellectual who prided himself on his intelligence and vision, Pierce was intent on influencing individuals and building elite cadres rather than a mass movement.[80] About a decade before Timothy McVeigh, his devotee was Robert Mathews, who, like McVeigh, modeled his actions after *The Turner Diaries*, creating a group called The Order that robbed banks, counterfeited millions of dollars, murdered an anti–right-wing talk show host, Alan Berg, and planned a massive assault on the power supplies of four major cities, which did not come to fruition as Mathews was killed in a showdown with federal agents. Given the fact that Pierce's most ubiquitous tract, *Who Rules America?*—which demanded that "Jewish control of the American mass media is the single most important fact of life"—was distributed in the Kanawha Valley, it is not far fetched to speculate that Pierce had hoped to find a predecessor to Mathews and McVeigh during the textbook controversy. This might explain why Kanawha County bombers considered not only schools and buses but also television and radio towers as targets, according to Delbert Rose's testimony in the 1975 grand jury hearings. Perhaps Pierce's conspiracist, apocalyptic denouncements of a Jewish-controlled media had made as much sense to Delbert Rose as Marvin Horan's Christian, apocalyptic fears of Judgment Day had.

Be that speculation as it may, what *is* certain is that Pierce's interest in West Virginia, however tangential initially, reflected—if not escalated—the local Klan's and Dietz's public rededication to anti-Semitism. After Klansmen were pictured at Witcher Creek making a Nazi salute to the burning cross, and about the same time that George Dietz rejected Robert Welch's brand of anticommunism in favor of blatant anti-Semitism, Pierce denounced George Wallace for the same reason: he had made no acknowledgment that the purported Jewish control of the mass media and the government was the fundamental problem facing society. There was, then, a concentrated discursive shift occurring among the ultraright, which does not necessarily indicate communication or collusion among Kanawha County Klansmen, Dietz, and Pierce, but does suggest that the Old Right, with its emphasis on economics and racial segregation, was waning. In its stead arose a New Right, the subject of the next chapter, and a revitalized ultraright with a visionary, anti-Semitic vengeance. Pierce's taking notice of the Kanawha County textbook controversy in the mid-1970s prefigured his eventual relocation to West Virginia, the Appalachian image of which merged with his white supremacist vision.

Ten years after the textbook controversy, Pierce bought 365 acres of farmland in Pocahontas County, West Virginia, with $95,000 in cash.[81] Many have claimed that the money was loot from *Turner Diaries*-reader turned bank-robber Robert Mathews, who reportedly admitted to one man that he had given a large amount to Pierce. Why would a white supremacist move to West Virginia? Most people presume automatically that in moving to West Virginia, "Pierce shunned the burgeoning black population of Washington" for a place where you could "count on your fingers and toes the number of blacks" in residence.[82]

But there were more tactical reasons. As anyone familiar with the now declassified cold-war era military bunker beneath the opulent Greenbrier resort about 120 miles south of Charleston in White Sulphur Springs knows,[83] the rural south of West Virginia is strategically situated amid sheltering mountains and in proximity to the nation's capital. If for no other nefarious reason, this proximity was important because Pierce would continue to conduct business in D.C. or its suburb of Arlington, from which he was relocating.

Another tactical reason for choosing Pocahontas County was its natural network of underground caves and freshwater sources. To Pierce's mind, white revolutionary survivalists could utilize these resources as the race war progressed. In addition to the obvious apocalypticism of *The Turner Diaries*, there is other evidence that Pierce was preparing for large-scale, cataclysmic warfare. He built a water system in caves that channeled spring water through 500- to 1,000-gallon stainless steel canisters so that the condensation would be collected, resulting in an uncontaminated water supply. He also learned to breed rabbits and freeze-dry the meat as a quickly renewable source of food (rabbits can reproduce litters of twelve or fourteen in six weeks).[84] Thus this second tactical point of choosing West Virginia for its natural resources blends geographic reality with apocalyptic fantasy and well-wrought tropes of Appalachia.

The advantage of moving to West Virginia was as symbolic as it was tactical. Pierce's relocation to West Virginia associated him and his mission with some key ideas of Appalachia that were prominent in the 1970s and beyond.[85] First, largely because of the War on Poverty imagery that proliferated in the 1960s, Appalachia was assumed to be "the locus of perfect victimization" in which white people had supposedly been persecuted for more than a century, an idea that fit perfectly with Pierce's siege mentality, his conspiracist notions about the Jew-controlled government. Second, the idea of Appalachia also operated as "a wild land. . . populated by inconsequential savages," those hillbillies whose saving grace was resisting what Pierce saw as society's corruptions. Third, the idea of Appalachia also operated under the assumption that the region was populated by racially pure "contemporary ancestors, country cousins in need of uplift" and, if Pierce had his way, racial awakening. In addition to these cultural assumptions, Pierce exploited the assumption of Appalachia as a folk culture. No doubt mirroring the Nazi exploitation and racialization of the German *volk*, Pierce's desire to create a "new people" meant narrating himself and others as part of Aryan culture, the images of which resembled Appalachian tradition, or at least those images of Appalachian tradition that were being produced and marketed in the 1970s.

The symbolic advantage of moving to West Virginia in the 1980s was that the 1970s had seen an increase in interest of Appalachian "folk" ways. The back-to-the-land movement brought people to West Virginia who were seeking a primitivistic escape from the pressures of modern life and corrupt ways. Such seekers of authentic living in Appalachia read the new

Foxfire books, manuals for getting back to nature that in the 1970s became a phenomenal celebration of mountain folkways. Beginning in the 1970s, Charleston officials created a yearly gathering of Appalachian folk culture on the capitol grounds that became known as Vandalia. Thus an interest in Appalachian identity flourished in the 1970s. People came to West Virginia with a desire to dodge anything inauthentic, to return to what was supposedly real, to get back to the land that was deemed "almost heaven, West Virginia" by singer John Denver, to relinquish the corruptions of American life, with Watergate and Vietnam topping the list. Living in the mountains, building your own cabin, buying a hand-carved stomper doll, or sampling home-made apple butter or potato candy were ways to escape the corrupt commodity system, even if that meant buying real estate, purchasing the *Foxfire* volume that gave instructions on cabin building, or paying for the folk crafts and food that provided that sense of escape.[86] Throughout the 1970s, progressives and conservatives alike came to Appalachia and thereby participated, consciously or not, in a critique of the commodity system. Moving to West Virginia in the 1980s was an effective way for Pierce to present himself and his mission as an authentic, down-to-earth, wholesome, pure kind of enterprise. It was a smart way to narrate himself and his colleagues as good "folk."

This is not to say that William Pierce was particularly concerned with how others saw him; indeed, he was most reclusive and unconcerned with his public image. Rather, his promotion of (white supremacist) folk exploited a time and place that had experienced a renaissance of (Appalachian) folk culture. When Pierce did make public appearances, there was no hiding his extreme, racist, conspiracist views. But that did not stop him from presenting himself as just another hard-working, salt-of-the-earth, back-to-the-land man who called Appalachia home.

For example, in a documentary film on the National Alliance, Pierce appeared as a rugged individualist wearing jeans, work boots, and an outdoorsman jacket, seated on a small wooden stepladder outside. Behind him are the bare branches and dull green hills of southern West Virginia in late fall. "It's often difficult to coax the kind of people that we need away from the affluent life in the big city and get them out here where they have to use a pick and shovel and hammer and saw," Pierce explains.[87] Later the film shows Pierce providing fatherly instruction to a woman who is hammering a nail into the wall. Literally building community, Pierce tries to appear in the film as a benevolent dad.

Other scenes in the film depict the gendered dynamic of Pierce's operation in West Virginia. For example, Pierce is shown dressed in shirt sleeves and tie, holding an issue of *National Vanguard* magazine, the successor publication to *Attack!* The cover of the magazine he is holding is a woodblock-type image of a girl with braids in a peasant blouse looking out over idyllic hills to the rising sun. The cover reads "Toward a New Consciousness, a New Order, a New People." These images blend the icon of the Germanic-looking girl with the icon of the Appalachian countryside. Thus Nazi folk imagery is mapped onto Appalachian imagery. Pierce positions himself as the protector of the girl on the magazine cover, who represents the dawning of a new people on a free land, as well as the patriarch of the barely English-speaking Eastern European women who, according to the film, came to live with him on the Pocahontas compound. In this way, Pierce's National Alliance idealized the mountain region as it was idealized in nineteenth-century local-color fiction, representing Appalachia as a land that is gendered female, as a domestic space that can be invaded by outsiders, an area of purity in need of paternalistic protection.

Another aspect of this gendered perspective is the National Alliance's promotion of not merely a protective but also a vengeful masculinity. In a book review of Robert Howard's "Conan" novels, *Attack!* claimed that they

> exemplify Aryan heroic vitalism at its best and transmit basic Aryan archetypes. . . . The two dozen or so Howard paperbacks now available are primarily valuable because they provide a stimulus which, in an effeminate age, seeks a response in the essential virility of the White race—a virility which can lift us out of our present degradation and disunity and bind us into a tight throng of warriors who, possessed of the hard ferocity of all the ages, in a brightening fire of hate and blood-vengeance will wipe out every restraint and obstacle in our way.[88]

Pierce's promotion of such pulp fiction is based on his belief that whites "should have an acquaintance with the folk traditions, the legends and myths, and the lives of great heroes of his people." Indeed, Pierce believed that "racial identity is based on more than history; the soul of a people is in its legends and myths."[89] Howard's novels qualified as good reading for Pierce's revolutionaries because the Conan character featured in them is part of the pagan tradition that feeds the "pan-Aryan religiosity" of the National Alliance.

A non-Christian pagan influenced by Francis Parker Yockey, Pierce espoused a pantheistic brand of white supremacism. Over the years, Pierce was compelled to articulate his spiritual beliefs in terms of "cosmotheism," a neologism that Pierce created to label his synthesis of "Darwinian evolution, Teutonic mythology, and the 'scientific' findings of early racial theorists" of the late nineteenth and early twentieth centuries.[90] Pierce's cosmotheism saw "each race and species assigned a specific role in relation to the Whole. While the Negro is content to idle and the Jew acts as ferment of decay, the white man is guided by the Divine Spark within him ever upward toward the Creator, who is a living part of his Being."[91] With such lofty derivations of early twentieth-century racial theories, Pierce could not abide what he saw as more mundane, lower-class articulations of race relations. For example, although Pierce was born in Atlanta and was a descendent of a Confederate soldier, he eschewed the South-will-rise-again rhetoric of the Klan, disdaining the "loud-mouthed, beery rednecks letting off a little ritualized steam about the 'goddam niggers.'"[92] Likewise, Pierce rejected the British Israelism of the nineteenth century and its late twentieth-century manifestation, Christian Identity, which presumes that the Caucasians are the lost tribes of Israel and, in effect, that whites are the "real" Jews according to the Bible, the real chosen people of God.[93]

Despite his elitist disdain for the Klan and Christian Identity, Pierce is generally regarded as the contemporary white supremacists' intellectual leader and spiritual father. What allowed him to appeal to those he openly disdained was not only the shift to anti-Semitism and seeing Jews and ZOG as the common, fundamental enemy. He won followers with his emphasis on narrative, on telling stories that shared an overall apocalyptic tone and promoted a kind of racial masculinity that transcended the ideological and class differences among various white supremacist factions.

It makes perfect sense, then, that Pierce would spend resources promoting a reading list and providing volumes to readers through his National Vanguard Books catalog, as well as trying to create new "Aryan" legends for the twentieth century and beyond, namely *The Turner Diaries* and, later, *Hunter,* his second novel, in which a white supremacist sniper murders mixed-race couples. As we know from the conclusion of *The Turner Diaries,* Pierce's vision was a post-apocalyptic agrarian utopia where "the air seems cleaner, the sun brighter, life more joyous" because the country is devoid of nonwhites. Pierce's move to West Virginia, imbued as it was with the symbolic ideas of folk Appalachia, not only fit his fantasy narrative but also helped others to envision and tell it, too.

Narrating True Sons of Appalachia

By others, I do not mean only Pierce's disciples, McVeigh and Mathews. I mean scholars and reporters who have unwittingly perpetuated the ideas of Appalachia as a land of pure whites or inhabited only by whites, as a virgin wilderness in which one tests oneself or relinquishes the supposed corruptions of modernity. In so doing, writers metonymically create the image of residents of West Virginia—including Pierce—as a natural force with which to be reckoned. For example, in a scholarly examination of Pierce's belief in "cosmotheism," sociologist Brad Whitsel makes much of the setting of the National Alliance's headquarters with particularly evocative words:

> This article seeks to address the religious and philosophical underpinnings of a potentially militant separatist society located in a *remote* portion of the *Appalachians*. William Pierce's West Virginia-based Cosmotheist Community, situated near the town of Marlinton in rural Pocahontas County, is home to a small group of people who feel that their truth is *timeless*. Tucked away near the Monongahela National *Forest*, this *settlement* follows an unsettling philosophy which attributes the demise of America to Jews and non-whites. (Emphases added)[94]

Although Whitsel's introduction is absolutely factual and perfectly academic (rather than salacious) in intention, his choice of words—"remote," "timeless," "forest," "settlement"—calls up a concise concentration of images that resonate with centuries of ideas of Appalachia as a region that is stuck in the colonial past, isolated culturally, and opposed to modern ways. But West Virginians, least of all William Pierce, are not any of those things. In addressing the spiritual dimensions of the National Alliance, Whitsel admirably attends to an underexamined aspect of Pierce's work; Whitsel is in line with interdisciplinary scholarship that is at pains to take "extremists" seriously, to analyze closely apocalyptic narratives, and to consider carefully millenarian or millennial movements without dismissing them as pathological paranoids spouting "Bible babble."[95] He also, however, foregrounds the mystique of Appalachia, rather than cosmotheism or spirituality, by titling the article, "Aryan Visions for the Future in the West Virginia Mountains." In this emphasized geographic setting and symbolic context, Pierce's "eccentric spirituality" seems implicitly related to the mountains. But as much as he capitalized on the ideas and imagery of Appalachia, Pierce's strategic relationship with the mountains—with their craggy hillsides, underground caves, and old coal mines—was far from romantic or spiritual: "All the homosexuals, race-mixers, and hard-case collaborators in the country who are too far gone to be re-educated can be rounded up," Pierce said, "packed into 10,000 or so railroad cattle cars, and eventually double-timed into an abandoned coal mine in a few days time."[96] Such a mountain grave is hardly sacred or spiritual. Whitsel's emphasis on the "West Virginia mountains" functions unwittingly as a titillating juxtaposition of romantic images of Appalachia with the revealed truth of deviant racism thriving in Pierce's compound. As an author, Whitsel takes his reader behind the "craggy hillside that obscures the view from the road" to reveal eccentricity, hatred, and racist deviance.

A more conscious, heavy-handed example of this typical treatment of examining life in the mountains is a journalistic exposé of George Dietz's early computer "bulletin board" network. Tim Miller takes his reader through "hilly farm country," painting an idyllic picture with a sordid revelation: "The dusty mountain road winds through a leafy tunnel formed by overhanging trees, past goats chewing on meadow grass. There, tucked in a cranny of the bucolic valley, is a quiet farm where the message once preached by Adolf Hitler is now propagated by an Apple IIe."[97] Dietz, of course, had no objections to such a scene. On the contrary, he reported that "since this article appeared, the number of calls to the Bulletin Board System has tripled!—Thanks, Tim Miller!"[98]

This response is hardly surprising given Dietz's own deployment of symbols and myths of Appalachia and its "mountain folk." In "Triumph of the Will takes to the hills," *White Power Report* purported that

> West Virginia is an unusual area of White Power, as most counties have few or no Black invaders in residence. In other words, this is time-capsule country in which the biggest event ever to happen, aside from the Civil War, was the Hatfield-McCoy Feud. Most of the Whites preface their remarks on race by saying, "I saw a colored fella once . . ." Thus, the impact of 20th century race war has largely bypassed these White hillfolk and so, it was with small expectations that the "Triumph" team from Reedy made its foray into the woods with movie screen and projector.[99]

Like the projection of film onto screen, Dietz projected whiteness onto "hillfolk." Dietz clearly saw his white supremacist venture as a modern one, saw these "sturdy and taciturn mountaineers" as the timeless, backwoods, contemporary ancestors and country cousins needing white racial uplift. Like Pierce, Dietz's investment in West Virginia as a place to foment "race war" was dependent on and perpetuated a narrative of Appalachia in which "mountaineers" are portrayed either as innocuous fugitives from a foolish, effeminate, corrupt, modern world, or as much more dangerous deviants, perverts, or warriors.

Sometimes the mountaineer acts in both capacities, serving as a trickster hillbilly with the liminal capacity to cross corporeal and temporal boundaries. One report of the textbook controversy published by John Birch Society's *American Opinion* magazine projected a familiar nineteenth-century figure onto a textbook protester who did not appreciate media representation. The *American Opinion* article romanticizes a tiff with reporters:

> It is true that a C.B.S. television crew was roughed up, with one man having his nose bloodied when the newsmen barraged into a rally of concerned parents. The protesters had just been worked over pretty badly by local television coverage and weren't overjoyed at the thought of being pushed around again. We were told that the network boys had been instructed by a mischievous local that a good way to ingratiate themselves would be to greet the protesters by calling them "Creekers," a regional epithet not lightly endured from strangers in those parts. Whether it was this that put the C.B.S. nose out of joint, we have no idea, but we will wager that somewhere Dan'l Boone (who once lived hard by the Kanawha River) was smiling a smile as wide as the Cumberland Gap.[100]

Transcending the boundaries of time, the unnamed, liminal, "mischievous local" becomes Daniel Boone or is revealed to have been in some essential way already always Daniel Boone, a contemporary embodiment of his mountaineer spirit. By invoking Daniel Boone, the writer activated a classic American narrative of Appalachia and Appalachians, positioning his readers as rooting for, if not identifying with, the frontier legend.

It is in this regard—of invoking legends, and familiar "folk" narratives, and positioning readers in relation to them—that makes a writer for *American Opinion* no different than William Pierce, despite the ideological and political differences between the John Birch Society and the National Alliance. Texts by both writers operate similarly, by narrating not only a plot but a subject position for the reader.

As literary and cultural studies have shown, narrative plays an important role in the social reproduction of individual and community identity. To say that William Pierce builds bombers and not bombs is to acknowledge that he had a particular skill in creating narratives, such as *The Turner Diaries*, so that readers are not only convinced by Pierce's rhetoric and racist ideas but see themselves as part of his apocalyptic fantasy and the "Aryan race" and, thus, begin to act accordingly. Pierce understood that "racial identity is based on more than history; the soul of a people is in its legends and myths." This emphasis on legends, myths, and soul is not incompatible with what scholars say about ethnic identity. How we know who we are is by what kind of story, or narrative, we collectively tell ourselves and others.[101]

The stories of Ed Miller, George Dietz, and William Pierce show how the textbook controversy was an occasion in which right-wing agitators as well as Kanawha County protesters were compelling people to ask, Who are we? What is our relation to the government? What is our relation to the new national story told in the books proposed for our children? How will our children be narrated by the books? Who will our children be if they read these books? Who will "we," as a people, be? With their involvement in the textbook controversy, however tangential, Miller, Dietz, and Pierce were posing these questions to the residents of Kanawha County in an overtly racialized way. Their definitions of the "true sons of Appalachia" were based on biological determinism; to be a "true son of Appalachia," one was expected not only to demonstrate a particular bloodline but also a particular racialized and gendered relationship to land, to heritage, and to God. Miller, Dietz, and Pierce—like many of the protesters—were trying to define the local community and the nation. This is not to say that all whites in Kanawha County or all protesters of the books were racists. On the contrary, they were not. But among the protesters of the books, white supremacists were most consciously trying to forge subjectivities. So, looking at them helps us understand this process, which is important because it precludes the fatalistic idea that the battle over books was a natural uprising.

Seeing the 1974 textbook controversy as an inevitable "clash of values" ignores the efforts of George Dietz and William Pierce to exert influence over the conflict and ignores their effects. To ignore these white supremacists is to cling desperately to the idea that the textbook controversy was the result of a never-evolved fundamentalism of "yesterday's people," a backward biblical literalism indigenous to the Kanawha County mountaineers, as old as the hills in which they lived. On the contrary, the textbook controversy reflected and advanced the very contemporary formulation of a post–civil rights white supremacism.

Pierce and Dietz were not necessarily collaborators but their messages to the textbook protesters in Kanawha County were fundamentally the same—both were arguing that the supposed conspiracy afoot in the textbook adoption was not simply communist but Jewish as well. This message was reinforced by Ed Miller's fellow Klansmen who protested books by day and by night added a "Heil Hitler" salute to the cross-burning ceremony at Witcher Creek. What white supremacists in the Kanawha Valley experienced in 1974 and 1975 became more common on a national scale throughout the 1980s and 1990s. With Dietz's and Pierce's propaganda machines liberated from the guises of the John Birch Society and George Wallace's American Party and operating at full capacity, a new narrative was forged, and with it new racialized subjectivities. What resulted was a nazi-fication of the Klan and the new unification of white supremacists under the banner of the Aryan Nations. The media created by Dietz and Pierce—beginning with the leaflets printed directly for the textbook protesters or targeted at them, the periodicals (*Liberty Bell*, *Attack!*, *White Power Report*), the electronic bulletin board systems that linked white supremacists worldwide,[102] the highly influential fiction (*Turner Diaries*, *Hunter*), and the book catalogs (National Vanguard Books and the Liberty Bell library)[103]—all these are evidence of a newly formulated racist Right, a postmodern white supremacism that sent swastikas into cyberspace and positioned readers as revolutionaries in an apocalyptic race war.

The stories of Ed Miller, George Dietz, and William Pierce thus are representative of most of the protesters only in the sense that they saw the book protests not as a mere opportunity (to recruit or exploit residents of Kanawha County), but as a *necessity* for building the kind of community they thought was key to the future of the United States of America. "Our children" became the symbol for these forward-looking movements of the citizens of Kanawha County, West Virginia, and for right-wing movements that built on the momentum of, and in some cases actually modeled themselves after, the textbook controversy.

In order to secure a focus on the child as the symbol of the American future, a mother was necessary. That is the role that Alice Moore played. Not a white supremacist, Alice Moore was nevertheless, I will argue, always implicitly racialized in her role as someone who could make protesting books and other forms of political activity as natural as a mother's love. As the next chapter shows, the politics of maternal love, so overshadowed by the ultraright's virile masculinity in its narration of the true *sons* of Appalachia, was born again in the New Right.

FIGURE 8. An unflattering caricature of Kanawha County Board of Education member Alice Moore. Taylor Jones, *Sunday Gazette-Mail*, March 30, 1975. Reproduced with permission.

CHAPTER THREE

Sweet Alice and Secular Humanism

Unlike George Dietz, Ed Miller, and William Pierce, Alice Moore was universally portrayed as a central figure if not the sole instigator of the textbook controversy. Representations of her were as diametrically opposed as media takes on the conflict as a whole: she was either reviled or revered. An illustration of her printed in the local newspaper revealed Moore to be a distortion of womanhood, with a slack-jawed face with a look of intolerance and suspicion (see figure 8.) Such a caricature portrayed Moore as ignorant, dull, and dumbfounded rather than how she really was: articulate, outspoken, and attractive. Generally speaking, it was the working-class white man—the fiery fundamentalist preacher or the victimized coal miner—who played the part of the hillbilly in national and international media. Alice Moore was usually criticized on different terms, in relation to her living up to the idea of a southern lady.

Much like the feminists of her time, whose politics she opposed, Alice Moore was disdained as someone who was breaking the rules of traditional femininity. Referred to as "Sweet Alice" by admirers and opponents alike, Moore hailed most directly from the Mississippi middle class.[1] Regardless of the biographical actualities of Alice Moore, it is as a caricature of southern white womanhood and as a political persona that "Sweet Alice" deserves scrutiny.[2] As a political persona, Sweet Alice emblematizes the shift that Christian conservative women were making in the 1970s. Although she did not feel as though she was breaking any taboos, Alice Moore nevertheless transgressed unspoken rules of passive femininity and Christian humility. In the process, she helped shape a discursive strategy that distinguished the New Right from the Old Right. The arguments made by Sweet Alice ultimately refashioned the Old Right's fears of conspiring communists and racial integrationists, replacing them with a new conspiracy featuring secular humanism, which served as the mobilizing narrative of the "southern strategy" that brought the New Right to power and ushered in the culture wars.

The "southern strategy" was a way to ensure that voters in the South, especially those enamored of George Wallace, the segregationist governor of Alabama who ran for president in 1968, would support the GOP rather than the Democrats. Richard Nixon deployed several tactics of this strategy, including supporting only selected aspects of affirmative action in order to split people between civil rights, which appealed more to blacks, and labor issues, which appealed more to working whites.[3] There was a psychological aspect of this strategy as well. Political analyst Kevin Phillips, whose research enabled the southern strategy in the late 1960s and early 1970s, "bluntly recognized the role [that] fear in general, and white fear of blacks in particular, would play in guaranteeing the emerging Republican majority."[4] A strategy based on racialized fear was as cultural as it was political, and as the Right continued its resurgence throughout the 1970s and beyond, it became focused on cultural practices that one scholar suggests amounted to a "southernization of the right." In *Up from Conservatism*, Michael Lind explains that "the southernization of the right has meant more than the 'southern strategy' devised by Goldwater and Nixon and perfected by Reagan and Bush—a strategy for luring white southerners away from the Democratic coalition. It means the adoption, by the leaders and the intellectuals of the American right, of a 'culture-war' approach to politics."[5] Lind focuses on male leaders and intellectuals of the Right, overlooking the crucial roles that women and womanhood played in organizing and strategizing the "culture wars" to the Right's benefit. Alice Moore was part of a whole history of conservative activists who profoundly shaped the culture wars as women and mothers.

Beginning with the local perception of Moore as "southern womanhood at its finest," and moving on to an examination of previous and subsequent right-wing women, especially Connaught Marshner, in this chapter I demonstrate how gender was an important aspect of the resurgence of the Right, how "Sweet Alice" was part and parcel of the southernization of American politics, and how the Kanawha County textbook controversy, especially as extolled in Marshner's book *Blackboard Tyranny*, was a historical and strategic pivot point that resulted in relinquishing Old Right red-hunting and fashioning a new narrative for a New Right.

Southern Womanhood at Its Finest

Having lived in North Carolina, Tennessee, and Alabama previously, Alice Moore came to Charleston, West Virginia, from Mississippi in 1967.[6] Before the textbook controversy ever erupted, she agreed to interviews with Charleston television reporters, speaking out on two occasions in 1973 to oppose evolution and abortion, which made headlines due to the Supreme Court decision in *Roe v. Wade* that year.[7] Earlier in 1970, she had won her election to the Kanawha County school board on the basis of opposing sex education. Moore's forthright passion during school board meetings served her well because her interlocutors were neither familiar with the rhetoric that she used nor accustomed to having white middle-class women like Moore act so assertively. Audio recordings of meetings reveal how people reacted to her with incredulity and confusion before they saw her as any kind of adversary or instigator.

In the April 11, 1974, meeting, when Moore made her first objections to the proposed language arts curriculum, people responding to her were caught completely off guard by her insistence. On routine issues discussed before book adoption, such as a debate on whether or not to allow students to have a field trip to King's Island, an amusement park in Ohio, Moore was a sharp commentator and responsive to the various points of view voiced on the matter. She freely conceded some points after their deliberation and gave in to some demands she initially opposed. But when discussion of the new language arts curriculum ensued, she was uncompromising. Her early objection to the books was a quick reference to "anti-American social science books" in which "everything in America is denigrated." After she said this, there was an awkward silence. No one seemed to know how to respond. Then Moore laughed liltingly, almost apologizing—"I don't want to sound ungrateful" for all the work the committee had done for selecting this new curriculum. Moore's back-peddling apology was met with nervous laughter from the room, which sounded like profound confusion: Why was she bringing up social science? What was un-American? What was she talking about?

As the meeting progressed, Moore issued a steady stream of accusations with little patience for responses from the selection committee responsible for recommending the books. She disregarded out of hand criticisms of the most blatant contradictions and non sequitors in her arguments and the most logical rebuttals against them. For example, when she suggested that the dialectology lessons were a new feature of the books that indicated a real threat to students, she was told that she was mistaken because those lessons had appeared in the old language arts curriculum as well. This elicited no thoughtful reconsideration on Moore's part; instead, she immediately claimed that even one lesson was too much.

After forty-five minutes of questions and answers disregarded, the meeting during which everyone expected to adopt the recommended books ended. All five of the board members, including Moore, voted for adoption. But she had cast aspersions not only about the quality of the curriculum but also about the motives of the publishers, writers, and, most surprisingly, the local teachers who made up the selection committee.

Some suggested that Alice Moore's behavior that day and subsequently was accommodated because of the gendered conventions of the time and place. To say she was "sweet Alice" was to emphasize, sarcastically or not, Moore's femininity. As Nell Wood, the chair of the textbook selection committee, attested, "she was a beautiful woman, soft-spoken, with a Mississippi accent. She served on a board of education with four men who were southern gentlemen, with people who found it very difficult to look a beautiful woman in the eye and say, you're a liar, you are manipulative, you are using things for your own benefit, even when they knew that."[8] Wood grew up in a coal-mining community in Wyoming County and obtained her teaching credentials at Concord College in Athens, West Virginia.[9] Her perspective therefore was that of a working-class West Virginian who saw Moore and the four men on the school board as distinctly "southern." Moreover, in calling them "southern gentlemen" Wood was noting their class, acknowledging their genteel tendency to honor women of their same socioeconomic stature. Along the same line, Wood's mention of the Mississippi accent can also be read as noting Moore's southernness, implying a contradistinction to the so-called twang of the West Virginia dialect, which is universally perceived as a marker of less education and more economic and cultural impoverishment. Begging the more involved questions of the relationship between southern, Appalachian, or West Virginian identities, Nell Wood's explanation for why Alice Moore's objections were so accommodated is that the male board members saw Moore as embodying the ideal of "southern" femininity. Wood was not the only one who judged Moore in terms of gender and sexuality. But rather than analyze the dynamics of femininity at work in Moore's self-presentation, others simply demonized her for it.

For example, in the made-for-television movie script based on James Lewis's experiences in the controversy, Alice Moore is caricaturized as having a "honeyed voice" and being conniving. The dialogue and directions hyperbolically make the same points Nell Wood made about Moore's style of speaking and how male board members were accustomed to view her through the lens of southern conventions and expectations. But the script exaggerates them to suggest that Alice Moore was a media-crazed narcissist and exhibitionist:

PAGE: Sweet Alice is about to arrive.
JIM: I can't wait.
PAGE: Southern womanhood at its finest. The first voice against the books, and the easiest to listen to.
JIM: Does she get flowers every time?
PAGE: Usually they're already on the table.

At the Door:
The crowd parts, and ALICE MOORE enters like the beauty queen she could have been. In her early thirties, she's a minister's wife, mother of [four], and the only woman on the school board. The room starts to APPLAUD. She raises a politician's hand of happy acknowledgment. Her blouse is buttoned high and tied with a bow, but she's wearing a short skirt that shows off damn good legs. She inhales the fragrance of her bouquet.[10]

This portrayal of Moore goes too far in exploring her cultural capital as an attractive, middle-class white woman. Although it is absolutely evident that Moore was conscious of her appearance, likely it was a consciousness born out of political aspirations to promote conservative and fundamentalist principles. She was not the narcissist that a television production would make of her. It is a mistake to attribute Moore's self-presentation to female vanity.

In fact, Moore's involvement in the controversy jeopardized her feminine status. This is clear in one newspaper account that commented on Moore's change in hairstyle, which had become a bland bun rather than a coif full of curls because, as the bold print announced, she was "Just Too Busy For Rollers."[11] Moore explained that she did not have time to sit under a hair dryer with curlers. On one hand, the observation documents Moore's political goals as a priority over a beauty regimen. On the other, such a comment serves to ridicule Moore as a woman whose political involvement was taking a toll on her looks, her feminine self-presentation.

Days earlier, a columnist for the same paper had suggested that Moore's look was as calculated as it was unfeminine. Juxtaposing her with the "nubile Lolitas demonstrating against suggestive literature while wearing shorts that are definitely suggestive," *Gazette* writer L. T. Anderson delivered a slut/prude dichotomy:

> The reverse of this [irony of young protesters in suggestive dress], also highly amusing, is the sight of Mrs. Moore in her frequent television appearances with her hair pulled back from her forehead so fiercely that it gives headaches to viewers, and with her visage otherwise converted to her flock's notion of what a God-fearing woman should look like. Of course it could be an imposter there on the screen. Mrs. Moore has been in the Gazette newsroom several times, and on those occasions her hair was curled prettily at the temple, and her practice of the womanly arts instinctive.[12]

If a woman does not present herself "prettily" her "womanly arts" are failing her; she is an "imposter." Moreover, according to Anderson, Moore had to squelch her natural instincts as a woman in order to appeal to a "God-fearing" audience—"her flock" of fundamentalists.

Even advocates of Moore suggested her femininity was suspect due to her political action. One letter sent to school board member Harry Stansbury remarked, "It does seem quite a shame that among yourself, Mr. Issacs, Mr. Kinsolving, Alice Moore, Dr. Underwood and Mr. Stump there is only one real man and that is Mrs. Moore."[13] Clearly such a letter was meant to shame those men who were apparently being emasculated by a woman willing to take the lead. But the underlying logic points to a real problem that conservative Christian women faced as much as feminists: the idea that the public sphere and political debate were realms reserved for men, not women.

Such political involvement was taboo for a woman unless, that is, she did it as a mother. In fact, Moore won her 1970 election to the school board with the slogan, "Put a mother on the school board." Moore had four school-age children. She let that basic fact speak for itself and operated as a mother in a particularly matter-of-fact way. She did not, for example, speak in sentimental terms about her specific children, did not bring them to meetings or hold up pictures of them, nor did she refer to their experiences in school or her experiences in rearing them. But her understood maternity was integral to her credibility and her purpose, which was not only to object to books but also to the "alien philosophy" that they purportedly promoted. An album of songs produced by Avis Hill featured lyrics that heralded "Sweet Alice" and bemoaned "Our Lost Heaven," a song that riffed on John Denver's hit "Country Roads," which had become the unofficial anthem of West Virginia in the 1970s. Denver's lyrics were replaced with words indicating how important the idea of motherhood was to the fight against the textbooks: "Our lost heaven, West Virginia, dirty textbooks, broken-hearted mothers."[14] Another song, the "Ballad of Kanawha County," included an episode about "an angry mountain mama."[15] Although these songs sentimentalized protesters as mothers both mad and mournful, Moore did not present herself as a brokenhearted mountain mama, but rather as an insistent, strategic protector of the educational system and its ability to uphold the American "heritage" against alien "indoctrination." In this way, Moore was distinguished from other mothers pictured in the news. Unlike "Sweet Alice," working-class mothers were most often depicted as angry and anguished, overcome by emotion, overwhelmed and victimized.[16] These were not the faces of "southern womanhood" so epitomized by Alice Moore, who "did not venture into the coal mining portion of the county" but "rallied the mothers of the affluent western portion of" it, and did not consider herself part of the mass protest, only a beneficiary of it.[17] She said, "I draw back, I get a little embarrassed by . . . crowds, by marching in parades, by emotionalism, by anything like that, by marching in the streets, but I am grateful for the people who did, for without them, we would have had no attention."[18]

As Avis Hill's record album makes clear, what the female working-class protesters and middle-class Alice Moore had in common was a claim to motherhood. Someone perceived as a southern lady rather than a mountain mama, Alice Moore acted as if her natural duty was to challenge the state in defense of "our children" rather than wringing her hands over her own, specific offspring. Coolly, she wrote a letter of explanation of "citizens' rights on bad textbooks" that situated her maternity first and foremost. The letter began, "As a concerned mother . . ."[19]

Previous Sweeties

With such a middle-class maternal justification for her cause against local government bureaucracy (that is, the school board), Moore's political involvement somewhat resembled the U.S. "mothers' movement" of the 1940s. Like Moore's unsentimental presentation of motherhood-as-civic-duty, middle class and wealthy women interested in retaining an isolationist stance and avoiding war with Germany also positioned themselves in a monitoring, if not adversarial, relation to the state.[20] Like Moore, these women balked at overly sentimental gestures, preferring instead to make impassioned arguments and to ally themselves with professionals. For example, Moore would appear as a spokeswoman but would not picket the school board building, kids in tow, as many of the working-class mothers did. Both the "mothers' movement" and Alice Moore, furthermore, were highly suspicious of the government agencies they were trying to influence or expose as corrupt colluders in subversion and indoctrination. Moore distrusted and denounced various agencies, including the federal office for Health, Education and Welfare, the National Council of Teachers of English, and the National Education Association (NEA) when it came to town. She saw an overarching threat, a particular "alien philosophy" spreading among these and other such institutions, aiming to take over the minds of children.

Although the politicization of motherhood, therefore, preexisted Alice Moore in the form of the mothers' movement, it is not accurate or fair to equate them, since the leaders in the 1940s movement were actually profascist, blatantly supportive of Mussolini and Hitler. They were also flagrantly anti-Semitic, while Alice Moore was not. More to the point, mothers' movement leaders saw their maternity in particular relation to the state. They produced the boys who would become the men of government, the leaders of the state; to go to war was directly counterproductive to their womanly contribution: "War would negate the work of mothers: homemaking and nurturing sons from cradle to manhood."[21] Although Moore's stake in motherhood was similarly a maternal preservation of "our children," it lacked the kind of overt claim of reproducing for the state that fascistic women took pride in.

We must therefore take into account the distinction between conservative and profascist women in their political deployment of motherhood. Historian Glen Jeansonne's comparison of mothers' movement leader Elizabeth Dilling and conservative activist Phyllis Schlafly is instructive here:

> In the postwar period women were attracted to the right, but the moderate right was more successful in gaining women than was the bigoted right represented by the likes of Dilling. The best-known leader of the women's postwar right, Phyllis Schlafly, resembles Dilling in being a staunch anticommunist who publishes prolifically and leads an upper

middle-class lifestyle. Because of these similarities, she has been compared to Dilling, a comparison that is unfair to Schlafly. A child of working-class parents, Schlafly is a lawyer who wrote a best-selling defense of Goldwater's 1964 campaign and ran two unsuccessful races for Congress, activities that distinguish her from Dilling. Although her views are inflexibly conservative—she stresses family values, opposes feminism, and was instrumental in the defeat of the proposed Equal Rights Amendment to the Constitution—she has none of the anti-Semitic or subversive tendencies of the mothers' movement, and her views reflect those of many women. Moreover, none of the major leaders of the postwar women's right wing base their ideology on anti-Semitism.[22]

Jeansonne points out these important differences between prewar, pro-fascist "mothers" and postwar conservative activists such as Schlafly and, to extend his analysis, Moore. Although Jeansonne makes excellent points to keep in mind regarding the vast political differences between someone like Phyllis Schlafly and someone like Elizabeth Dilling, it is also worth considering how what they have in common—a tremendous capacity for simplifying complicated concerns and reifying them as a black-and-white issue—could accommodate ultraright views (such as anti-Semitism).

On this point, cultural studies scholar Linda Kintz's examination of Schlafly slightly but significantly tempers Jeansonne's defense of her: "And though it is not fair to accuse Schlafly of anti-Semitism without more concrete evidence nor to suggest guilt by association, the rigidity of her monolithic anticommunist framework, which prevents nuanced investigation, makes her argument far too easily available to those who believe in conspiracy theories about international Jewish interests."[23] What Kintz is saying is that Schlafly's absolutist presentation accommodates, rather than articulates, anti-Semitism. Although this adjustment to Jeansonne's perspective no more indicts Schlafly herself as an anti-Semite, it does recognize that in the postwar period right-wing women, especially conservatives such as Schlafly, were aiming not for "nuanced investigation" but for dichotomized presentation.

Kintz claims that this obliteration of ambiguity and mandate for super-simplified "clarity" is the hallmark of conservative mothers who became active after World War II. Moreover, "The effectiveness of this rhetoric of simplification lies in the fact that its clear structure can be easily used in a variety of different circumstances [such as anti-Semitic conspiracy theories] with very little adjustment, and it easily fits into an absolutist religious binary of good and evil," which easily accommodated Christian fundamentalism.[24] Alice Moore's objections to the new language arts curriculum, much like Schlafly's objections to the Equal Rights Amendment, allowed for a variety of followers because of her "rhetoric of simplification," which accommodated anti-Semites such as George Dietz, the influential neo-Nazi who supported the protesters, fundamentalist preachers such as Avis Hill, and countless women who applauded the pluck of Sweet Alice.

In the persona of Sweet Alice we therefore see one conservative, middle-class woman's effort to cross the border into the political realm from the postwar domestic sphere. This was all the more unlikely a transgression—hence an effective strategy—because she was a southern woman who was not expected to make political arguments with her "honeyed voice." On top of that, it was an unlikely transgression because Christian evangelicals were taught that the public, political sphere was not only the domain of men but ungodly, corrupt men whose time would be better spent proselytizing. Although Moore had never been denied access to political debate—indeed her family routinely "talked politics" at the dinner table—she nevertheless felt compelled to clear her decision to run for school board with the elders of the church that employed her husband.

Much has been written about how white evangelical Christians became politically active in the 1970s and 1980s. Of course, white Christians were politically mobilized in the 1950s and 1960s, too, but there was a mass mobilization in the 1970s.[25] Sweet Alice spoke the rhetoric of conservative women who came before her, such as Schlafly, and paved the discursive way for those who would follow.

Especially in her insistence that her fight was about "control over our children's minds," Moore's campaign reflected women's efforts to thwart progressive education policy since the 1950s. For example, a grassroots effort to vilify the United Nations educational organization UNESCO was led by "a career anticommunist crusader" named Florence Fowler Lyons in 1952. Claiming that the program was not educating students to appreciate peace and international perspectives, but indoctrinating them, Lyons warned of an "alien enemy attacking innocent child minds . . . diabolically rooting up your children's faith in God, flag, country, and home."[26] Sweet Alice maintained the exact same narrative of child-targeting conspiracy, but blamed HEW rather than UNESCO because HEW issued the mandate for multiethnic textbooks: "HEW and the federal government promote this stuff. HEW does whatever it pleases. Congress doesn't control it. The voters don't control it. Parents have no lobby, no influence, no control over their children's education."[27]

Like Lyons, Moore saw the attack on children as being as insidious as a disease. This obsessive insistence on the toxicity of the books themselves aggravated Moore's colleagues on the school board, who nevertheless patiently waded through every amendment she proposed to motions meant to accommodate protesters. A good example of this is the November 8, 1974, school board meeting, which was held in the Charleston Civic Center so the public could attend and witness the extent to which the board was willing to go to be accountable to the public. By this time, some students had missed as much as nine weeks of class and truancy laws had not been enforced. The school board met with the intention of passing a mandate they hoped would resolve the issues and get students back in classes. To address specifically the charge of "indoctrination," the board passed a measure saying that students could submit a letter from parents who objected to any book in order to excuse the child from reading it. To make it all the more encompassing, one school board member moved to add to the measure this statement: "No teacher is authorized to indoctrinate a student to follow either moral values or religious beliefs which are objectionable to either the student or the student's parents." Moore tried to amend this several times to include "educational materials," implying each time that the texts themselves, regardless of teacher or student intention, could do damage to the students because they deliver an "alien philosophy." Like the anticommunist crusader Lyons, Moore spoke as if she felt that alien way was omnipresent and pervasive. Moreover, Alice Moore took ownership of the supposedly targeted children, sounding the alarm to save "our children." Lyons, who was not a parent, could not make such a claim.

Alice Moore's fear of the indoctrination of our children reflected other conservative campaigns aside from Lyons and the anticommunist attack on UNESCO. The idea of brainwashing, which had originated in the Korean War, gained notoriety with the 1958 appearance of E. Merrill Root's anticommunist *Brainwashing in the High Schools.* This book had a particular influence on women in the South; a year after its publication, the Daughters of the American Revolution "released a list of 170 objectionable texts," which inspired regional chapters of the DAR to compile local lists of suspicious books. Women "unearthed forty-four 'subversive' books in Mississippi; in Georgia the total swelled to sixty-nine. Alabama's DAR, rather than simply comparing book titles, established its own textbook study committee. The panel found subversion lurking in every corner of the curriculum, especially in literature anthologies." Like Alice Moore, these southern ladies saw language arts as the means to seduce children to "socialistic" ideas.[28]

Moore said she first got involved in protest with the issue of sex education. Denying she had any political involvement prior to Kanawha County, Moore told the story of how she became politically awakened to a leading cause of conservatives in the Southwest:

> My little girl started school in Mississippi. I had some doubts when I was told to help her to read by showing her the pictures and asking her to guess at the word on the basis of what the picture looked like. It kind of sounded odd to me, but I went along because I thought they knew what they were talking about. After I got up here [i.e., relocated to Charleston, West Virginia], and I read in the paper that they were going to introduce this sex education program, and I went up to the school board to see exactly what it was, because I had read something about some of them being pretty far out. I decided I would go up and know what this one was, so I would know what I was talking about. When I saw it and I realized that they were pushing the idea of social drinking, they were pushing the idea of the democratic family, and that children should question or challenge their parent's authority, that children should be asked in the classroom to reveal their personal private information about their family to debate the various family values and this type of thing, and I saw that this was a lot more than simply teaching biology.[29]

This statement attests to Moore's familiarity with campaigns to ban or monitor sex education: she "had read something about some of" the sex-ed programs as "being pretty far out." Such anti–sex-education literature had been circulated from the sunbelt, where some of the most publicized battles against curricular materials occurred in the late 1960s and early 1970s.

In Texas, for example, Norma Gabler and her husband Mel quickly gained a reputation for opposing textbooks. Their operation of reviewing curricula and mobilizing parents was an increasingly sophisticated one, and Moore's familiarity with it in 1974 indicates not only their effectiveness but also her active awareness of conservative political organizing. In fact, in a statement to *U.S. News and World Report*, Moore basically admitted to her predetermined opposition to the language arts curriculum, shattering the illusion that her alarm was a natural and spontaneous response to the books themselves or to the adoption committee's recommendations in April 1974: "When I knew the book selection was coming up last spring, I got in touch with the Gablers. They told me some of the things to watch for in the books. I wrote for their reviews."[30] In addition to the Texas mother Norma Gabler, in Anaheim, California, Eleanor Howe was another mother who, like Alice Moore, capitalized on that maternal status to lend an air of authenticity to her opposition to sex education. Basing her objections in terms of her parental rights, much like the Gablers, Eleanor Howe prefigured Moore's success in mobilizing the parents of Kanawha County.

Moore's specific tactics and rhetoric resembled anti–sex-ed campaigns around the country. In particular, Moore's frequent claim that exercises in the textbooks elicited from students information about parents and family deemed too private to share reflected anti–sex-ed campaigns that preceded the Kanawha County controversy. For example, Rhoda Lorand argued that education about menstruation was "an appalling invasion of girls' privacy."[31] In a December 12, 1974, meeting, Moore said the new curriculum would amount to "child taps" that invaded the "privacy of child, home and family." Also, anti–sex-ed campaigns of the time often reproduced precisely what it ostensibly meant to prohibit: pictures of genitalia said to be educational materials distributed to students. One of the most inflammatory flyers distributed in the summer of 1974 included a large image of a penis that protesters suggested was included in the language arts textbooks. The claim was quickly proven false; the graphic material had come from a book in a school library that was not required or recommended reading and was in no way part of the language arts curriculum.[32]

This tactic of decontextualization and "cut and paste" was a direct echo from the Anaheim, California, protests, where opponents also "claimed that sex education materials were pornographic, and they would read these aloud during school board meetings. . . . Often, however, the materials in question were not used with students but were in fact teacher resources, library books, or in some cases even doctored documents."[33] Alice Moore employed this tactic to great effect, despite teachers' objections that she was reading the passages out of context.

The arguments and tactics of the textbook controversy were therefore derivative of decades of what scholars have variously called "housewife activists," "kitchen table activists," and "suburban warriors."[34] These conservative spokeswomen were very influential. One scholar claims that the 1950s grassroots work to vilify UNESCO, for example, "fueled the 'back to basics' movement and launched the career of Dr. Max Rafferty."[35] Rafferty, in turn, fanned the flames of conservative women with publications such as *What They Are Doing to Your Children*, distributed in 1964. This was quintessentially Old Right discourse characterized by anticommunist conspiracism.

As McCarthyism became increasingly discounted as "hysteria" from the 1950s and red-baiting earned people the reputation of extremists, the anticommunist rhetoric of the Old Right had to be reconfigured. Conservative women had exhibited in the 1950s and 1960s the cold war anxiety that education policy was really ideological indoctrination into an "alien" communist way of life.[36] Communism was the root of the problem, and presumed commie teachers were part of a large-scale domestic subversion of American values and institutions, large and small. Subversion of the family was but one result—along with "sexual deviance" such as pornography, homosexuality, and feminism—of pervasive communist influence that was reputed to have infected the federal government and the military. But in the 1970s, Christian conservatives saw it a slightly different way.

From Communism to Humanism

As Frances FitzGerald reported in a 1981 *New Yorker* article, "by the nineteen seventies fundamentalist preachers from Billy James Hargis to James Robison and Jerry Falwell had reversed this causal sequence: the feminists, the pornographers, and the militant homosexuals were destroying the American family, and its destruction would (in Confucian sequence) lead to the destruction of the nation by Communist armies."[37] A communist takeover thus became the portending result, not the unacknowledged origin, of America's ills. Sexual deviance dropped out as a catch-all phrase for the threat to the family; in its place was secular humanism, which functioned as a code for liberal ideology that was supposedly anti-Christian. Shifting the cause of American decline from communism to humanism, conservative discourse also focused more on the family and the disruption of domesticity. Consequently, women played an increasingly important role as the Old Right left McCarthyism behind and emerged as the New Right.

Most researchers interested in the role that secular humanism played in this transition focus on the sex education battles of the 1960s and various curriculum disputes of the 1980s, without examining what happened in between. For example, education historian Jonathan Zimmerman moved from a discussion of banning sex education in 1968 to similar battles in the 1980s, noting that "critics now charged that sex education—formerly viewed as an enemy to religion—actually convey[s] a religion of its own—secular humanism."[38] He thereby noted the distinction but did not trace the shift, attributing this change in representing secular humanism to "New Right groups like Moral Majority," which "had brought this argument into the popular lexicon" by the early 1980s.[39] This alacritous move from the 1960s to the 1980s is characteristic of scholarship dealing with the work on movements that oppose secular humanism.[40] This does not explain the difference between complaints about secular humanism that accompanied the anticommunist campaigns against sex education in the 1960s and the idea of secular humanism as a conspiracist narrative, which helped shape the New Right's construction of cultural conservatism in the 1980s and beyond.[41] Alice Moore was a transitional figure who moved from the Old Right to the New Right as she went from opposing sex education as a communist plot to opposing the language arts curriculum as a secular humanist conspiracy. She helped pave the way for the Sweet Alices of the Reagan era, those "concerned mothers" who read about Kanawha County and learned to relinquish anticommunist language and leave red-baiting behind.

Particular organizations were responsible for the tactics that Alice Moore shared with previous "sweeties" in opposing both sex education and the language arts curriculum. Many accounts of Alice Moore's campaigns recognize the influence of the John Birch Society. Materials from a John Birch Society front group called MOTOREDE, which was a shortened form of Movement to Restore Decency, and MOMS (Mothers Organized for Moral Stability) "played a prominent role in Alice Moore's successful campaign for the Board of Education. At least two members of her campaign committee (Citizens for Parent Action) were admitted John Birchers."[42] But MOTOREDE was launched in 1969 by the John Birch Society, several years after the Christian Crusade made sex education an "auxiliary cause" of its anticommunist campaigns. No other account of the Kanawha County textbook controversy recognizes that Billy James Hargis's Christian Crusade not only began the anti–sex-education campaigns but also had a relationship with Alice Moore.

The director of the Christian Crusade's Department of Education, Gordon V. Drake, published a book in 1968 that was based on previous pamphlets, radio addresses, and lectures. In *Blackboard Power: NEA Threat to America*, Drake suggested that parents should do exactly what Alice

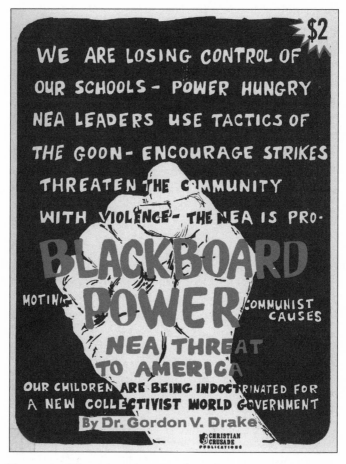

FIGURE 9. The title and cover of Gordon Drake's *Blackboard Power* (1968), featuring the Black Power salute of a raised fist, linked communism with the racial integration of schools and other goals of progressive education, epitomized by the NEA. Image courtesy of the Wilcox Collection of Contemporary Political Movements, Spencer Research Library, University of Kansas.

Moore did, namely "*Expose* and *depose* through school board pressures those teachers and administrators who do not reflect your community's mores" (see figure 9). Drake made this instruction relevant by providing a "sensational description of sex education as an anti-Christian, un-American, Communist plot that had been birthed from the bowels of Hell."[43] Specifically, that anticommunist plot focused on the National Education

Association, thereby harkening back to the 1950s campaign led by Florence Lyons. Drake added the innovation of smearing the Sex Education and Information Council of the United States (SEICUS). In addition Drake claimed that the NEA wanted to exchange "the traditional moral fiber of America" with a "pervasive sickly humanism." For the Christian Crusade as well as for the John Birch Society, however, this "sickly" pathology was only a symptom of the larger, more pervasive, dreadful disease of communism, which both groups denounced loudly, publicly, and unequivocally. By 1975 warnings about humanism were being widely circulated.

But were they warranted? Was there not, actually, a movement promoting secular humanism in the 1960s? What evidence was there of "sickly humanism" in Kanawha County?

As Chip Berlet and Matthew Lyons have noted, secular humanism was indeed a real movement that "developed in the United States during the late nineteenth century as a descendant of the rationalist philosophies of the Enlightenment." In terms of its principles, secular humanism "argues that ethical behavior can flow from the human intellect and a self-conscious conscience. Its attitude toward God and religion ranges from hostile to indifferent." But there is a difference between the actual principles of secular humanism and the perceived politicization of those principles as something far less innocuous than an intellectual movement. Just as there is a difference between anti-Communism as a way of opposing actually existing political parties and organizations whose members self-identify as Communists and anticommunism as a way of opposing imagined communist threats, there is a difference between opposing secular humanism as a matter of philosophical disagreement and opposing secular humanism as a matter of fear and suspicion of a secret conspiracy. According to Berlet and Lyons, "While historically there has been an organized humanist movement in the United States since at least the 1800s, the idea of a large-scale quasireligion called secular humanism is a conspiracist myth." Rather than a religion or even "quasireligion" in its own right, secular humanism is actually an intellectual movement. But Right-leaning people began to attribute to secular humanism omnipotent powers and ambitions of mythical proportion, to oppose it as if it were a "pervasive" conspiracy.[44]

The beginning of this attribution, according to religious studies scholar Martin E. Marty, was in relation to the case of *Torcaso v. Watkins*, a footnote of which listed secular humanism along with Buddhism and Taoism as a religion. "Here may be an instance where one can date precisely the birth of a religion: June 19, 1961," Marty said, noting the day of *Torcaso* with irony. In a 1987 article he debunked the idea of secular humanism constituting anything but a neologism deployed in the culture wars. "What clearly is at issue? My answer: politics, mainly. There's a war on for the mind and heart, the votes and the pocketbook of America, from the local school board and library board to the Supreme Court and the White House." What was happening was an overt political construction, "the manufacture of a term," secular humanism, that was deployed strategically to convince Americans that a conspiracy against Judeo-Christian principles was afoot.[45]

Indeed, those so convinced argued in McCarthyesque doublespeak both that secular humanism was a small evil cabal aiming to undermine the righteous religious majority of the United States *and* that secular humanism was an invisible, overpowering presence already in place and victimizing the few righteous religious folks who recognized the supposed tyranny. Of course, "The antisecularists cannot have it both ways. If secularists are in charge of everything, then America is not as religious as the religiously correct claim; if secularists are an insolent minority trying to erode the values of the majority, then they are not in charge of everything."[46]

People who believed and promoted the secular humanism myth referred to the 1933 document known as the "Humanist Manifesto I" and to the 1973 updated version, the "Humanist Manifesto II." "The critics of public education see a link between these 'humanist' documents and the religion of secular humanism, as they define it."[47] But such critics defined it in various and indeterminate ways so as to confuse and conflate "humanistic education" and even "the humanities" with secular humanism. Moreover, according to some, in arguing that humanism was biblical absolutism's evil Other, opponents of public education belied their own paranoia.[48] Instead of the paranoia thesis, Martin Marty recognized that opponents of public education were right that textbooks and schools did a poor job of teaching about religion in general because "of an atrophy of imagination among textbook writers and the school boards that buy books," but "not because a dedicated set of votaries influenced by documents called *Humanist Manifestos* have engaged in a conspiracy to keep all religion, or 'other' religion at bay."[49]

Alice Moore had no problem espousing these conspiracist notions in various interviews and at many meetings. She believed that an "alien force" was spreading throughout the country, but she did not refer to the force as "*secular* humanism." She said, "All this Humanistic philosophy—that no higher authority outside man exists. Most behavioral scientists are pushing this for the schools, but it is alien to Christianity, which teaches that there is an outside authority that determines right or wrong. These people want to use schools as change agents to make a 'humanistic' society, without Christianity."[50] The reference to behavioral scientists is likely derived from a critique of one of the signers of the 1973 Humanist Manifesto, the famous behaviorist B. F. Skinner, and to the related fear that students were becoming programmed into communism by behaviorist means. This fear was aroused beginning in 1969 with the wide distribution of the film *Pavlov's Children (They May Be Yours)*, which linked "sex education to communism, warn[ing] that sex education was part of a one-world conspiracy to 'reduce morality of all to the standard of the most immoral.'"[51] Likewise, Moore deplored the idea that the new textbooks supposedly asked students "to debate moral relativism."

According to religious studies professor Clayton L. McNearney, who methodically analyzed all the letters to the editors of Charleston newspapers printed during the textbook controversy, the parents who joined Moore's opposition to the books tended to believe that "a specific theology informs the approach taken in these textbooks." But those parents and letter writers had

> some difficulty describing this theology. At times the claim is made that 'atheism' is a 'form of religion.' Other times they might insist that 'humanism' is itself a 'narrow teaching,' i.e., a particular or sectarian point of view. More commonly they fulminate against the 'situation ethics' *advocated* by these texts. As they use it, the phrase 'situation ethics' covers a multitude of sins, but it is meant primarily to refer to the 'non-judgmental atmosphere' of the textbooks. Whether we describe this atmosphere and approach as naturalistic, rationalistic or humanistic, the important point to note is that under whatever name it relativizes all claims to the Absolute.[52]

Especially in focusing on situation ethics and moral relativism, letters to the editor were reflecting if not quoting directly the literature from previous right-wing campaigns led by the Christian Crusade, the John Birch Society, and others.[53] The fact that literature from both organizations was available at American Opinion bookstores explains how such publications came into Kanawha County. As chapter 2 detailed, George Dietz, who printed thousands of anti-textbook flyers for protesters, operated the local American Opinion bookstore in Reedy, West Virginia, just about an hour outside of Charleston.[54] Moreover, protesters' mention of humanism and Moore's particular demonizing of "Humanistic philosophy" rather than communism was right in step with the shift made in contemporary publications such as the 1972 Christian Crusade pamphlet, *The Sinister Assault on Family*, which singled out humanism as the shadowy force behind "indoctrination" that heretofore had been primarily attributed to communists. Opposition to secular humanism was ushering in the family values discourse of cultural conservatism and the New Right.

One reason for this shift was the success of exposés of the Christian Crusade printed in a variety of popular magazines such as *Look, Life, Redbook*, and *Reader's Digest* in the late 1960s. These magazines criticized Drake, the Christian Crusade, and the John Birch Society for using McCarthyesque "smear sheets and scare tactics."[55] Once the anti–sex-education campaigns were revealed as a bunch of red-baiters, the jig of fomenting discontent among parents who would pay for materials and speakers who could "prove" the existence of conspiracy was up. In 1969, when Drake refused to tone down his anticommunist zeal, Hargis fired him and "announced a fifty percent decline in Crusade's income" only a month later.[56] Clearly the 1960s anti–sex-education campaigns were lucrative—until they were widely exposed as an outdated routine, the Old Right anticommunism of Joseph McCarthy.

This discursive shift away from McCarthyesque anticommunism is evident in issues of the *Christian Crusade Weekly* that dealt with the West Virginia textbook controversy. The Tulsa-based Christian Crusade capitalized on Kanawha County. They featured Moore in their publications, brought her to Oklahoma to give a lecture, printed her talk, sold tapes of the lecture, and sent out direct-mail fund-raising letters that highlighted Kanawha County. Publishing articles on the textbook controversy by nationally known anticommunists Max Rafferty, Charles Secrest, and Billy James Hargis as well as reports and interviews from West Virginians Marvin Horan, Linda Paul, and Alice Moore, *Christian Crusade Weekly* linked the textbook controversy in Charleston to the new John Marshall Fundamental School in Pasadena, California, where conservative parents were demanding education free from "open campuses, modular scheduling, unstructured learning, ongoing relevance or the other bilge that passes for the wave of the future."[57] Despite the idea of *going back* to basics and thwarting what was seen as needlessly futuristic modes of education, these articles nevertheless reflected and promoted a conservative wave *of the future* by playing up the godlessness of the books and downplaying the new curriculum itself as a communist conspiracy.

Two headlines in the issue that reported Alice Moore's visit to Tulsa suggest this shift. The primary, front-page headline was "Public Schools Undermine God's Law." On page four there is a shorter article about how the Communist Party newspaper, the *Daily World*, was reporting on Kanawha County, headlined "Communists Enter the Textbook Controversy."[58] Entering rather than spearheading the controversy, communists were seen as an adjunct to the attack on the family, not the instigators. The old cry of communist infiltration was giving way to warnings of a conspiracy against "God-given moral absolutes on which our nation was founded," an attack aimed at "tear[ing] down the relationship between children and parents."[59]

It was not until after the Kanawha County conflict that the specific term "secular humanism" gained widespread popularity and currency as *the* name of the dreaded conspiracy against "our children."[60] After the Kanawha County controversy died down in 1975, a slew of publications appeared that heralded secular humanism as the real threat to school children, displacing the overt anticommunism that had characterized earlier attacks on public education. The most influential of these publications were from new organizations and institutions that constituted the New Right.[61] Key among these was the nascent Heritage Foundation, which was founded in 1973 and closely connected with the Kanawha County textbook controversy in the news:

> The media again stressed the Heritage–New Right connection when the foundation's legal counsel, James McKenna, paid frequent visits to Kanawha County, West Virginia, to help parents who objected to the liberal textbooks chosen for their schools. The struggle [of] the Kanawha County parents against West Virginia's educational establishment (and the National Education Association) was prominently featured in *Conservative Digest* and other New Right publications. Further evidence of Heritage's tilt to the New Right was provided by its publication, in late 1976, of a *Critical Issues* study entitled "Secular Humanism and the Schools: The Issue Whose Time Has Come," by Dr. Onalee McGraw. The thirty-page pamphlet was described as "a case study of the growth of humanistic teaching in the public schools and the efforts of local parent groups to stymie the humanistic trend." It quickly went into a second printing and became one of Heritage's most popular early studies.[62]

McGraw's tract was geared toward a Washington, D.C., audience, focusing prominently on the implications that secular humanism had for policy. Even her discussion of local parent groups, specifically that of Frederick, Maryland, served the larger purpose of delineating policy points about particular aspects attributed to secular humanism. For example, McGraw provided terminological or historical "background" and then a statement on "policy" regarding particular topics (such as situation ethics, group therapy, sensitivity training) that were said to constitute humanistic education.

McGraw's work thereby encouraged campaigns in "local communities, in the Courts, and in the halls of Congress," where the Heritage Foundation decided around this time to channel its energies.[63] McGraw's pamphlet was clearly designed to prepare policymakers and members of Congress to push legislation prohibiting "the government from establishing a religion of secularism by affirmatively opposing or showing hostility to theistic religion, values, and beliefs."[64] Congressman John Conlan (Republican from Arizona) offered such a bill in May 1976 that passed the House but not the Senate. McGraw and the Heritage Foundation succeeded in making the secular humanism conspiracy a credible narrative for policymakers whose constituents would no longer stomach Old Right rhetoric. As Martin Marty explained, what McGraw, Conlan, and

> the millions who buy books by militant clergy of their outlook contend is that all alternatives to 'traditional theism' amount to a competitive religion of Secular Humanism. When a textbook does not mention the God of the Bible, they say, it necessarily leaves a void which it must fill with the Religion of Secular Humanism. If so, argue plaintiff parents in courts and complaining parents to school boards, at least give us "equal time." Why not give privilege and, in effect, subsidy to, the traditional religion of the vast majority, a religion that currently comes under the banner of "Judeo-Christian?"[65]

Indeed, McGraw's next publication for the Heritage Foundation was about subsidizing school choice, which had originally been "a key element in the southern strategy crafted by Richard Nixon to win the votes of the followers of George Wallace."[66] In the early 1970s, campaigns for school choice did not appeal primarily "to religious-right voters but to former southern segregationists who did not want their children to attend racially integrated schools, and to northern white ethnics who sought an alternative to court-ordered busing for their children."[67] But by the 1980s, with the new narrative of secular humanism securely backing it, school choice was safely revived not as a racist throwback to the days of segregation but as a measure to save "our children" from educators. In this way, secular humanism became the new mobilizing narrative of the Old Right's Southern strategy, courtesy of New Right institutions such as the Heritage Foundation.

Another sign of the displacement of anticommunism with anti–secular humanism is the 1977 John Birch Society publication of *The SIECUS Circle: a Humanist Revolution*. In the John Birch Society's 1969 *Sex Education Problems*, SIECUS was smeared as a commie plot. But after the Christian Crusade, after the textbook controversy, after the Heritage Foundation, even the John Birch Society blamed humanism more prominently than communism as the "revolutionary" force threatening America.

And, as Alice Moore's and Onalee McGraw's presence attests, it was important that women—those Sweet Alices—led the way in promoting this new narrative of secular humanism, lest that other irritation from the late 1960s and early 1970s, namely feminism, get in the way of the New Right.

Reagan's Sweet Alice

The best example of how leaders of the New Right capitalized on Kanawha County and replicated the formula of Sweet Alice and secular humanism is Connaught Coyne Marshner, who was married to William Marshner, a prominent New Right leader and one of the architects of cultural conservatism. In 1978, after years of shuffling "back and forth between the Free Congress Committee [which her husband helped create] and the Heritage Foundation, wherever her services were most needed," the ubiquitous "conservative gadfly" Connie Marshner published *Blackboard Tyranny* (see figure 10).[68] Like Gordon Drake's similarly titled *Blackboard Power*, Marshner's book featured secular humanism. Unlike Drake, Marshner also featured Kanawha County and claimed Alice Moore as a hero.

Marshner was a consummate "Sweet Alice" in the sense that her conservative political identity was inextricable from her gender expression as a feminine, not feminist, woman. According to a *Washington Times* reporter, "Marshner's straight-laced style, however, is in stark contrast to her rhetoric. She and her associates don't chain themselves to gates, splatter blood on historic buildings or go on hunger strikes. Hers, the New Right style,

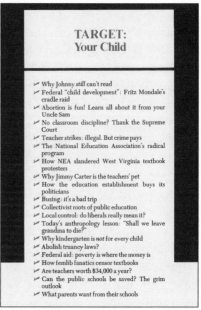

Figure 10. Repackaging Old Right anticommunism in a New Right vein, Connie Marshner's *Blackboard Tyranny* (1978) put Drake's arguments against the NEA in a familial context, championing West Virginian Alice Moore as a concerned mother and declaring "your child" a "target."

is reserved, coolly intellectual, well-organized, politely gracious—never strident." In addition, Marshner "almost always wears dresses, no more makeup than a nun in modern dress and her speech is as immaculate as her attire." Opposed to feminist principles personally and politically, going so far as to lobby against day-care centers and a bill against domestic violence, Marshner claimed that "being female and feminine . . . was no liability."[69]

In fact, in *Blackboard Tyranny*, which is geared toward invigorating a "parent's rights" movement against the "education establishment," Marshner went to great lengths to counsel women on how to present themselves and organize against secular humanism, which she saw as the reason for poor test scores, illiteracy, and rebellious teenagers. In particular, she cautions against excessive emotions, of the kind that were seen as the female hysteria of working-class mothers in Kanawha County:

> Above all, *do not become emotional.* Emotional parents, particularly mothers, seldom get anywhere with a bureaucrat. If you are all worked up, steel yourself and let your anger make you forceful. Do not allow

yourself to be handled like a frenzied feline—by being mentally put into a cage. If the administrator dismisses you, in his own mind, as an emotional female of no significance, almost automatically he will dismiss your case as trivial. That is easy for him: you have showed yourself incapable of speaking in cold, hard facts.[70]

Delivering "cold, hard facts" supplied by New Right institutions such as the Heritage Foundation and textbook monitors Mel and Norma Gabler, Marshner's readers were tutored to follow the rules by which Alice Moore, not her working-class counterparts, played.

Since Marshner had "organized a training seminar for the Kanawha County textbook protesters in 1975," it is difficult to say just who first taught whom the rules of performing as Sweet Alice.[71] Clearly Marshner's political activism preceded her going to Kanawha County, and Moore's objections were made well before Marshner's arrival, but the visit was likely a give-and-take to and from Washington, D.C., and Charleston, West Virginia. As much as Alice Moore may have learned from Connie Marshner, Connie could have learned from Alice.

In the PBS documentary series, *With God on Our Side: The Rise of the Religious Right in America*, the episode featuring the Kanawha County textbook controversy directly precedes an episode exploring Marshner's campaign to disrupt Jimmy Carter's 1980 White House Conference on Families (WHCF). The sequence suggests that one led to another historically. But there is evidence that Marshner's campaign against the WHCF was actually modeled after the West Virginia textbook controversy. Presenting herself not as a political strategist and affiliate of right-wing think tanks, but as a "concerned mother,"[72] Marshner seemed to reprise the role of Sweet Alice in Washington, D.C., attempting to re-create on a national level the uprising that had occurred in Kanawha County. Even though she was well known in Washington conservative circles, "probably because of her low-key style, she is not as recognizable as [Phyllis] Schlafly," and so she could credibly perform the Sweet Alice role.[73] Therefore, although she served officially as the chairman of the National Pro-Family Coalition on the White House Conference on Families, sharing that responsibility with Schlafly, Marshner not only "developed the strategy for sending pro-family delegates to the conference" but also appeared less as a high-profile political activist and more as a concerned mother.[74]

Sociologist William Martin detailed how Marshner developed that strategy for sending "pro-family" delegates to each of the three regional conference sites (Baltimore, Minneapolis, and Los Angeles) that comprised the WHCF. Marshner "and her growing network attempted to capture as many spots as they could. Their first effort, in Virginia, was phenomenally successful; mobilized through churches, Bible study groups, parents' organizations, and other pro-family bodies, they packed the convention and walked away with twenty-two of twenty-four elective positions."[75] They were less successful in the other two cities, but nevertheless Marshner's motive was clear: she was obviously determined to load the conference with conservatives.

During the first day of the conference, these delegates overwhelmed the process by demanding, often in the exact same language, a definition of "family" in conservative Christian terms, and objecting to the Equal Rights Amendment, abortion, and gay rights. One woman reportedly admitted, "I came to read the script" that had been provided to her by leaders of a Mormon contingent. During the second day, Marshner staged a walkout, complaining to the media that "WCHF organizers stacked the deck against pro-family representation"; she called it explicitly "a liberal stacked deck."[76] The walkout was not a spontaneous act of dissent, but part of what critics labeled a "cynical agenda" to make it appear that good Christian folks had come dutifully and open-mindedly to the conference, were repelled by its process and discussion, and felt morally obliged to denounce it.[77]

Evidence of this cynicism included the fact that "had Marshner's band of angry warriors not de-camped, they could easily have defeated" a resolution that "lent the conference's endorsement to the ERA, abortion on demand, and gay rights," which had passed by only a single vote.[78] Moreover, profamily delegates in Minneapolis had been instructed by their peers "to vote in favor of the pro-abortion resolution. They explained that since the resolution had passed by only a single vote in Baltimore, if the Minneapolis conference took a pro-life position, it would undermine the dissenters' claim that the conference was biased against conservative views." In this way, Marshner's involvement with the White House Conference on Families appeared to be a bust for conservative forces but actually was a huge success. It was

> the first serious attempt since the 1930s to build a grassroots alliance between culturally conservative Protestants and Catholics. Marshner, a Catholic like Phyllis Schlafly and Paul Weyrich, later called the campaign against the WHCF an instance of "applied ecumenism" in which

Catholics "tutored" sometimes-wary evangelicals and fundamentalists in the ways of practical politics. As Marshner also recalls, the conservative campaign against the WHCF was "primarily a woman's movement." Marshner in retrospect sounded as proud as any feminist when she remembered the "moms" prodding sluggish clergymen in action.[79]

Attacking the WHCF was, said Marshner, an excellent "training ground for pro-family activists" whose actions convinced the media that "this place is stacked" with liberal, not conservative, delegates.

In this triumph it is important to note a particular irony that links Marshner's strategy back to Alice Moore's six years earlier. Marshner had successfully blamed the conference organizers for "stacking the deck," even while she had, according to *Conservative Digest* and William Martin, devised and overseen the strategy for getting participants to the conference in an effort to emphasize conservative issues. She herself had attempted to "stack" the conference and then turned around and blamed her opposition for doing the same. It was a political case of the pot calling the kettle black.

Back in Kanawha County, Alice Moore did something similar when a citizens' review panel was proposed as a compromise between opponents and supporters of the books. Members of the school board were to appoint citizens to serve on the panel. At first Moore approved the idea, then rejected it, then agreed to it again. In the process of this vacillation, she admonished a fellow board member, Douglas Stump, for reneging on a promise to pick a "minister known to be opposed to the books" and declared the panel was stacked against her. An editorial in the *Charleston Gazette* summarized Moore's fluctuation then astutely analyzed the situation:

> What piqued our interest throughout the off-again, on-again performance of Mrs. Moore was the show of innocence with which she declared the review panel was stacked against her position. Mrs. Moore has proved that she is an experienced in-fighter. She isn't so naïve as to suppose that pro-textbook board members would appoint reviewers predisposed to an antitextbook view. We may be certain that Mrs. Moore didn't, herself, pick reviewers at random. She publicly upbraided Stump for declining to choose a panelist favorable to the Moore view. By all signs, then, Mrs. Moore was busily seeking to stack the panel in her favor even as she sulked about similar strategy on the part of other board members.[80]

Commentators who saw fit to provide actual political analysis of Moore's actions and not simply malign her in the sexist fashion of the day understood that "stacking the panel backfired" on Sweet Alice.

But it did not backfire on Connie Marshner. This same strategy of blaming your opposition for "stacking" a panel or a conference while disavowing your own attempts to do the same with a remarkably disingenuous "show of innocence" succeeded in Washington six years later. It seems that Marshner, who had visited protesters in Kanawha County, improved on Moore's stacking strategy for a larger scale action with national implications. She was a Sweet Alice for the Reagan era.

Obfuscating the strategy she developed to raise such a ruckus, Marshner represented the conservative campaign to disrupt the WHCF proceedings as a natural, organic uprising. In the year Ronald Reagan appointed her chair of the President's Commission on the Financing of Elementary and Secondary Education, Marshner wrote, "From the beginning of Carter's White House Fiasco," which she said was directed by "feminists and anti-family bureaucrats, with some help from the homosexual movement," "parents and concerned family members resisted."[81] Highlighting the range of the dissenters, Marshner suggested that the protest had been a spontaneous one, never mind her orchestration of it, and endowed the protesters with a singular motive: "Traditional conservatives, fundamentalist Christians, Mormons, traditional Catholics, Protestants, Orthodox Jews, blue-collar/working-class housewives and ministers of all faiths began to show up at state WHCF meetings to protest and attempt to reverse the coming of the secular humanist state."[82] Secular humanism was the reason to protest. It was the reason, according to Marshner's *Blackboard Tyranny*, that a parents' movement was needed and why women must appear to lead it.

Blackboard Tyranny not only demonized secular humanism as the "boogeyman of the Christian right,"[83] but also claimed the impulse to oppose it as a "natural right" and Christian duty of parents. Defining secular humanism precisely as a religion, Marshner also portrays it as an infectious disease, spread in the classroom, which explains generational tensions and family discord:

> Mothers have long observed that after the first child starts school, the rest of the family starts catching more colds and flus. But other forms of disease are not so evident. What about the personality traits that start developing? What about the dissatisfaction with family rules and routines?

What about boredom with learning, loss of curiosity about ideas and the world at large? Why do children suddenly begin to complain about responsibilities toward little brothers or sisters? Why do they resent doing accustomed chores? Why does off-color language or unfamiliar slang suddenly crop up in a child's conversation?[84]

Marshner's answer to these questions is that the "Education Establishment" turned schooling into social work long ago.

According to Marshner, the ills of "modern education" began with John Dewey, who ushered in behavior modification as a replacement for learning.[85] But the "messianic roots" of the Education Establishment were planted early on, when Horace Mann suggested that American schools should help develop democracy, instead of preserve the republic that our forefathers sought to establish. The implication is that education became a way of indoctrinating children into an egalitarian democracy, rather than a God-abiding republic.[86]

According to the footnotes in *Blackboard Tyranny*, Marshner basically lifted this explanation of "the messianic character of American education" from Rousas J. Rushdoony's 1972 book of that title. Using Rushdoony, Marshner thus suggests that the architects of nineteenth-century U.S. education—and the education "professionals" of today—aimed to replace the messiah of Jesus Christ with a different, incompatible, and conflicting "messianic" religion, secular humanism. In this regard, the "Education Establishment" is basically anti-Christian, and so parents' rights to oppose it, according to Marshner, "are not mere legal creations" but "come from God by way of the natural law; the existence of the family unit presupposes parental rights; continuation of civilized society presupposes the existence of the family unit."[87]

This particular articulation of natural rights also derives from Rushdoony, who in 1973 argued that the nuclear family is the basic unit of government under God's covenant, and that Christians should strive to apply the Bible as law to obtain "the only true order."[88] Similar to Marshner's definition of secular humanism as a religion that is by default anti-Christian because it is not Christian, Rushdoony's theology demanded that "all law is religious in nature, and every non-Biblical law-order represents an anti-Christian religion. Every law-order is a state of war against the enemies of that order, and all law is a form of warfare."[89] Thus, Rushdoony's vision was inescapably apocalyptic; that is to say, Rushdoony saw every society that is not based on the Bible to be inevitably and ineluctably at war with the theocracy that he aims, through the glory of God as prophesied in the Bible, to establish. Although Marshner eschewed such apocalyptic rhetoric, some of that sensibility appeared in her letter encouraging Christians to "reverse the coming of the secular humanism state."[90] If we extend the shared logic of Marshner's *Blackboard Tyranny* and Rushdoony's *The Messianic Character of American Education*, this purported advent of the "secular humanist state" is concurrent with, and the opposite of, the coming of Jesus Christ.

Marshner's drive to inspire and choreograph a parents' movement against public schools was clearly in step with Reconstructionism, the theology attributed to Rushdoony, who is generally perceived as being far to the right of mainstream evangelicalism, far more dogmatic than American expressions of Christian fundamentalism, and a dangerous advocate of a theocratic state. Followers of Rushdoony, known as "theonomists," "reconstructionists," or "dominionists," have been called "our version of the Taliban."[91] One of Reconstructionism's most influential tenets is that of "dominion," the idea that Christians must create a Christian society here on earth *before* Jesus Christ returns. Based on the Book of Genesis, this is not a purely Reconstructionist idea, but one that Reconstructionism has widely disseminated among many Christian Right thinkers, including "the late Frances Schaeffer, whose book *A Christian Manifesto* was an influential call to evangelical political action that sold two million copies."[92] Marshner knew Schaeffer, and quotes him in the introduction of her overtly antifeminist tract, *The New Traditional Woman*, her own manifesto for politically active Christian women written after *Blackboard Tyranny*. Putting the idea of dominion in layperson's terms to diminish suspicion of political engagement, Marshner told a *Christian Life* reporter that people should "get involved with clean politics. It is simply prejudice that believes politics is dirty and ill-informed. Christ commanded us to occupy until He comes, not to hide cringing in out-of-the-way places. Therefore, let us occupy—let us take control of all the areas of human endeavor, with government among the first."[93] That is why Marshner sought a parents' movement. According to Marshner, Christ commanded her to occupy and control all the areas of human endeavor—apparently with the help of armies of Sweet Alices.

Women were crucial to this effort of Christian occupation and control. Spending "little of her time lobbying directly," Marshner "spends more time training other lobbyists," particularly "mothers and grandmothers."[94] She saw the "'awesome potential' of the New Right women" in her college days at the University of South Carolina in the late 1960s.[95] But it was what she saw in Kanawha County that was the real turning point in her efforts to nationalize the fight against public education. For Connie Marshner, "the first inkling that most of the nation had anything resembling a parents' rights movement came in late 1974, when the Kanawha County (West Virginia) textbook controversy made front-page headlines."[96] Omitting from the story her own training session for protesters and the fact that a Heritage Foundation colleague, James McKenna, was a legal counsel for the protesters, Marshner spun a purely populist tale of one mother who stood her ground against the education bureaucracy and inspired thousands to join her in the process.

Marshner's *Blackboard*

In *Blackboard Tyranny*, Marshner's story of Kanawha County begins with the supposedly shadowy hiring of Kenneth Underwood, a suspiciously "new [school] superintendent . . . who was described by his friends as a 'dedicated humanistic educator.'" Hoping to raise the red flag of secular humanism from the start, Marshner provided no source for the quotation and no explanation that the speaker may have been confusing "humanistic" with "humanist" or "the humanities." This is a distinction she did not hesitate to make years later, however, when conservatives balked at the 1985 appointment of William Bennett as secretary of education. In a *Conservative Digest* essay, Marshner defended Bennett's suspected associations with the National Endowment for the Humanities and a Humanities Study Center in North Carolina by explaining that "when a scholar is called a 'humanist' in the old sense of the term, it means that he studies the humanities. . . .A 'humanist' studies the things of culture, as opposed to a 'scientist,' who studies things of nature."[97] Ken Underwood got no such explanation because it would have impeded Marshner's narrative of secular humanists invading West Virginia.

Marshner's narrative of the Kanawha County textbook controversy proceeded to make inaccurate claims and spurious omissions that belied her intentions and alliances. First, she discussed the book selection procedure as something out of the ordinary. She wrote, "The professional textbook committee appointed by Superintendent Underwood waited until five days before the appropriate board meeting to send in its recommendations."[98] But in fact committee members volunteered for the task of textbook selection, which was generally perceived as "a hell of a tough job, and it takes a lot of time and dedication."[99] The superintendent may have appointed her in the sense that a committee was officially called for, but Underwood himself did not choose Wood or the other teachers to serve on the committee. Moreover, all five of the textbook selection committee members were raised and educated in West Virginia.

As for the timing of the recommendations, they went according to schedule. It is true, as Marshner says, that Alice Moore "persuaded the board to withhold authorization for purchase" but not because the board had not "seen the books for itself" as she purported. As noted in chapter 2, the books had been on display at the board of education and in public libraries for at least four weeks before the selection committee made its full report and recommendation. Moore herself said that she "did not take advantage of an opportunity to go up to the Board to see [the books] because of a lack of time,"[100] but they *were* available for review by both board members and parents. Marshner continued to purport that despite Moore's success in postponing purchasing, "Superintendent Underwood went ahead and signed contracts with publishers to buy the books," suggesting that Underwood was the "humanistic" villain behind the purchasing of harmful books rather than a bureaucrat following the state mandate to order books by a particular date.[101]

Marshner's overall characterization of the conflict as one pitting "the citizens" against "the bureaucracy" or the "educational professionals" completely elided the fact that in Kanawha County (and elsewhere) the school board members *are* citizens. At work in this false duality was the simplifying technique of conservative mothers that Kintz elucidates, an imposition of "clarity" that conveniently unmuddies the waters, that ignores and denies the complexity of any given situation. So when Marshner reported that the coal miners' strike was the point at which "the NEA sent in some investigators to see what was the matter," she not only got her chronology wrong, but also she avoided revealing the more complicated situation, which was that Roscoe Keeney, leader of the West Virginia Education Association, *asked* the NEA to come to Charleston. Keeney's organization was the same group that parents rallied to oppose the Kanawha County school board by calling for the ouster of the principal at Ruthlawn Elementary School. In creating the monolithic education "bureaucracy," Marshner lumped together Kanawha County teachers and administrators, never recognizing that the relationship between these parties was sometimes unified and sometimes opposing, depending on the issue. Moreover, she positioned teachers as uniformly in opposition to parents, which was not the situation in the Ruthlawn case because the parents joined with disgruntled teachers, contacting the WVEA to join forces against Underwood, who had not taken action on their complaints about the controversial principal.[102] Marshner's dichotomy of "the bureaucracy" and "the citizens" is inaccurate in the case of Kanawha County.

Lest Marshner's populist conspiracy be mistaken for a tale about class conflict, in which the distinction between elite "professional" bureaucrats and the high-school-educated Alice Moore, with her working-class counterparts, might endorse a socialist analysis she would abhor, Marshner never mentioned Nell Wood or others on the selection committee. As both a "citizen" with working-class roots and an "educated professional," Wood would completely disrupt Marshner's populist narrative—unless, of course, Marshner took the view of one book protester who denounced Wood. She was not considered one of the "good teachers in this county who were reared in Cabin Creek or some other coal mining town" and who understand "the problems of the people surrounding them and how to cope with and resolve their problems. This does not mean Nell Wood (who is from a mining town)," the anonymous protester acknowledged, "because she has no doubt been brainwashed by Dr. Underwood."[103] Marshner could have publicized this view of Wood, but in doing so she would have risked acknowledging that some of the teachers in fact were from the working class, and that all the selection committee members were raised and educated in West Virginia, and were therefore not the outsider, "elite" professionals she monolithically demonized.

Also in this effort to avoid a class-based analysis, Marshner focused not on the economic exploitation of the protesters, but rather on their cultural values as the cause of their lower social status. Marshner sarcastically reported that the NEA's "learned conclusion was that the hillbillies were bigoted Bible-thumpers who really needed multiethnic, pluralistic books to bring their children into the modern world." Elsewhere, Marshner wrote, "whereas it had once felt comfortably superior to the uncultured hillbillies, the board was now despised by the very people it had previously patronized."[104] It was the matter of culture, then, not class, that allowed Marshner to fashion the story of Kanawha County as a successful right-wing tale.

Key to diverting attention away from the plight of the protesters as exploited people fed up with lack of representation in an economy based on absentee corporate owners was Marshner's emphasis on Elmer Fike and his middle-class, conservative reasons for protesting the school board. Marshner's examples of Fike in *Blackboard Tyranny* fit neatly with her attempt to demonstrate that the NEA is a "totalitarian" agent of secular humanism. "The founder of the Business and Professional Peoples' Alliance for Better Textbooks of Kanawha County, West Virginia is a grandfather whose own children long ago finished college," Marshner reported. "Yet Elmer Fike's interest in education has stayed high because, as a businessman, he is acutely aware of the failure of schools today to graduate employable students."[105] Marshner again mentioned Fike's organization as a key player because of their ability to publicize and mobilize: "The Business and Professional Peoples' Alliance for Better Textbooks was organized, and bought a full-page ad in the *Gazette*, quoting extensively from the profane books."[106] In *Blackboard Tyranny*, Fike and Moore are the only protest leaders named. There is no mention of the leaders who hailed from the working class—Avis Hill or Marvin Horan—and certainly no hint of Klansman Ed Miller or neo-Nazi George Dietz who printed up so many flyers and stoked the flames of the protest with the magazine *Liberty Bell*.

For Marshner, Kanawha County was pivotal in the fight against public education because "West Virginia woke up the rest of the country." The practice of setting up citizens' review boards was one favorable result, she wrote.[107] As was her way, Marshner portrayed the "parents' movement" as a grassroots effort that was entirely natural and spontaneous—not a matter of political agitation and organization by top conservative strategists. Moreover, the organic "West Virginia battle did more than alert the country to the textbook crisis," she claimed. "Because it was so publicized, parents who had been toiling unrewarded in their local areas suddenly realized that they were not alone. After the media made West Virginia a national issue, stories began to filter in from Michigan and Maryland and New York and Pennsylvania—and many other states. Parent groups got in touch with each other across state lines."[108] Here Marshner completely omitted the fact that the Heritage Foundation became a clearinghouse for those groups and was the organization that brought them together. "As early as 1975, the Heritage Foundation formed the national Congress for Educational Excellence to coordinate the activities of roughly 200 text-book-protester organizations nationwide," most of which were probably established as John Birch Society MOTOREDE chapters.[109] Connie Marshner attributed the parents' movement to the Kanawha County text-book controversy, not to the efforts of her Heritage Foundation: "Without West Virginia as a catalyst, it might have been years before parent activists recognized their potential impact."[110]

It was Marshner's goal to politicize parents, especially mothers, ever since she was "at the forefront of a successful drive to get then President Nixon to veto a bill which would have established federal day care centers."[111] Due in part to her efforts, Marshner witnessed an overwhelming response against the proposal. "There was more mail than on any other issue before or since—including Watergate," she said. "I realized then that there are real women out there in the real world who are concerned about family values. Until then, they were basically isolated from the political process."[112] Since then, Marshner planned to bring women into politics, as per her mandate from Christ, to "occupy" and "control."

In light of this background, we can surely say, as Marshner did, that West Virginia was pivotal, but not because the textbook controversy brought conservative mothers and Christian parents together on its own merits. Rather, it was because people such as Marshner created a narrative in which the Kanawha County textbook controversy served as a pivot point. The simplicity and seeming universality of the story was not lost on those who examined the textbook controversy. As one commentator explained,

> There was a hero or in this case a heroine, and there was a victory where the forces of good—depending, of course, on your perspective—won out over impossible odds. The villains included the school board, the administration—particularly the superintendent—and the books. The heroine was Alice Moore. The fact that she was a school board member, a lone dissenting voice—the little woman, the little mother standing her ground against seemingly overwhelming odds—imbued her, in the eyes of her supporters, with the aura of a crusader. The victory was a stunning one—the multiethnic, multicultural materials—all 325 challenged titles— were removed [at least for a while] and the superintendent was forced to resign. No wonder Kanawha County became the rallying cry for the next four years.[113]

Fashioning the narrative in this populist fairy-tale way, Marshner conveniently left out the fact that Alice Moore, Elmer Fike, and the rest of "the citizens" were much aided by Marshner, McKenna, and other cultural conservatives, including Robert Whitaker and Robert Hoy, whom I will discuss in chapter 5, and Robert Dornan, another conservative crusader who lent his political savvy to the textbook protesters in Kanawha County before becoming a member of the House of Representatives. It was in his capacity as a member of Congress that Dornan supplied a laudatory preface to *Blackboard Tyranny*, which ironically obscured such political maneuverings, opting to portray Kanawha County as an inevitable clash of absolutes and Alice Moore as the Rosa Parks of a new movement.

This tendency toward hiding influence and alliances—which later would be called "stealth politics" and attributed to the Christian Coalition of the 1990s—was a tactic Marshner sought to pass on to other conservative mothers in 1978. In *Blackboard Tyranny*, Marshner instructed her readers not only to control their anger but also to hide their suspicions. "Avoid letting the teacher think you feel she's just a pawn in the hands of a monolithic NEA conspiracy," cautioned Marshner. "Parents can learn a great deal by volunteering inside a school, if they find the time to do it. Substitute teaching on a regular basis is also a good way to gather intelligence." Gathering intelligence about the formidable, pervasive "disease" of secular humanism in the schools might tip the reader from cloak-and-dagger mode to all-out hysteria, so Marshner commanded: "Don't be paranoid. Don't assume that the [school] commission members are all evil schemers who have signed the Humanist Manifesto. . . .You cannot expect them to be knowledgeable: assume they are innocent of nefarious intentions until they prove the contrary." When it comes time to take action, such as launching a "systematic letters-to-the-editor campaign," "the crucial thing here is not to give the *appearance* of an organized campaign."[114]

Equally crucial, according to *Blackboard Tyranny*, was to relinquish the conspiracist language and tactics of earlier anticommunist campaigns. For example, Marshner cautioned her reader against conducting "smears," which were significant tools of 1950s McCarthy politics, although she did not name the tactic as such. Mothers were right to be suspicious of their children's teacher, but should "never slur her intelligence or competence," Marshner instructed. Lest this be heeded as simply a getting-more-with-honey-than-vinegar matter of strategic etiquette, Marshner wrote, "The last thing you or your youngster needs is for your son to be overheard telling his classmates that you think Miss Johnson is a crypto-pinko." Mothers were also told that "in 1971, during the child-development campaign, the phrase 'Sovietizing of American youth' pigeonholed its users as right-wingers. Now that may not be so terrible in itself. However, a more desirable impression to give would have been that of nonideological objection to federal child care." In other words, it was not inaccurate to suggest that American youth were being subjected to communist plots and propaganda, but this particular "ideological" posture was no longer, in 1978, a "desirable" stance. Regardless of the validity of anticommunist ideas, Marshner implied, using the tactics and the language of the McCarthy era will not work effectively. Marshner never instructed her readers not to believe the anticommunist ideas; she basically suggested that they hide them and create a more palatable "impression."[115]

Red-baiting simply would not do, and neither would repeating those anticommunist conspiracy theories with anti-Semitic overtones. Again Marshner referred obliquely to anticommunist rhetoric but did not deny it. Without denouncing particular narratives of anticommunist conspiracies but certainly alluding to them, Marshner encouraged her readers to avoid them in their new "parents' rights" quest against secular humanism:

> There is nothing arcane or obscure about parents' rights. Therefore, if your parents' group is working for a candidate and trying to attract supporters, it makes no sense to waste time on arguments over possible sinister implications of the symbols on a one-dollar bill. There is no need to advert to secret languages and secret meanings and secret societies that are controlling the country and destroying the world. There are enough perfectly obvious examples of educationist totalitarianism in everyday school life all over the country. Trying to explain the local school board's stupidity as part of a worldwide conspiracy makes extremely difficult a job that would normally be fairly easy to anyone who approached the point by appealing to the commonsense of those who pay the tax assessments dictated by that school board. Enough said.[116]

In dismissing discussions of "symbols on a one-dollar bill," Marshner was referring to various conspiracy theories regarding supposedly Masonic and Jewish imagery on the back of dollar bills, including the pyramid and its banner heralding "Novos Ordo Seclorum," which translates as "New Order of the Ages," reflecting the revolutionary spirit of the founding fathers who designed the seal, and the grouping of stars placed above the eagle's head on the right-hand side of the bill. Mistranslating the Latin as "New World Order," some right-wing conspiracists associate the pyramid with Freemasonry, rumored at various historical points to be an anti-Christian plot devised by Masons such as George Washington. Because the thirteen stars, symbolic of the original colonies, are spatially situated so that one could draw a six-pointed shape resembling the Star of David around their perimeters, other conspiracists claim this as evidence of a

Jewish-controlled financial system. Further purported evidence for this: turn the bill upside down to see how the tail feathers of the bird resemble a menorah.

Such anti-Semitic interpretations of imagery on U.S. currency were promoted throughout the twentieth century by various right-wing writers, as we have seen. Marshner's request that her activists stop talking about "secret languages and secret meanings and secret societies that are controlling the country and destroying the world" clearly referenced conspiracy theories like those that had West Virginia Klansmen believing that Lady Bird Johnson and Franklin Delano Roosevelt were secret Jews ushering in the Zionist Occupied Government. But Marshner's was not a request to stop conspiracist thinking, just to refocus it. *Blackboard Tyranny* encouraged readers to drop the conspiracist language of bygone eras and, nevertheless, to adopt the conspiracist narrative of the 1970s and beyond: secular humanism.

Marshner did not invent the idea of secular humanism and was not the first to suggest it was a totalitarian conspiracy moving primarily through the U.S. education system. She was hardly the best known or the most powerful conservative to articulate a defense of children from a supposed new class of elitist educators and government bureaucrats who worried "that families were coming between the professionals and the children whose future they wanted to form."[117] This populist idea of a pernicious, sinister class of people preceded Marshner and succeeded her. But that is not to say that her work was insignificant because it was unoriginal. On the contrary, it was very significant.

What Connie Marshner and her New Right cohort achieved with the story of secular humanism was a "neoconservative version of the new-class theory," a populist narrative that had so much power it made the Kanawha County textbook controversy a right-wing triumph rather than a leftist uprising of working-class people. On the national level, the new-class theory operated ubiquitously as a narrative of secular humanism to the point of cliché:

> Although it was never plausible and has been convincingly discredited, the neoconservative version of the new-class theory has become one of the clichés of the Republican right. The reason is that it gives the appearance of social-scientific validation to the apocalyptic conspiracy theories of the mostly southern and western Protestant fundamentalists upon whom conservatives now depend for votes. By talking about a new-

class conspiracy of "amoral elites" trying to brainwash "our children," Ivy
League intellectuals on the right like Kristol and Novak and Bennett and
Kirkpatrick appear to be giving credibility to the deepest nightmares of
deluded working-class white evangelical Protestants.[118]

Connie Marshner was therefore not the first or the best known conservative to promote secular humanism as a new narrative for the New Right.
But she, unlike the Ivy League intellectuals, did more to reach out to the
non–Ivy League crowd, to the mothers in whom she saw not a "deluded
working-class" but "real women isolated from the political process."
Marshner centralized the New Right women, following the example of
Kanawha County, where Alice Moore occupied the center of attention.

Marshner saw that in West Virginia in 1974 a woman with a capacity to
characterize an issue in terms of super-simple clarity and conspiracy occupied the center of dissent. This was the role of Sweet Alice, a political
persona that New Right strategists attempted to replicate on a national
scale in the form of a parents' movement. To mobilize this movement,
Marshner deployed a new narrative, one close enough to the Old Right's
anticommunist conspiracies but devoid of red-baiting rhetoric and salacious stories of secret societies seeking world domination. This was the
New Right's new narrative of secular humanism, a story of urgency but
not hysteria, a story told by the cool "southernized" voices of Sweet Alices,
those mothers who sought to protect "our children" from the supposed
evils of a post–civil rights world. For the Sweet Alice of the Reagan administration, Connie Marshner, that post–civil rights world was all about
ethnicity. "Ours is an age of neo-ethnicity," she declared. "Blacks are proud
to be blacks, and want their public education system to foster that pride in
their offspring; Chicanos want Chicano language, customs, and attitudes
taught to their children. Middle-class whites do not agitate for 'white
studies' courses; the equivalent demand is for traditional American and
Christian values."[119] For Marshner and the New Right, "traditional
American and Christian values" equaled the "neo-ethnicity" of whiteness
without calling it white.

By the time Alice Moore was campaigning for reelection to the school
board in 1976, her image was as solidified as the concept of secular
humanism, and the reverence of her had trumped the revilement. In a
political advertisement, her photograph is a carefully constructed image to
show Sweet Alice as holy, pure, and feminine even in her untraditional role
as a middle-class working woman (see figure 11). The photograph features

Figure 11. Campaigning for reelection, Moore appeared in a holy
light. Political advertisement, Charleston Newspapers. Reproduced
with permission.

a white light shining down so strongly from above that Moore's raven
locks look almost blond. Her long, quadrupled strand of pearls indicates
femininity, fertility, fidelity, and affluence. Her eyes are directed upward;
she is looking to the heavens. And we, as viewers of the photograph, are
looking up at her. She is the quintessential conservative woman of the
1970s, the epitome of Marshner's "new traditional woman": inherently a
mother, indubitably a politician, irrepressibly a Christian. The advertisement lists Moore's expectations of the Kanawha County schools, which
include respecting "family privacy and our right as parents to rear our

children according to our own moral, ethical, and religious beliefs without interference." There is no longer any need to pose this expectation in terms of opposing multiracial literature or protecting white women and children from the words of black writers such as Eldridge Cleaver. The whiteness of "our children" is understood, just as the whiteness of Sweet Alice is coded in her pearls and in the heavenly light that makes her hair look anything but black. In 1976, Alice Moore was reelected to the Kanawha County Board of Education by a landslide.

WHITE FOR PURITY was the way a textbook protester explained why she pinned a white carnation on the Rev. Avis Hill as he was released from jail Friday and was greeted by about 50 supporters. She said the carnation symbolized that even though the minister had been in jail he wasn't a criminal.
(Gazette Photo by Leo Chabot)

FIGURE 12. Symbols of whiteness functioned during the textbook controversy much as they did at the turn of the twentieth century, signifying the purity of one's soul, the innocence of one's actions, and a spiritual essence that transcends bloodline or biology. Leo Chabot, *Charleston Gazette*, October 19, 1974. Reproduced with permission.

CHAPTER FOUR

Reproducing the Souls of White Folk

The previous chapter discussed how Connie Marshner's *Blackboard Tyranny* aimed to inspire mothers to assume the prescribed role of defender against secular humanism—in effect, to see themselves as Sweet Alices, feminine conservative Christian activists. In this way, *Blackboard Tyranny* is an excellent example of how political discourse narrates subjects as victims with an untouchable American core—a protester's soul—that compels them to fight back. If people were already possessed of this fighting spirit then books such as *Blackboard Tyranny* would not need to exist. But there is a need for such instruction because political discourse actually creates the political subjects it is said merely to represent.

As we have seen, *Blackboard Tyranny* downplayed the political mobilization it took to heighten conflicts over the Kanawha County textbooks or the White House Conference on Families, attempting to make them appear solely organic and naturally arising from the American people. Acknowledging this is not to say that Marshner, McKenna, and their New Right cohort were particularly nefarious, dishonest, or engaged in a clandestine conspiracy. And it is not to say that outsiders were simply leading Kanawha County protesters around by the nose, duping them with their apocalyptic or conservative ideology. There was nothing particularly secret about New Right initiatives in the 1970s or since. On the contrary, the political aims of the New Right have been quite apparent and loudly stated. Acknowledging how *Blackboard Tyranny* represents political work as personal conviction, then, is simply acknowledging how political identities are not merely reported or awakened by discourses surrounding protest but actually forged as new subject positions.

In this chapter I take seriously the idea of forging or "reproducing" political identities or subjects rather than awakening a dormant but already existing discontent. Just as we explored in chapter 1 how the images and ideas of Appalachia, namely the hillbilly, are redeployed and "reinvented," here we will discuss how Appalachians are reinvented or reproduced as protesters, and specifically as political subjects who support right-wing ideologies and are engaged in right-wing campaigns. Given an opportunity and impetus—the textbook controversy—to discuss forthrightly what it meant to be a Kanawha Countian, an Appalachian, or an American, all of the protesters reiterated an established tale of victimhood and captivity while retaining the right to fight back. As we saw in chapter 3, this narrative of victimhood cast secular humanism as the bogeyman and cast Jews as the culprit behind an impending total tyranny. As we saw in chapter 1, however, scholars and journalists routinely saw these protest narratives as a matter of class consciousness. In this chapter I examine "soul" and other invocations of spirituality as the discursive connection between the right-wing apocalyptic narrative of impending tyranny and the narrative of class consciousness that is often associated with left-wing politics and was attributed to protesters of the textbooks in Kanawha County.

Protest based on the idea that one's soul is at stake is the hinge on which working-class protesters swung away from identifying as economically exploited people, middle-class protesters swung away from Old Right rhetoric, and both factions of the textbook protest swung toward identifying as victims of a cultural assault. By hearing and telling a story of how their children's souls were at stake, working-class protesters became aligned with conservative and/or right-wing discourses that spoke less and less about communism and integration and more about secular humanism or ZOG. The narrative of soul reproduced new political subjects for a post–civil rights conservatism that claimed to be colorblind, and a post–civil rights white supremacism that claimed that Jews, not blacks, were the white man's worst enemy. Of course, invoking "soul" in the 1970s for political purposes was something black nationalists were more practiced at than white conservatives. So this chapter necessarily examines the racialization as well as the politicization of fighting for the soul of "our children" and the soul of the nation. I begin by exploring how nationalism and national identity has been racialized historically, recognizing in the textbook controversy some persistent patterns from the early part of the twentieth century.

The American Race circa 1974

In the early twentieth century, immigration issues incited much talk along the lines of what it meant to be American and what it meant to be white, prompting people such as Theodore Roosevelt to embrace what we now might see as contradictory claims. As president, Roosevelt both took pride in America as a melting pot and spread fear about a white "race suicide." Roosevelt did not see a conflict in believing both in "Anglo-Saxon and Teutonic superiority *and* in the grandeur of a 'mixed' American race."[1] In fact, that very phrase, "American race," was a favorite of Roosevelt's and it effectively became a euphemism for "the white race" despite his outspoken admiration of theories of evolution and race that portrayed miscegenation as a positive thing. The trick was keeping the "mixing" to a minimum, lest cultural and genetic traits taint an otherwise robust national "racestock." "The 'American race' could absorb and permanently improve the less desirable stock of 'all white immigrants,' perhaps in two generations, but only if its most desirable 'English-speaking' racial elements were not swamped in an un-Americanized Slavic and southern European culture and biology."[2] Culture and biology went hand in hand as issues of immigration became inextricable from issues of race, which in turn became inextricable from issues of citizenship and belonging in America. The mélange of issues provided "an opportunity, the chance to create a new ideological entity—the American race. And this new entity (the American race) has substituted so successfully for its predecessor (the white race) that most Americans are genuinely shocked by any assertion of what looks like the old biological racism."[3] The shocking charge of "racism" is rightfully so fraught with insinuations of poor character and nefarious motivations that it is difficult to recognize and discuss rationally just how central being white is, historically at least, to being American without offending white people's sense of dignity and fairness. But the discursive and ideological legacy of those early twentieth-century conversations does indeed link the two.

Tracing the links between being white and being American through some of the classics of modern American fiction as well as in domestic policies and theories of race suicide during the 1920s, literary scholar Walter Benn Michaels argued that Teddy Roosevelt's ideology of the "American race" persisted beyond that era:

In fact, insofar as the question, Are you white? has been and continues to be successfully replaced by the question, Are you American?—insofar, that is as a question supposedly about biology has been preserved as a question supposedly about national identity—one might say that the very idea of American citizenship is a racial and even racist idea, racist not because it embodies a (more or less concealed) preference for white skins but because it confers on national identity something like the ontology of race.[4]

Here is revealed a logic that suffuses the comment about textbook defender James Lewis.

Recall from chapter 2 the discussion of *The Liberty Bell*'s essay, "A Message to All True Sons of Appalachia." Specifically, an embittered resident of Kanawha County warned that "we don't want and don't need Lewis' of any color around here." The implication of this remark is that the enemies of the so-called true sons of Appalachia *are* "colored" and that Jim Lewis's whiteness should not fool anyone: he is just as "colored" as people readily perceived to be "colored." This kind of statement not only comments on race but also on character, much like another old saying spoken to a white person from a white peer in mock surprise: "That's mighty white of you!" The effect of this phrase is to suggest that whatever "you" are doing, it is not usually what "you" have been doing. It is damning by faint praise. It is suggesting that you have not been acting white except in this instance. Likewise, the comment about James Lewis suggested that he was not acting white—he is therefore not really white—even though his appearance, his color, indicates that he is Caucasian. Race becomes more a matter of character, and less a matter of melanin. "A Message to All True Sons of Appalachia" insisted that character is biologically bound to bloodline, to ancestry, specifically to "Godly" "Germanic and Scotch-Irish" lineages. So, according to that logic, it is absolutely possible to be "colored" white and not be a "true son" of Appalachia, or, once the logic is extended, a true white man. Hence James Lewis can be "colored" white but not be a "true" white or a true son of Appalachia despite his appearance as a blue-eyed, sandy-haired, fair-complexioned man.

Just as Lewis's color was not enough to prove that he was a "true son of Appalachia," "white skins" were not enough to prove that one is American, even if one were speaking English and living in America. There must be more than biology, that stuff that provides mere appearance. There must be something more like an ontology of the white race, which means something demonstrable even in its invisibility. Proving one belonged to the American race in the early twentieth century was as tricky as proving one was a "true son of Appalachia" circa 1975. Clearly, one's color was no proof; white skin did not reveal the presumed character beneath it.

Posing the problems of belonging and being white in the late nineteenth century and early twentieth century are thus similar to posing the problems of belonging and being white in Kanawha County in 1975. How does one demonstrate one's "true" self? How does one at the beginning of the century demonstrate one's membership in the white race, the American race? How does one in the last quarter of the century demonstrate one's self as a truly "concerned parent," as a true American who insists on banishing "anti-American" textbooks, or as a "true son of Appalachia"? How? Symbols help. Alice Moore's aforementioned election photo deployed important symbols of femininity and whiteness: those pearls and that white light beaming down on her. Klansman Ed Miller also deployed historically resonant symbols when he appeared on the capitol steps wearing white robes. This example warrants further commentary.

Michaels argued that the white sheets worn by the original members of the Ku Klux Klan had a symbolic function of making visible what was largely invisible: membership in the white race, that particular character that color could mask. Understanding this entails, first, understanding how race became something other than mere biology. Tracing the cultural logic of the Klan back to the novel that helped popularize it and make it a modern, middle-class organization of businessmen and concerned mothers in the early twentieth century, Michaels found that identity as a white person is "based from the start on a racial principle that transcends visibility"—that goes beyond the idea of appearing white or of being "colored" white. Going back to the 1905 Thomas Dixon novel, *The Clansman*, Michaels hit on the somehow more ethereal and, paradoxically, the somehow more solid "racial principle" that allowed the Ku Klux Klan to rise up as whites and, in rising up *as* whites, to be known and recognized as whites.

That racial principle, according to *The Clansman*, "consists of 'the reincarnated souls of the Clansmen of Old Scotland.'" Like the "Message to All True Sons of Appalachia," *The Clansman* emphasizes Scots-Irish lineage as what Michaels called the "souls of white folk." But the appearance of white skin is never enough to prove one's lineage or membership in the so-called white race because a more invisible character must be proven, or claimed, too. This more invisible character is not lineage but a spiritual quality, a "soul" according to Dixon, whose tale of two white families, the Camerons and the Stonemans, during the Civil War narrated a spiritual union that goes beyond kinship to create the Ku Klux Klan. Michaels explained it well in a close reading of the novel:[5]

> Identity in *The Clansman* is always fundamentally spiritual. Thus, for example, marriage and "the close sweet home-life" can make people more "alike in soul and body" than can any physical relation. "People have told me that your father and I are more alike than brother and sister of the same blood," Mrs. Cameron writes to her daughter, "in spirit I'm sure it's true." This is why the Civil War, customarily represented as turning brothers into enemies, is represented in *The Clansman* as turning enemies into brothers. The identity of soul that brings the Stonemans and Camerons together transcends biology, replacing the natural unity of the family with a spiritual unity that, unlike the family, is genuinely indivisible. And this is why the Klan is more than a clan.[6]

Michaels went on to link the novel's view of the Klan as something spirit-like and soul-like with the nineteenth-century-law's view of a man whose racial identity confounded state courts.

Like the Supreme Court's 1896 decision in *Plessy v. Ferguson*, which said that Homer Plessy's color was not enough to discern his race (Plessy was one-eighth black and seven-eighths white, and thus "colored" under Louisiana law), *The Clansman* insisted that belonging to the white race is not literally apparent, it is not written on the body, but is of the soul, and therefore it is a spiritual essence that must be *made* visible. Michaels described how Aleck, a character in the novel, reflected the author's logic:

> Aleck's account of [the Klansmen dressed in flowing white robes and appearing as ghosts or] as 'Sperits' corroborates Dixon's; his superstitious fear of the spirits must thus be understood as a response to the terrifying representation of an essentially invisible racial identity, an identity that can't be seen in people's skins (it couldn't be seen in Homer Plessy's), but can be seen in the Klan's sheets. The purpose of the sheets, then, is not to conceal the identities of individual clansmen for, far from making their visible identities invisible, the sheets make their invisible identities

visible. The Klan wear sheets because their bodies aren't as white as their souls, because *no* body can be as white as the soul embodied in the white sheet.[7]

This cultural logic of "the souls of white folks" as a personal invisible character or property therefore extends beyond Dixon's famous novel about the Ku Klux Klan into the legal realm. And, as many scholars of race relations and critical legal studies in the twentieth century have made clear, this cultural logic of the invisible property of whiteness extends beyond the nineteenth century.[8]

But rather than review that scholarship, we can see that cultural logic of the "souls of white folks" and its invisible whiteness at work in images of the textbook controversy. Consider not only the way Alice Moore looks up to the heavenly light shining down on her as an example of imagery that succeeds in making visible the spiritual essence of a white woman's worth. Also consider the imagery involved in making visible the spiritual essence of a white man whose moral worth and righteousness was questioned. When Avis Hill, the minister who moved from protesting textbooks to protesting busing, was arrested for blocking school buses in Kanawha County and then released from jail, a woman pinned a carnation on his lapel (see figure 12). The caption read "white for purity" and thereby served as a symbol of what Hill could not prove or make visible himself, his innocence. Or, as the woman said, "the carnation symbolized that even though the minister had been in jail he wasn't a criminal."[9] Hill was not a Klansman; in fact, he suggested that his home and family may have been targeted by the Klan because he "wouldn't openly endorse them."[10] But a similar cultural logic at work in enrobing a body in white is operating in pinning a white carnation to Avis Hill's lapel. The whiteness of the sheets and the whiteness of the carnation signify what has been invisible and what must be made apparent because the body alone is no proof: the purity of one's soul, the innocence of one's actions, the spiritual essence that transcends one's bloodline or biology. This is what Walter Benn Michaels meant by the "souls of white folk": it is the essential character that is supposedly unsullied by moral ambiguity or racial impurity.

But if the Ku Klux Klan's white robes meant all that in the nineteenth century and the early twentieth century, what is the significance of the decision of the fifth-era Klan of later years to replace their robes for army-type fatigues? As we learned from the story of Ed Miller, who did appear in Klan regalia on the West Virginia state capitol steps in 1975, those white robes became less prominent throughout the 1970s. The symbolism of the Klan changed with its focus. Donning paramilitary garb in the 1980s and 1990s, the Klan deemphasized blacks and announced that the Zionist Occupied Government was its archenemy. The sartorial shift signaled the besieged mentality of the Klansman as a New (white) Warrior, akin to the Patriot militia movement but not exactly like it, akin to the National Alliance, but not exactly like it.[11] All three promoted vigilante action, whether it was the Klan's Greensboro Massacre of 1979, the Order's bank robberies and counterfeiting of the 1980s, or the Oklahoma City bombing of 1995. Like the white robes, which never were relinquished by all Klansmen, the camouflage fatigues worn by some fifth-era Klansmen ironically did not serve to hide anything—they were not meant to conceal one's body at all—but rather to render visible what the Klansmen understood as largely invisible (thanks to the media, according to Klan logic) and what they felt they knew to be "true": they were white men at war.

In tracing from the nineteenth century to the twentieth century this sartorial practice of rendering visible what is invisible and thereby claiming an identity as or a belonging to the white race and/or the American race, Walter Benn Michaels made a parallel between Thomas Dixon's *The Clansman* and William Pierce's *The Turner Diaries* that shows how even the blatant white supremacism of the late twentieth century articulated race as a cultural and spiritual, more than a biological, property. Michaels argued that Earl Turner turns the project of the mass killing of nonwhites "into a technology for identifying white people" in which "spirit and consciousness not only supplement blood, they supplant it."

> Indeed, in *The Turner Diaries*, the term "technology" is taken literally; The Order defends itself against infiltration by administering injections of drugs and monitoring the response with electrodes, a "method of interrogation" that "leaves no room for evasion or deceit." In this test for whiteness, the difference between physiology and ideology (between, say a blood test and a loyalty oath) evaporates, as both are subsumed by a "spiritual thing" that is something "more" than biological and something more than political or social as well. To join the Order is thus, as Turner says, to be "born again," and to die for it, as Turner does, is to accept its

offer of "everlasting life." In the nuclear holocaust that ends *The Turner Diaries*, the reincarnated souls of the Scots clansmen are reincarnated again.[12]

Michaels moved us back from the twentieth-century National Alliance and The Order in *The Turner Diaries* to the nineteenth-century Klansman.

Another connection can be made between the ultraright, white-supremacist idea of race as something now more spiritual than biological and the New Right idea of race as something also free from the ideological constraints of old-fashioned biological racism. What allows historian Amy Ansell to argue that the New Right has ushered in a new racism is the same thing that allows Michaels to argue that the founder of the National Alliance wrote a novel in which blood is supplanted by spirit and consciousness. As Ansell says about the New Right's take on race: "It is a form of racism that utilizes themes related to culture and nation as a replacement for the now discredited biological referents of the old racism."[13] Similarly, even while conceding the obvious point that "the commitment to a biological racism seems as strong here [in *The Turner Diaries*] as ever," Michaels adds that "its strength is at the same time a mark of its remoteness from middle-class American culture, which, substituting character for skin, has largely repudiated biological racism."[14] The only similarity between "middle-class American culture," the New Right, and the virulent white supremacism of the National Alliance was this repudiation—however tenuous or steadfast—of biology and blood as the ideological bases for race. In staking their claims as true Americans of the twentieth century, they all narrated themselves as beyond a biological essence but never beyond the spiritual realm, the realm of "spirit and consciousness" that has supplanted blood as proof.

As blood has, throughout the twentieth century, ceased to be the telltale identifier of white racial identity and supposed biological superiority, the spiritual realm has become all important. This emphasis on the spiritual eliminates or at least shortens that "remoteness from middle-class American culture" that some may take comfort in while considering the avowed white supremacism promoted by someone like Pierce. Some middle-class Americans as well as some scholars who study ultraright movements distance themselves from blatant white supremacism by suggesting that its ideology is extreme, esoteric, or downright weird in addition to being morally repugnant. But other scholars draw our attention to the way these "extreme" ideas about race are part of the literary and cultural narratives that have come to define Americanness.

Walter Benn Michaels's essay again provides a good example. He traced the idea of "good breeding" throughout American novels such as *The Great Gatsby* and *The Sun Also Rises*, arguing that characters in classic fiction reflect and perpetuate more overtly political concepts, such as the national "racestock," the fear of an "alien tide" of immigration, and white "race suicide," which were circulating among policymakers and congressmen. Like Dixon's less acclaimed novel, these examples of "great literature" were, of course, products of their time. Specifically with regard to issues of race and breeding, Michaels argued that Hemingway, for example, "made use of this threat [of immigration] to imagine not so much a *race* whose purity would be defined by its sterility (this is what Dixon did in imagining white men who could reproduce themselves racially without reproducing themselves biologically), but an *aesthetic* defined by breeding without biology."[15] Just as policy-making court decisions such as *Plessy v. Ferguson* and middle-class organizations such as the Ku Klux Klan substituted character for color as a marker of race, bourgeois writing created literature that emphasized social graces as telltale signs of race. Lest we presume reductively that he was saying Hemingway and Fitzgerald were merely reprehensible racists, Michaels closes his essay with the caveat that "it is no more appropriate to think of American racism in the 1920s as fundamentally literary than it is to think of American literature in the twenties as fundamentally racist." He then went on to claim that "it is race and literature both that have contributed to the meaning of the term 'American.'"[16] In other words, overtly political discourses about the white race and the need to preserve it are aestheticized in "great" works of literature that have contributed to the very definition of American culture. Michaels is only one among several scholars who has successfully argued along these lines.[17] The distance between nineteenth-century and early twentieth-century racism is hardly remote from the very middle-class leisure activity of reading novels, the specific kind of literature upon which the nation has staked its claim as a cultured society.

This perspective that literature has the power to shape and convey racial ideologies is, paradoxically, both compatible and incompatible with some objections raised against the textbooks in Kanawha County. On one hand, many protesters were making claims that sounded similar to those of scholars such as Michaels—that literature is a conduit of racial ideologies. Local chemical company owner and conservative commentator Elmer Fike, for instance, wrote that the textbooks "pit black against white, accentuating their differences and, thereby, stirring up racial animosity."[18] On the other hand, there is a difference between arguing that literature promotes racial ideologies and saying that it actually incites racial unrest.

Fike's writings in particular demonstrated how middle-class protesters could credibly claim a lack of hostility toward people of color and still perpetuate racialized sentiments unintentionally. Moreover, Fike's writings exemplify the post–World War II version of "the American race," that idea that white culture is what constitutes America. In his writings we see an increasing reliance on the spiritual and the cultural, which is defined *in opposition to* what is seen as antispiritual and lacking culture, namely secular humanism and literary writings about black life.

Adamant that protesters did not deserve the label of "racist" that was flung their way, Fike pointed out that his group of "protesters supported the only black running for the Legislature" in West Virginia and that, as president of the Business and Professional People's Alliance for Better Textbooks, he had spoken to the local chapter of the NAACP. In Fike's writings, opposition to the books was not based on any resistance to or personal animosity against black individuals, but on bona fide political disagreement. His encounters with the NAACP revealed those political impasses.

For example, Fike wrote that at the meeting of the NAACP he was "shouted down when he tried to read a passage from George Schuyler, the black author" who began his writing career with essays published in the NAACP's *The Crisis* and later renunciated progressive politics with membership in the John Birch Society. In other words, Schuyler had shifted radically to the right in his lifetime, to a conservative position to which Fike could relate. Therefore, wrote Fike, "the protesters do not object to authors because they are black"; black conservatives were all right with Fike. In asserting that the fundamental difference between the protesters and the proponents of the books was a matter of political orientation, Fike was at his most credible.

A sharp writer with rhetorical panache, Fike elsewhere discussed an encounter at the NAACP meeting during which the political and epistemological impasse between white conservatives and black liberals was evident. One of Fike's repeated gripes with the books was that they do not offer "hope" for minorities. For an example, Fike recounted a story in one of the textbooks by George Parks, in which an African American man who graduates at the top of his college class can only find employment as "a red cap in Grand Central Station in New York." Instead of seeing this as an example of systematic barriers to economic equality that justify affirmative action measures, Fike interpreted the story as a negative message that instills no hope and ignores "today's world of affirmative hiring practices that force employers to hire Blacks or other minorities ahead of anyone else."[19]

Data from the era calls into question Fike's impression of affirmative action. It may be true that more minority workers were hired because of the 1964 Civil Rights Act, which "initially made real progress in reducing employment discrimination, lessened the gaps between rich and poor and between black and white workers, and helped bring minority poverty to its lowest level in 1973." But the recession of that year, 1973, initiated a series of layoffs that disproportionately affected people of color. For example, "In cases where minority workers made up only 10 to 12 percent of the work force in their area, they accounted for from 60 to 70 percent of those laid off in 1974," according to the U.S. Civil Rights Commission report of 1977.[20] Fike's impression that affirmative action had eliminated barriers to stable employment for blacks was thus statistically false; the early 1970s actually "initiated a reversal of minority progress and a reassertion of white privilege" in employment practices.[21] Despite this, Fike's writings suggest that affirmative action made writing about economic disadvantages the same as dwelling in hopelessness.

Parks's story about the black graduate who ended up hauling luggage in Grand Central Station was, to Fike, "typical" of the textbooks that "hold out so little hope." During the aforementioned NAACP meeting, Fike offered up Schuyler as the antidote to Parks because the former "points out the essential ingredient, 'they must have feelings of hope.'" As the meeting adjourned, "a young black man came up to" Fike and "asked why I disagreed with the author George Parks who taught there was no hope for the Blacks. I noticed a college ring on his finger and asked where he worked. He named one of the prominent chemical companies in the area, and I asked him what his job was. He answered, 'chemist.'" Fike's tale of the encounter ended there, suggesting that the young man was disingenuous in his supposed stance of rejecting "hope" and conservative by-the-bootstrap mentality. His own middle-class status as a chemist apparently signaled to Fike the "hope" the young man had presumably had in order to achieve his college ring and his impressive employment.[22]

True to his conservative orientation, Fike thus eschewed any structural analysis of the barriers to equality for the majority of African Americans. Again, Fike was at his most convincing when he argued and implied that a basic difference of political opinion, rather than outright bigotry, personal prejudice, or intended racism, motivated his objections to the books. By understanding racism as personal prejudice or an individual's hatred of people of color, Fike was justified in rejecting the charge that in opposing the books he as a protester was a racist.

But as his reading of Parks's story indicated, Fike's conservatism left no room to entertain another understanding of racism. Institutionalized racism, in which no individual or singular group of individuals consciously deploys the various barriers to social or economic equality, did not figure into Fike's take on this ugly idea. "A racist," he wrote, "is defined as one who advocates racism—a belief in the superiority of a particular race and its right to domination over others. The KKK certainly rates as a racist organization."[23] Equating racism with conscious hostility toward people of color or organized white supremacism, Fike and other protesters who were repelled by the Klan's involvement in the textbook controversy were angered to have their rationales dismissed out of hand with the razor-sharp pejorative of "racist." That is not to say, however, that, especially in Fike's case, racial discourse did not come into play.

Fike's rebuttals to charges of racism ironically resonated with overtly racist ideas of the time. "The protesters," wrote Fike, "do not object to authors because they are black, but they do believe convicted criminals and revolutionaries like Eldridge Cleaver should not be recognized."[24] As noted previously, repeated references to Cleaver misled people to believe that his book, *Soul on Ice*, was required reading and not an optional supplementary text for college-bound senior high school students. In promoting "racial animosity," according to Fike, the books were "an attack on the American system that has made this country the envy of the world"—an attack led not by black nationalists, but rather by "avant-garde liberals."[25] Fike leaves to the imagination what the relationship was between "revolutionaries like Eldridge Cleaver" and the white "avant-garde liberals." But apparently his suggestion is that the white avant-garde was the real foe and the militant blacks were mere symptoms of the larger liberal disease. In this way, Fike's implication was what neo-Nazi William Pierce and Klansman Robert Miles argued outright: blacks are too lazy, corrupt, stupid—or, to use Fike's term, "hopeless"—to be the real threat, the masterminds behind a cultural attack on America. So even while denouncing organized white supremacism as abhorrent and claiming that his group was the "moderate" one, Fike's discourse resonated fully with those sentiments deemed extreme. Nevertheless, this racialized sentiment was subsumed by Fike's increasing adherence to the New Right focus on cultural assault, religious plight, and spiritual degradation.

Fike's involvement in the textbook controversy shows how a seasoned conservative came to relinquish his Old Right thinking for the rhetorical strategies of the New Right. At one point, Fike claimed that the textbook "controversy is more nearly between the avant-garde liberals and the conservatives who want to *preserve* the American heritage." *Preservation* of the economic and social status quo was the hallmark of the Old Right style of conservatism. The New Right, on the other hand, grew to promote social change on its own terms; preserving the status quo was not enough. The Old Right emphasized economic imperatives while the New Right ushered in cultural conservatism. The textbook controversy compelled Fike to emphasize the political differences between liberals and conservatives in cultural rather than economic terms. Well known for writing critically about labor relations and industry regulations, and for touring with a lecture titled "Can the Free Enterprise System Survive?" Fike became convinced that "these books are part of an overall program to destroy the Judeo-Christian culture of the United States."[26] He thus shifted his emphasis to religious culture, instead of the economic system, as the imperiled foundation of America. Although he was hardly imbued with the same kind of millennialist rhetoric that the working-class protest leaders such as Marvin Horan and Avis Hill deployed, Fike nevertheless began to see the textbook controversy as a battle on religious grounds.

This was especially evident in a report from *Christian Crusade Weekly*, in which Fike was portrayed as a textbook protester who was grasping fully for the first time how effective arguing on religious grounds might be. Like Alice Moore, Fike began to see the fight before them as one against secular humanism, defined not only as a cultural attack on all things American but also as an alien religion. In fact, the *Christian Crusade Weekly* article succinctly illustrates how the discussion during a "hearing" hosted by Fike's anti-textbook group moved from Old Right anticommunism to the New Right conspiracy narrative of secular humanism as the underlying problem with the language arts curriculum. To put the local controversy in a national context, the forum included speakers who advocated resistance to "progressive" education by offering "traditional" schools in Prince Georges County, Maryland, and Pasadena, California. Here is part of the report published in *Christian Crusade Weekly*:

> The Rev. Carl Dabney told the hearing that by ridding the schools of the controversial texts, Kanawha County would be "making its biggest and best contribution towards getting rid of this stinking mess of international communism." Mrs. Donna Singer, a teacher at Anne Bailey Elementary School [in St. Albans, just west of Charleston], said Mr. Dabney's theory did not go far enough. "I think it is Satan himself who is behind this," she asserted. The Rev. Darrel Beach, speaking on behalf of Concerned Citizens of the St. Albans area, charged that the texts were being used to promote a humanist philosophy. He declared that the humanists are "trying to get rid of three things—faith in God, patriotism, and family life." Prof. Berbusse [from Fordham University in New York] commented that recent rulings of the U.S. Supreme Court have placed "secular humanism" in the same category as organized religions. He defined secular humanism as "a faith in man as such and separated from any conventional religion." Berbusse declared that "since humanism is now considered by the Court to be a religion, it must be prevented from being established by government." Elmer Fike, leader of the Business and Professional People's Alliance, asked Prof. Berbusse if Kanawha County text opponents would have a chance of winning a case before the U.S. Supreme Court if they contended that secular humanism was being taught to students in the controversial texts. "I think you may have the material if you can get a crackerjack lawyer," the Fordham professor replied.[27]

Moving from the anticommunist sentiments of Dabney to the anti–secular humanism comments of Beach and Berbusse, the discussion mirrors the general discursive shift from Old Right to New Right articulations of the textbook controversy. The discursive bridge between the two was the fearful Christian angst over satanic influence. Thus, even someone so ensconced in middle-class privilege and Old Right entrepreneurship as Elmer Fike became focused on the specter of cultural assault instead of the threat of the economic demise of the "free market," and began framing his concerns over the textbooks in terms of a battle for the "Judeo-Christian culture of the United States." The New Right narrative of secular humanism prevailed and references to spirituality and religion escalated even among protesters such as Fike who did not claim a Christian fundamentalist identity.

In adopting the narrative of secular humanism and cultural attack, Fike's discourse accommodated some racialist ideas and resonated with the working-class protesters' millennialist rhetoric. Although it is fair to absolve Fike and other protesters of the charge of racism insofar as that pejorative indicates an active, personal hostility toward people of color, it is also fair to acknowledge how Fike's embrace of spiritual and cultural attack went hand in hand with his condemnation of black "hopelessness" on one hand and black resistance on the other. Fike's gradual emphasis on the spiritual (that "Judeo-Christian culture of the U.S.") depended on an articulation of what was deemed lacking spirit or antispiritual: not only the supposed secular humanism that New Right supporters and some evangelicals involved in the protest were objecting to but also the hopelessness of blacks supposedly showcased in writings by George Parks and Eldridge Cleaver. The faithful (textbook protesters upholding "Judeo-Christian culture") and the faithless (the language arts curriculum that dwelled on the "hopelessness" of life, in particular black life) were thereby racialized in Fike's remarks, regardless of his intentions.

With an increasing emphasis on cultural and religious/spiritual analysis of the textbook controversy that relied on such racial undertones, Fike, a white conservative who never stopped arguing against health and safety regulations, environmental protection, and unions, ironically became political allies with those white working-class protesters who could possibly benefit from health and safety regulations, environmental protection, and unions. While the working-class protesters were bemoaning the loss of "the souls of our children," the professional-class protesters, exemplified by Fike, were likewise arguing to save the "Judeo-Christian culture" of the nation and appealing to parents: "While giving our children the things we didn't have, let's not forget to give them the things we did have."[28] Before exploring in more depth the discussions by working-class protesters along these lines, it is important to explore how, discursively, references to the spiritual are related to the formation of ethnic identity and political affinity.

Evoking Soul, Left to Right

Equating the textbook protest with a fight against a cultural attack on the religious foundation of America was Fike's conservative articulation of what others, mainly evangelicals, claimed was a battle for the soul of the country. Invoking the soul of the nation, or the soul of the people, or the souls of our children in order to make particular political claims is a discursive practice with a history. Historically, invoking soul has had the discursive power to transform the goal of fighting against victimhood or tyranny from a goal of emancipation to that of domination. Invoking spirituality or soul is connected to ethnicity in such a way that it allows white people to claim that they are victimized even when they do not have a history of alienation, exploitation, or oppression. Understanding this helps us to see how the liberal and leftist narratives of soul can be quite compatible with right-wing apocalyptic references to spirituality, which is important as we consider how the working-class protesters in Kanawha County became aligned with conservative, right-wing forces at the local and national levels. To this end, theoretical discussions by comparative literature scholar Rey Chow are helpful in understanding how the protesters invocation of "soul" is intimately associated with ideas of ethnicity and domination.

What is applicable about Chow's anti-Marxist discussion is how it reveals, in writings that theorize working-class resistance, the significance of the "soul" as that kernel of humanity that resists the victimization it perpetually suffers.[29] Tracing this idea of humanity or soul through theories of class consciousness and capitalism, Chow shows an inextricable link between labor and the ethnic. Briefly, as summarized in a review of her book, *The Protestant Ethnic and the Spirit of Capitalism*, Chow's argument

discusses ethnicity as a form of class consciousness and struggle via Georg Lukacs, inflected by Leonard Tennenhouse's concept of the "resistant captive." Because Lukacs' model leaves the subject as both commodity and non-commodity, the modern ethnic is caught in the position of captive, "whose salvation," Chow argues, "lies in resistance and protest, activities that are aimed at ending exploitation (and boundaries) and bringing about universal justice." Here Chow adds Max Weber to the picture, since, in contrast to Lukacs—who sees protest and resistance as the emergence of class consciousness—Weber views protest and resistance as constituent of the capitalist spirit. In Chow's view, capitalism and the ethnic are symbiotic.[30]

Thus Chow's work illuminates how protesting captivity, alienation, and exploitation can become a way of seeking not emancipation or liberation from such (capitalist) oppression, but of seeking continued domination through the enhancement of capitalism.

This analysis flies in the face of standard Marxist takes on how working-class protesters are always inherently in opposition to, not complicit with, capitalism. For example, if we examine Georg Lukacs's writings through the lens of Chow's analysis, we can see that invoking the soul—saying that we must save the soul of the nation, for instance— triggers a narrative in which "captivity is transformed through (the proletarian's) resistance to capital into class consciousness and thus emancipation."[31] But if we examine Max Weber's theories, again as Chow suggests, we see instead that invoking soul triggers a narrative in which "captivity is inseparable from a form of power that is distinguished by its twin capacity for sustaining victimhood (as a way to legitimize social protest) and for transforming victimhood into the very means of cultural domination."[32] Chow's work helps explain how proletarian protest can sustain instead of fight capitalism, and playing the victim can ironically set you up to rule over others.

This description of victimhood is very appropriate for understanding how conservative and right-wing discourses invoke soul. Because it does not depend on demonstrating "past injustices" and a *history* of alienated labor, but rather a capacity to "monopolize and capitalize on victim-hood," this narrative of the captive-yet-resilient soul can be deployed by those whose history is, as a matter of fact or of design, one of cultural domination.[33] Consider, for example, the blatant narrative of soul that William Pierce circulated in *The Turner Diaries* and his other National Socialist writings. His use of spirituality—of being born again, of "race-soul"—was forthrightly about "transforming victimhood into the means of cultural domination." He quite blatantly sought domina-tion. Since the supposed takeover of the white world had not entirely transpired, he did not seek liberation. His perceived victimhood was one situated in the future, in the "post-white" world, as cultural critic Mike Hill would say, that he imagined. Yet, his apocalyptic perspective narrated Earl Turner, Robert Mathews, Timothy McVeigh, and other readers or members of the National Alliance as victims of Jewish rule and the Zionist Occupied Government. Banking on the future, rather than history, of white people's alienation, Pierce and other millennialist white suprema-cists positioned themselves as victims even as they sought domination.

As our earlier discussion of the American race suggested, the souls of white folk are narrated beyond the blatant white supremacism of someone such as Thomas Dixon or William Pierce. Walter Benn Michaels's theory of the soul of white folks as the invisible, essential character that is unsullied by moral ambiguity or racial impurity can be refined by the narrative of soul as an internal essence that is not a static property or character but a more dynamic process, a "mode of power found and engendered *inside* the self," a mode of power in which people can occupy a position of victimhood and a position of domination simultaneously.[34] Seeing the souls of white folks as a mode of power, rather than as a static property, helps to explain the liminality of conservative and right-wing invocations of the soul, a narrative of spirituality that depends on an apocalyptic future of alienation, not necessarily a history of alienated labor. A white, right-wing invocation of spirituality puts an apocalyptic emphasis on the future, projecting white people forward into a postwhite world only to send them back to the future of avoiding that demise.

Recall how Connie Marshner narrated Alice Moore and subsequent concerned mothers, those Sweet Alices, in her book *Blackboard Tyranny*. Marshner not only presented Moore as an exemplar but also provided her readers with instructions in the proper social graces (how to dress, how to talk, how to control emotions so as to appear sweet and concerned rather than paranoid and menacing) that would make them effective political agents fighting against their captivity by the "tyranny" of professional educators and secular humanists. Moreover, by framing her conspiratorial story of captivity by the education establishment with references to R. J. Rushdoony, Marshner situated her readers in the apocalyptic framework of dominionism, which is *not* a fixed timetable but a vague injunction to act now before the unknown but imminent timing of the Second Coming. Here is another case in which a captivity narrative transforms victimhood into the means of cultural domination. For Marshner and Rushdoony, dominion was absolutely tied to the spiritual; recall that Marshner told the *Christian Life* reporter that "Christ commanded us to occupy until He comes," which she interpreted as do any number of devotees of dominionism—to live and act according to biblical time, to the dispensations of millennialism, as well as to chronological, man-made time. *Blackboard Tyranny* turned this biblical injunction into a political one by assuming Christians should "take control" and "occupy until He comes," by narrating its readers as active, concerned mothers with the properly feminine social graces, and by, in effect, breeding Sweet Alices in the distorted, double temporality of apocalyptic millennialism.[35]

In this way, Marshner's conspiracist narrative of being held captive by a "blackboard tyranny" was utterly compatible with domination. Moreover, protesting secular humanism became devoid of the anti-Semitism and anti-integration of the Old Right; overtly stated racial concerns evaporated as a politics of Americanness merged with the spirituality of a right-wing apocalypticism. Seeing Marshner's apocalyptic story as the narrative of soul illuminates why and how blatant racial concerns gave way to invocations of Americanness *and* allowed her to transform her presumed victimization by a secular humanist "tyranny" into an entitlement to "occupy" for Christ, to dominate the cultural and political institutions of the nation.

The fact of Marshner's femininity—and the deft deployment of maternal politics she advocated—was an asset to this endeavor because "when whiteness feminizes," according to Chow, what results is a "tendency to monopolize and capitalize on victimhood."[36] Chow's critique of white Western feminism in this regard is all the more compelling when applied to conservative American women evangelicals such as Marshner and Moore, who defied traditional gender roles but deplored feminists' aims of equality or liberation from the male-dominated, male-privileged, or male-oriented world. Reading "representations of 'woman' *cross-culturally* by foregrounding the issue of ethnicity, including the ethnicity that is whiteness,"[37] Chow explores the complicity of white feminism with a "racialist hold on victimhood itself as cultural capital."[38] This discussion certainly echoes much criticism by women of color who have taken Euro-American feminism to task for its blindness to white privilege. But Chow adds a new element to this critique by paralleling it with the significance of ethnic protest in the contemporary late capitalist world. Her innovation in suggesting that ethnic protest is complicit with capitalism, her recognition of whiteness as an ethnicity, and her examination of how "woman" is deployed to capitalize on victimhood go a long way in explaining why and how white evangelicals such as Marshner and Moore became politically active in the ways they did after the 1960s.

Because of the progressive, even leftist, union politics that are historically associated with West Virginia, scholars have represented the textbook controversy by imposing a Lukacsian narrative of class consciousness. The alternative that is open to us when we read Rey Chow is to represent the textbook controversy in terms of a Weberian narrative in which the soul can be commodified, and invocations of spirituality can be absolutely compatible with capitalism. We can see why the Kanawha County textbook controversy played out the way it did if we look at the textbook controversy from the perspective that Chow prescribes for examining representations of ethnicity—that is, as protest that (1) corresponds with capitalism by relying on an "economic-spiritual framework of labor"; (2) solidifies an ethnic sense of "the people" that is articulated as alienated labor rather than racial identity; and (3) uses "woman" as a means to "monopolize and capitalize on victimhood."[39] We can see why alliances emerged among local populists and political elites. In other words, it explains why the historically progressive and leftist politics of the working class of Kanawha County became aligned with a conservative right-wing politics *and* why the blatant, race-based objections to the multiethnic curriculum by and large gave way to objections based on "our" American or Appalachian heritage and culture.

Thus, in understanding this right-wing narrative of soul as one that does not depend on a history of alienated labor but on an apocalyptic future of alienation, we can now return to Kanawha County with fuller attention to the textbook protesters' invocations of spirituality. They used the language of soul in order to express their concerns over belonging to the local community and the nation at large. In often conflating the local and the national in the figure of "our children" who needed saving from multiracial literature, working-class protesters' language reflected the equation of white ethnic identity with national identity, that legacy of the "American race." It was as a matter of what Michaels called breeding, of reproducing "our children" according to "our" ways, that many residents of Kanawha County saw themselves as protesters—Chow might say as ethnic protesters—who were saving the soul of the nation.

The Souls of Our Children

"You only have to look at the excerpts from the textbooks to realize that the most precious possession of a mother or father, their child's eternal soul, is endangered," wrote Kanawha County protester Linda Paul in the pages of the February 1975 issue of *Christian Crusade Weekly*. "O, God, help our nation when morally wrong is made legally right."[40] Linda Paul connected the souls of Kanawha County students with the nation's spiritual health. Like Alice Moore, who also was quoted in *Christian Crusade Weekly* and who gave a lecture for Billy James Hargis's Christian

Crusade audience in Tulsa, Linda Paul saw the textbooks as evidence of a conspiracy whose aim was to corrupt the children, hence the nation. For Paul and her readers, invoking soul tapped the "economic-spiritual framework of labor" that Chow says characterizes "the historical affinity between Protestantism and capitalist entrepreneurship."[41]

The rationale of this affinity, Chow says, "may be ultimately paraphrased as 'I protest, therefore I am': the more one protests, the more work, business, and profit one will generate, and the more this will become a sign that one is loved by God."[42] This logic seems apropos for Kanawha County middle-class entrepreneurs such as Elmer Fike, who both protested the textbooks and promoted free enterprise. But this logic also seems relevant to statements by working-class residents of Kanawha County whose culture of protest was well established by 1974. We can see this in letters addressed to the Charleston newspaper and to members of the board of education that frequently invoked "soul" in combination with "our children" or "the children" and deployed the language of *selling* one's soul.

One letter sent to board member Harry Stansbury admonished, "You can sell your soul to the devil if that's what you want to do. But the souls and minds of our children are not for sale." The letter, written by "a mother and a taxpayer," closes with a Bible verse: "What does it profit a man if he gains the whole world and loses his own soul." Pauline Tucker used this same verse in her letter published in the *Daily Mail*, extending it: "or what shall a man give in exchange for his soul." The language of the Bible verse matches the class antagonism of Tucker's letter, which disdains "people who are overly concerned with money and the impression they can make on other people" because such attention to money means they "are not at all concerned with what their children do or read or where they go, just as long as they stay out of their way."[43] She closed her letter by asking readers whether they would "exchange your children's soul for a so called education?" The editors chose this sentiment as a prevailing one, headlining the "Point of View" section "Trade a Soul for Education?" Such letters prompted readers to consider their souls in the context of trade. The new language arts curriculum was thus seen as a textualization of an ideological "assault" on children as the future of the nation, but it was put in an "economic-spiritual framework of labor."

Specifically, the lessons in dialectology, literature by people of color, and situation ethics featured in the books were deemed dangerous. These lessons were seen as mental labor that would do violence to the students of Kanawha County and would instill violence in them. Even one lesson of dialectology, according to Alice Moore, was too much. Texts were seen to be imbued with an inherent power. That power was supposedly aimed at the two elements of what Walter Benn Michaels called the souls of white folk: unambiguous moral character and racial purity. The books could taint the souls of white children, the soul being a marker of both good moral character as well as racial purity, hence racial loyalty. Introducing moral ambiguity into the world of children, as situation ethics were said to do, would damage students' moral purity. Introducing them to different dialects and multiracial voices would damage the racial purity of their thought processes, their mental labor.

There were several examples of these assumptions at work. The most telling example of how these assumptions were operating is the objection to Eldridge Cleaver's *Soul on Ice*. It was repeatedly singled out as an example of a text that not only *discussed* black-on-white violence but also could *reproduce* that racial violence *in* "our children." *Soul on Ice* was literature that could, according to protesters, do damage. It could incite black men to rape white women or white girls to mingle with black boys, and thereby taint the racial and sexual purity of Kanawha County females. These assumptions were also operating when Alice Moore suggested new guidelines for textbook selection. One of her demands was that any books promoting "racial hatred" be rejected.[44] Apparently she felt the entire curriculum, not just *Soul on Ice*, was full of hatred for white people. She admonished any opponents who belittled her claims by saying "now don't tell me these books don't say to go out and join the revolution and kill the white enemy."[45] Implicitly, she was claiming that the textbooks' multiracial writing could reproduce a bloodthirsty desire for racial violence in "our children." And it could, in effect, not only breed contempt for parents and America but also produce a new breed of brainwashed citizens.

Another example of these assumptions at work is found in the November 3, 1974, issue of *Christian Crusade Weekly*.[46] In a sidebar to an article about Kanawha County, excerpts presumably from the textbooks were printed under the heading "Black Panther Eldridge Cleaver Teaches Children Via School Textbooks" (see figure 13). The excerpt from *Soul on Ice* dominates the newspaper page visually. Dark bars reminiscent of censoring marks on peepshow broadsides designed to cover over explicit

Black Panther Leader Eldridge Cleaver
Teaches Children Via School Textbooks

At the nth degree of Ultrafeminine's scale of psychic lust (the contours of which few men or women throughout their entire lives ever in fact explore, resort being had to the forms of sublimation) stands the walking phallus symbol of the Supermasculine Menial. Though she may never have had a sexual encounter with a Supermasculine Menial, she is fully convinced that he can fulfill her physical need. It will be no big thing for him to do since he can handle those Amazons down there with him, with his strong body, rippling muscles, his strength ████████████████████

██

████████████████████ her psychic bridegroom can blaze through the wall of her ice, plumb her psychic depths, ████████████ melt the iceberg in her brain, ████████████████████

████████████████████████ —*Eldridge Cleaver*

(Note: The omitted words in text are too corrupt for a family newspaper.)

_____

All that is good and commendable now existing would continue to exist if all marriage laws were repealed tomorrow . . . I have an inalienable right to love whom I may, to love as long or as short a period as I can, to change that love every day, if I, please!—*Excerpt from a proposed textbook.*

_____

Edith is the "saved" broad who can't marry out of her religion . . . or do anything else out of her religion for that matter, especially what I wanted her to do. A bogue religion, man! So dig, for the last couple weeks I been quoting the Good Book and all that stuff to her; telling her I am now saved myself, you dig.—*Excerpt from a proposed textbook.*

FIGURE 13. An excerpt from Eldridge Cleaver's *Soul on Ice*, which was thought to represent the new language arts curriculum, appeared as censored pornography in the *Christian Crusade Weekly*, November 3, 1974.

material for the public's safety and titillation black out "words in text [that] are too corrupt for a family newspaper." For example, partially omitted is a sentence that begins with "he can handle those Amazons down there with him, with his strong body, rippling muscles, his strength"—and then the black bars. Presenting this pulpy excerpt as pornography in need of covering up, the *Christian Crusade Weekly* article then presents two excerpts that have marriage as a theme.

The first reads: "All that is good and commendable now existing would continue to exist if all marriage laws were repealed tomorrow. . . .

I have an inalienable right to love whom I may, to love as long or as short a period as I can, to change that love everyday, if I, please!" This quotation alerts readers of the *Christian Crusade Weekly* that not only marriage is being threatened, but that promiscuity, and, plausibly, miscegenation or homosexuality are being promoted. The second excerpt is: "Edith is the 'saved' broad who can't marry out of her religion . . . or do anything else out of her religion for that matter, especially what I wanted her to do. A bogue [sic] religion, man! So dig, for the last couple weeks I been quoting the Good Book and all that stuff to her; telling her I am saved myself, you dig." Here we can assume that readers would recoil at the bogus, predatory, and hypocritical nature of the black and/or beatnik narrator—you dig? Taken as a related trio, these excerpts echo the more succinct sentiments provided by Klansmen on the capitol steps who said that Kanawha County residents should worry about their daughters being seduced by black "bucks" and the quietly insistent disapproval by protesters who objected to the cover of a book displaying a black boy and white girl interacting in close proximity. The condemnation of so-called illicit sexuality and religious hypocrisy went hand in hand, judging from *Christian Crusade Weekly* issues of the time, which is why, by the way, Billy James Hargis was forced to resign as the Christian Crusade's leader when it was revealed in 1976 that he had been sleeping with female and male students enrolled in his American Christian College. More to the point, presenting these excerpts as representative of the language arts curriculum proposed for Kanawha County was in keeping with the general fear mongering and scapegoating of Eldridge Cleaver as the militant black menace that ostensibly wanted to get into "our children's" minds and white women's panties.

This analysis is very different from indicting the Christian Crusade, Alice Moore, and other protesters for being "racists" or "backward" fundamentalists who could not tolerate the inclusion of African American, Latino, and Jewish authors in the curriculum. In some cases—especially when the proposed curriculum was referred to as the "nigger books"— blatant racism and repression *were* undeniably the order of the day. But more generally, the textbook conflict was a process in which protesters reasserted their authority as white Christians without acknowledging (to others and perhaps to themselves) that race was a factor. Naturalizing the protest of multiracial texts and normalizing white Christians' sense of entitlement to protect their children from the violence that such literature could purportedly inflict were important aspects of the New Right.

Howard Winant and Michael Omi explain the obfuscation of racial concerns this way:

> The monitoring of books for public school adoption is another issue where a "hidden" racial dimension informs New Right politics. As early as 1975, the Heritage Foundation formed the national Congress for Educational Excellence to coordinate the activities of roughly 200 textbook-protester organizations nationwide. This effort capitalized on the feelings of many whites that their values and lifestyles were being neglected by "multicultural" texts. The New Right, for instance, can push a racial agenda merely by arguing for "traditional" lifestyles and families, for the return to a more homogeneous image of everyday life, purged of "secular humanism" and the rest of the unsettling ambiguities of the 1960s and 1970s. Textbooks focusing on Dick and Jane and Spot, and avoiding any mention of Ahmed or Chabrika, Fernando or Nguyen, effectively *re*-marginalize minority cultures without ever having to invoke the issues of race.[47]

Rather than invoking issues of race, textbook protesters as different as Elmer Fike, Avis Hill, and Linda Paul invoked religious culture and spirituality. Especially in expressing concern over "our" children's "eternal souls," such references to spirituality made the protest of multiracial curriculum not seem overtly political or racial, but only natural—as natural as a parent's love.

Invoking "soul" while arguing against writers who were exploring the very aesthetic of "soul" was a sharp irony. Beginning at least with W. E. B. Du Bois's 1903 *The Souls of Black Folk* and throughout the 1960s and 1970s, "soul" was touted as the essence of "blackness" in African American political and cultural endeavors.[48] Eldridge Cleaver's *Soul on Ice* was representative of this intellectual tradition. *Soul on Ice* played a significant role in the course of the controversy because Moore and others held it up as an epitomic example of what "our children" were expected to read. The role that *Soul on Ice* played in the conflict should not be overstated; it was not the root of the uprising or essential to its mobilization. The inclusion, however tangential, of *Soul on Ice* in the curriculum was hardly the single cause of Alice Moore's or anyone's objection to the books. So why concern ourselves with Cleaver's work? It is worth bringing up repeatedly because a variety of the protesters did *and* because of its own provocative invocations of spirituality in juxtaposition to violence. It was the book's violence rather than its spirituality that protesters emphasized as exemplary of the curriculum at large. Cleaver's book does discuss black-on-white violence and his rape of white women in particular as an "insurrectionary act." But it is important to understand that the trajectory of Cleaver's patchwork narrative moves from this remorseless confession and political analysis of his obsession with white women to a conclusion in which that obsession has been obliterated.

By the end of what may be considered a quintessentially modernist tale of alienation, Cleaver's mind is no longer "locked in Cold Storage" by a "cold, bodiless world of wheels, smooth plastic surfaces, tubes, pushbuttons, transistors, computers, jet propulsion, rockets to the moon, atomic energy"—a "mechanized, automated, cybernated environment" in which it is difficult for man to tell "where his body ends and the machine begins."[49] By the end of the book, Cleaver comes to a race consciousness and his "soul" is no longer on the anesthetizing "ice" of modern life. Consequently, instead of raping white women he invites black womanhood to "put on your crown, my Queen."[50] This move from demonizing to idealizing women, from rape to reverence, is surely no stride in feminist awakening. But it does attest to a move away from rape as a means to Cleaver's revolutionary ends.[51]

Moreover, he allegorizes his own social-political plight to harmonize the black mind and body, unleashed from modernity's and racism's numbing freeze, as America's "attempt to unite its Mind and Body, to save its soul."[52] So to represent *Soul on Ice* as merely, truly, or essentially a treatise on the raping of white women as an insurrectionary act of revolution is inaccurate. But that is what protest leaders did. Moore, Fike, Horan, and Miller all vilified the book as representative of militant, revolutionary writing that had no redeeming value and only promoted the rape and murder of whites. This vilification coming from Alice Moore recirculated the mythic southern trope of the black rapist as a general menace to white women. Opponents of the book who singled out *Soul on Ice* thereby effectively redefined Cleaver's soul as soulless, his blackness as ungodly. In a corollary move, moreover, the textbook protesters were claiming protective custody of their children's souls as the essence of *their* godliness and of their "whiteness." What the Kanawha County textbook controversy articulated was a intersection of two cultural traditions of "soul"—one pristinely and immanently white, fundamentalist, Appalachian, and Christian, and the other nonetheless pure as a manifestation of an African American aesthetic, black power, and urban social critique.

In fact, Eldridge Cleaver represented not just the curriculum's inclusion of African American writing and, therefore, its supposed threat of integration or revolution. More particularly, he represented black nationalists who sustained a critique of liberal education reform that was, ironically, on some levels very compatible with the protests by Appalachian whites in Kanawha County. Black nationalists, like some of the Kanawha County protesters, wanted local control over schools and disdained the federally run education programs that emerged in response to *Brown v. Board of Education*, the Supreme Court decision that mandated school desegregation. It took direct action by black students of Bluefield State College in 1960 to speed desegregation in West Virginia. "A series of nonviolent demonstrations and 'sit ins' spread to Huntington and Charleston and eventually led to a number of integrated theatres and eating-places in these and other major cities in the state."[53] Black nationalists argued *against* similar integration of schools because it often entailed the closing of black high schools and colleges and the championing of a supposedly race-neutral curriculum that favored Eurocentric, and eliminated Afrocentric, lessons and pedagogy. This was certainly the case in West Virginia.

As historian Joe W. Trotter notes, despite the 1954 ruling in *Brown v. Board of Education*, "as late as 1963, most African Americans [in West Virginia] continued to receive education within a segregated public school system. The tradition of all-black public institutions nonetheless gradually came to an end. As early as 1956, the state had terminated the Bureau of Negro Welfare and Statistics. Bluefield State College and West Virginia State College [which had been historically black] became predominantly white by the mid-1970s. At the same time, local school boards closed one black high school after another."[54] This trend was considered both "heartbreaking" and "deplorable" by members of the black community because "the artifacts, trophies, books, yearbooks and records now referred to as memorabilia were burned or placed away in boxes and forgotten."[55] From a black nationalist point of view, the rationale for closing black schools in West Virginia was the same deplorable rationale for including black writers in its secondary school language arts curricula—it was a move toward integration. But black nationalists such as Cleaver understood such liberal education reform to be detrimental to black history and power. It is ironic, then, that Cleaver's book, as a representative of a black nationalism that critiqued the new liberal education reform, garnered particular objection by white opponents of those very same reform measures in the form of the new language arts curriculum.

White defenders of the new books were stopped short when protesters brought up *Soul on Ice* because they likely considered black nationalists to be as questionable as the protesters. As we have seen, liberal residents of the Kanawha Valley demeaned the protesters in toto as illiterate, antimodern, fundamentalist, working-class, violence-prone hillbillies, despite their shared heritage and geographic home. In this way, the Kanawha County textbook controversy reflected and perpetuated national trends in debating education reform, in which both "black 'militants' and white 'rednecks' were defined together as extremists."[56] As critical race theorist Gary Peller argues, "in liberal education reform, the definition of what constitutes enlightened good sense was drawn in negative contrast to an image of the 'backward' and ignorant whites who opposed the racial integration of southern public schools, and whose lack of enlightenment was further symbolized by their embrace of the 'mythologies' of fundamentalist religion."[57] When liberal advocates of the books labeled the protesters "creekers" or "fundamentalists" it was an easy way to dismiss the more salient points of argument against the curriculum and the school board. As we saw in chapter 1, protesters in Kanawha County who recognized the new curriculum as a means of social reproduction of American subjectivity according to a particular, liberal ideology were absolutely right. Whether or not people opposed to such liberalism viewed that social reproduction as violence—and a *worse* violence than the dynamiting of the schools or white mob rule and its threat of lynching—depended on how much they saw "language arts" as a producer, and not only as a reflection, of "the people" and "our children." To put it in more theoretical terms, it depended on how much people saw what was happening as the production or reproduction of local ethnicity. The fact that opponents of liberal education reform were racialized either as "black militants" or "white rednecks" suggests again that what was at stake here was not only the teaching of language arts but also the production of ethnicity.

Whether the Kanawha County protesters were seen as "extremists" or "fundamentalists" or simply as "concerned parents," the common narrative that emerged was that not only they but also their (white) children were being victimized by the new schoolbooks, those textual stand-ins for the tyranny of "secular humanism," the menace of black "criminals and revolutionaries," or the "avant-garde liberals" destroying Judeo-Christian culture. Acknowledging this allows us to see that fighting the new language arts curriculum was tantamount to fighting the creation of a community that protesters might not recognize as their own. In other words, it was a fight against the textual reproduction of "our children" as non-Appalachian and un-American. Thus the protest reproduced "our children" and "the people" as immanently Appalachian, American, and white.

New Right leaders such as Connie Marshner sought to capitalize on this reproduction, encouraging people to fight the school board as a matter of "parents' rights," "natural rights," and "traditional American and Christian values." Well aware of the "community control" efforts in New York City and Detroit, Marshner made it clear that "militant community control, with its racial connotations, is not what middle-class parents want. Much can be learned from the community-control fight, however, and in some places middle-class parents might even go for a little ride on its coattails. It would be splendid indeed," Marshner envisioned, "for parents to have some say in the selection of principals, even more so in the election of teachers, but those goals are a long way off. More important to middle-class parents than control of the schools is control of their children."[58] Marshner thus redirected her readers from overtly racialized "community control" campaigns to put "children," clearly understood to be both middle-class and white, at the heart of the matter.

No available evidence suggests that any Kanawha County protester chose to align with overtly racialized efforts for "community control" over schools, those more progressive fights in New York City and Detroit happening in the late 1960s and early 1970s. They opted instead to centralize "our children" in the struggle instead of reforming the school system. Kanawha County protesters could have very successfully opposed a history of bad management by the school board by playing up the ousting of the principal at Ruthlawn Elementary School. Instead, the most resonant narrative told by the various factions of protesters was not one that reflected past abuses but one in which the books portended upcoming and total oppression. This is why the rallying cry more often included "our children" rather than "the students": connotations of growth, of future, and of promise are imbedded in the idea of progeny rather than the idea of learners. Like many other protest movements and political discourses before it, the Kanawha County textbook controversy relied on "our children."[59] And, as Lee Edelman put it, many protests contemporary with the textbook controversy focused on the "Child," that "fantasmatic beneficiary of every political intervention":

> Even proponents of abortion rights, while promoting the freedom of women to control their own bodies through reproductive choice, recurrently frame their political struggle, mirroring their antiabortion foes, as a "fight for our children—for our daughters and sons," and thus as a fight for the future. What, in that case, would it signify *not* to be "fighting for the children"? How could one take the *other* "side," when taking any side at all necessarily constrains one to take the side *of*, by virtue of taking a side *within*, a political order that returns to the Child as the image of the future it intends?[60]

Edelman's insights about the prevalence and absolutely unquestionable value of "fighting for the children" in protest culture are corroborated by Rey Chow's description of that protest culture as something that becomes in the late twentieth century complicit with capitalist, conservative, and ultraright ideologies. Relying on "our children" as symbolic of the future of America's character, right-wing protests have rallied against victimhood while conservative politics and policymaking have sought dominion economically and culturally.

Or as Ann Burlein has so powerfully demonstrated in her study of Pete Peters and Focus on the Family, "the Child" or "more exactly, adult images of children" serve as the linchpin between ultraright and Christian conservative discourses. Representations of children help to "reorient people's identities, histories, and worlds. Children act as affective magnets, attracting fears about sexuality and gender, race, class, and nationhood in ways that move people into the Right's orbit without requiring them actually to agree with its philosophical, doctrinal, or political positions."[61] Throughout the 1970s, 1980s, and thereafter, fighting for the children became the invocation of spirituality that heralded many a right-wing protest and conservative campaign.

The logic of protecting "our children" carried evangelicals from one conservative issue to another. Before Anita Bryant's 1979 campaign to "save our children" from "militant homosexuality" in Dade County,

Florida, and before Operation Rescue sought to "save babies" by block-
ading abortion clinics in the 1980s, there was the Kanawha County
crusade to protect "our children" from multiracial literature. We can
argue that the Kanawha County textbook controversy was historically and
politically significant because it was the conflict that led to the Heritage
Foundation's inauguration of a nationwide organization of textbook
protesters and was the model that Connie Marshner used for her attack
on the White House Conference on Families. But more significant is the
textbook controversy's discursive dynamic of reproducing the souls of
white folks in a way that the narrative of alienation turned right and a
new narrative of ethnic struggle emerged.[62] This was no originary
moment. But certainly it was a local turning point in which an established
grassroots protest culture favoring progressive changes in labor banded
together with the nascent New Right. It was a turning point that had
national implications for how far and how well the soul of the nation
became "our (white) children," and the fight to save them became
apocalyptic.

If the title of Eldridge Cleaver's memoir denotes the classic narrative
of ethnic struggle in which one strives to free one's people from the
numbing alienation of modern capitalism, the Kanawha County textbook controversy suggests another narrative of ethnic struggle in which
one strives to monopolize and capitalize on victimhood in the name of
the people but for the sake of dominating them, whether that domination is seen as a religious mandate or a racial one. Actual historical
alienation is not a necessary element of this second narrative but imagined or future alienation is. Kanawha County was a crossroads at which
lay these two narratives of soul—the captivity narrative of ethnicity as
alienated labor and the apocalyptic narrative of ethnicity as domination
through victimhood.

Cleaver's soul was blackness, that essential fighting spirit of black
nationalism. In Kanawha County there was a different soul. Its whiteness was just as essential a fighting spirit, but its protest was not
adamantly opposed to conservative capitalists. In what Connie Marshner
called "an era of neo-ethnicity," the Kanawha County textbook controversy was not the same kind of ethnic struggle as that of black
nationalism. It was, rather, the emergence of a new narrative of ethnic
struggle that Rey Chow delineates, one in which the soul is not uncom-
modifiable and protest is within, not outside of or resistant to, capitalism.
This narrative of white ethnic struggle uses "woman" to capitalize on

victimhood and "children" to connote the apocalyptic future of impending total oppression and the reason to thwart it now. Soul on *Appalachian* ice is ethnic struggle that is inside *and* outside of modernism and capitalism, that produces whiteness as an essential property and marker of character rather than of biology, that defies gender roles only to monopolize victim status, and that upholds protest as paramount for proving one's "true" self.

In reproducing the souls of white folk, the Kanawha County textbook controversy reconfigured conservative and right-wing struggle as matters of ethnicity, Christian heritage, and familial duty. This does not mean that the protesters or their allies were disingenuous or nefarious. Nor were they dupes or victims of outside organizers. But these ideas are important to explore more explicitly to clarify how the textbook controversy served as a turning point in the country's shift toward conservatism after the 1960s. The next chapter begins with the question of whether conservative and right-wing protesters in the 1970s exploited Appalachia as leftist volunteers were said to do in the 1960s.

FIGURE 14. During the textbook controversy, generations of protest merged as youth with long hair and bell-bottom jeans marched alongside right-wing demonstrators carrying Confederate and Klan flags. The local legacy of leftist resistance gave way to conservative campaigns in Kanawha County in 1974. *Sunday Gazette-Mail*, December 1, 1974. Reproduced with permission.

CHAPTER FIVE

The Right Soul

In 1979 Bill Best, a professor at Berea College in Kentucky, published a controversial essay in *Mountain Review* titled "Stripping Appalachian Soul." It was a psychological diagnosis of the trend of volunteerism that swept through the mountain South in the 1960s. Those left-leaning Volunteers in Service to America, charity do-gooders, progressive ministers, and red-diaper babies were motivated, according to Best, by a "moral code based on guilt. They feel that part of their material largess and relative social privilege have been gained, at least partially, at the expense of those 'less fortunate' (conceptualized in a remote, abstract, collective sense), and wish to partially assuage that guilt through the gift of sacrifice (time spent in service to others). They are being punished by consciences that will not let them rest easily without 'doing something.'"[1] Best's critical perspective on left-wing volunteerism has been lambasted as a weary rant that does not take into account the positive influences of such work, does not rely on any empirical or historical research, depends instead on pop psychology, and perpetuates divisions and stereotypes. For the academic "movement of Appalachian studies that was trying to overcome distinctions between insiders and outsiders, this article rubbed salt in wounds that were just beginning to heal. Subsequent issues of *Mountain Review* contained voluminous commentary on 'Stripping Appalachian Soul.'"[2]

But for all its flaws, Best's essay provides an interesting set of concepts with which to consider the right-wing organizers who came later. Chief among these concepts is the idea of Appalachian soul and "stripping" it. As absentee corporations stripped the mountains for coal, Best's essay suggests, leftist volunteers stripped mountaineers of their culture to capitalize psychologically on it. Could the same be said of right-wing protesters?

Stripping Soul

Best defines Appalachian soul as an essential quality that others extract in order to compensate for their own lack of wholeness:

> It is my contention that our helpers from the left come here more to be healed than to help—to partake of the psychic nurture that, for many reasons, escaped them or eluded them during their formative years. Appalachian 'Soul' is their 'Ace In The Hole,' just as surely as coal is 'Kentucky's Ace In The Hole,' because Appalachian Soul can help heal the split of the psyche caused by overindulgence in things material, quantitative, and conceptually abstract and the concurrent denial or suppression of feelings, spirituality, and the arts (as creative participants).[3]

Specifically, Best complains that volunteers fetishized Appalachian handicrafts and music, seeking out the most "pure" examples of mountain culture to compensate for their own lack of artistic endeavors. Best thus essentializes Appalachian soul as cultural characteristics that others lack—"sensuousness, emotion, and spirituality."[4] Such a sweeping definition of "Appalachian soul" in and of itself is less compelling than the insights Best produces by discussing what happens in the process he calls stripping soul.

Best portrays the process of "stripping soul" as a paradoxical means of making one look good and feel "whole" while making Appalachians look and feel lost. "Paradoxically (to again use my favorite term for this article), as the left strip our soul(s) in order to made whole, they get the good press, (because they so often control the press), and we end up again holding the bag—left again with the problems of reclamation."[5] Best's sense of injustice about this paradoxical process recognizes a time-honored dynamic in which the idea of Appalachia serves the needs of people who do not reside there. Scholars such as David Whisnant and Allen Batteau have historicized this dynamic with, respectively, case studies of various missionaries and settlement schools, and textual analyses of how Appalachia was "invented" repeatedly throughout the twentieth century in political, literary, and policy discourse. Best recognizes the repetitive nature of the game: "The public is misled because what is reported as happening is not really what happens. This, of course, is a situation which is not new to us. It's really just the latest chapter in a seemingly endless charade. Appalachia will again be discovered before long." Embittered by such a history of misrepresenting Appalachia and exploiting its people, Best proposes, "Let's do it ourselves next time."[6]

If we think about Best's bitter remarks in the context of right-wing, rather than leftist, involvement, we can extend his psychological analysis into a more overtly historical one. After years during which New Deal Democrats, New Left volunteers, and other soldiers in the War on Poverty pointed to the mountain South as an indicator of what was wrong and redeemable about America, the Right rediscovered Appalachia in 1974. The Old Right, losing electoral and policy battles throughout the 1960s, was suffering under an image of being too sterile in its focus on economics, too intellectual and well heeled, too anesthetized because of its upper middle-class privilege, and too hard-hearted in the face of new social movements that had claimed the moral high ground. Conservatives needed to shed that image. They needed exactly what Best said the Left got from "stripping Appalachian soul": an appearance of "sensuousness, emotion, and spirituality" but not so much emotionality that it would feminize them as hysterical and unreasonable. Applying Best's sentiments historically to the case of right-wing involvement in Kanawha County, we can entertain the idea that the textbook controversy was the Right's way of stripping Appalachian soul—of projecting onto, and extrapolating from, this thing called "Appalachia" an antidote for what conservatives saw as a profoundly divided American society that portended great strife and future alienation.

But unlike the Left which, according to Best, was motivated by guilt and the desire to be made whole, the Right fed on the idea of being torn asunder. They perpetuated a sense of being victimized by tyranny and of facing an oncoming onslaught of total oppression by secular humanists who were coming between children and parents or by Zionist occupiers who were disrupting the natural order. The Right's answer to such clandestine mayhem was the same as its prescribed means of proving one's authenticity in the face of an all-encompassing, if decentralized, tyranny like ZOG or secular humanism. For the Right circa 1974, the answer was not volunteerism but protest—spectacular, marketable protest that embraced technology and popular culture, perpetuated the apocalyptic narrative of saving souls before it is too late, and reproduced "our children" as white folk.

No wonder those in the nascent New Right came to Kanawha County. Since the days of the coal wars, protesters had been using that most effec-

tive rhetoric of fighting for the sake of "our children."[7] Moreover, despite
the actual multiethnic character of the coal industry and the mountain
South, its representation in fiction, government documents, and popular
culture reproduced the people involved as decidedly and defiantly white. It
was Alice Moore, a "concerned mother" from West Virginia, who became
a hero in Connie Marshner's book—not Alice Moore, a middle-class
woman who moved to Charleston from Mississippi and then became
involved in local politics. And once Marvin Horan had been indicted for
conspiracy in the school bombings, it was another charismatic, defiant,
working-class minister, Avis Hill, on whom Washington conservatives lav-
ished attention. Shall we then conclude with an echo of Best by suggesting
not only that right-wing protesters as well as left-wing volunteers have
exploited Appalachia and "stripped" its "soul" but also that, unless and
until mountaineers as a group arise to claim ethnic pride and resist a history of misrepresentation, the exploitation will continue?

A final look at Avis Hill's story provides a conclusion that is less grandiose and more nuanced, less a prescription for action and more a
description of process. Rather than prescribing what to do to prevent
such exploitation, Hill's story describes the historical and discursive process by which one man made the transition from an apolitical evangelical
to a member of the Christian Right. It is no coincidence that he redeployed the mountaineer image in the process and re-created Appalachia
as a result.

From Apolitical Ministry to Populist Militancy

No story better than Avis Hill's illustrates how the New Right narrative of
secular humanism, combined with political agitation from right-wing
populists, reproduced working-class, Christian fundamentalists as advocates
for right-wing causes. In an interview, Hill recounts not only his own
coming to faith and accepting Christ as his savior from a life of sin but also
extends that story to express how he became politically connected to the
New Right.

About a year after Hill was "saved" and experienced a conversion to
evangelical Christianity, "the Lord called me into the ministry" so he began
organizing meetings in the tent revival tradition that attracted "a tremendous outpouring of young people" in the St. Albans area, adjacent to the
city of Charleston. Hill was reluctant to join local political campaigns
because "I felt that God was wanting me in evangelism particularly."[8]

Taught for years to distinguish between politics and preaching, Hill considered elected officials to be unavoidably crooked: "If you're a good man that goes into office, he'll be crooked before he gets out." Like many Christian fundamentalists before the New Right and Christian Right gained any influence, Hill felt political campaigns to be worldly work that conflicted with his more godly work and that he should "let the politicians handle the politics and I'll handle church." But Hill was repeatedly approached throughout the summer of 1974 to become involved with local issues—"Oh, yes, a number of times." At first he rejected how "they were trying to get me involved" in the textbook controversy by remaining faithful to the worldview he was brought up with: "No, I really don't have time, I'm into the ministry. I'm into the work of the Lord and I'm evangelizing." So organizers that Hill does not name asked whether he would lead a prayer at the opening of the next protest meeting of about 250 people and it was there that he began to shift his opinion on working in local disputes.

Shown "the language of the textbooks had to offer," Hill began to reflect on his own daughter's educational experiences. In particular, he recalled how she received a failing grade for a report on creationism that she gave in defiance of the assigned report on evolution. At the time, Hill did not think much of the incident, but in the context of the textbook controversy, "then it dawned on me." According to Hill, "at that time, everyone was talking about a generation gap," which in light of his daughter's experience Hill began to see as a disconnection not between parents and children but between teachers and students, just as right-wing, anticommunist discourse had been saying for nearly two decades. But Hill's rendition of the *What They Are Doing to Your Children* and *Why Johnny Can't Read* rhetoric from 1950s and 1960s reflects the important shift that happened around the time of the textbook controversy. Instead of demonizing communists it blames secular humanism. In Hill's version of the New Right narrative, parents are "packing Johnny's lunch bucket, combing his hair, patting him on the head and say[ing], 'Honey, you go to school today now. You mind what your teacher says.'"[9] But parents are oblivious that, according to Hill, "the philosophy of the textbooks [is] secularism." The problem lay in having "the attitudes of evolution and all that is being thrown into their heads. And then coming home and the parents having another standard. So there was a generation gap. There was a pulling apart thing. And I thought, 'Hey, here's where the trouble is.' So that's the day I got involved" in the local campaign to protest books in Kanawha County.

In the context of secular humanism, Hill's daughter's encounter with evolution in school becomes something more sinister than a lesson in the history of science. The teacher's response becomes something more suspicious than the very common response to a student who fails to do the assignment. They become, instead, a sign of the conspiracy of "educational professionals" exercising their "blackboard tyranny." The New Right narrative of secular humanism reads the young Hill girl as a heroic resister to dreaded tyranny and the teacher as a nefarious accomplice for assigning a report on evolution, the single most influential scientific theory of the nineteenth century. Avis Hill, moreover, appears as the unwitting parent who sees the light about such tyranny at last, after numerous attempts to convince him to abandon his desire to keep "preaching behind the pulpits and in the churches and leave the politicking up to" the politicians.[10]

But more than local agitators came to call on Hill. When asked about whether Alice Moore's invitation to get Mel and Norma Gabler involved was a good move or not, Hill answered in a way that emphasized that conservative strategists came without invitations:

> Yes, I think [Moore's requesting the Gablers to come to Charleston] was a good move. I think it was a fine move. The fact of the matter, the reason why we probably went out of the state and brought people, not necessarily that did we go out and get them, but they came to us. . . . But they saw that there was an opportunity, a chance here in Kanawha Valley because of the Bible Belt and the fundamental beliefs of the people and the miners. Then they saw the opportunity for them. So they wanted to pull their alliance with us because we had the largest number of people [among other textbook skirmishes elsewhere in the nation]. But they came to us more than we came to them.[11]

Hill mentions the Heritage Foundation and discusses how he traveled to Boston, McKeesport (Pennsylvania), and other places where Washington conservatives aimed to aid grassroots uprisings.

In particular, Robert Whitaker and Robert Hoy of the Populist Forum helped Avis Hill connect politically with other groups nationally. The Populist Forum was a small organization, consisting primarily of Hoy, Whitaker, and Whitaker's wife, Brigitte. Its goals were to mobilize or agitate on the local level, connect those smaller uprisings regionally, and build bridges internationally among what Hoy referred to as "populist militants."[12] The Populist Forum's projects and members were involved in both New Right conservatism and ultraright white supremacism.

Hoy, for instance, not only had a key role in Avis Hill's protesting work but "was also meeting with nationalist groups influenced by national socialism."[13] This led to praising "various neo-Nazi nationalist movements in *Spotlight,* an anti-Semitic newspaper controlled by the quasi-Nazi Liberty Lobby in Washington, D.C. Hoy's photographic essays and articles for *Spotlight* have praised neo-Nazi skinhead groups, the fascist National Front in Great Britain, and other similar groups." Despite this engagement in ultraright activities, Hoy was welcome in the New Right. For example, he "contributed an essay to *The New Right Papers,* where he called for 'seizing the time' to make a right-wing 'revolution,' noting that Americans had 'made one revolution in 1775. If no alternatives are offered, they can make another one today.'"[14] Although such "revolutionary" rhetoric may have been seen as alarmist to some Washington conservatives, New Right readers were encouraged to entertain it as "an alarm worth hearing."[15]

In his essay in *The New Right Papers,* which was edited by his Populist Forum partner Whitaker, Hoy explains his approach to local groups, including the Kanawha County textbook protesters:

We spent several years trying to channel the energy and resentment of many sporadic uprisings against the establishment into some kind of enduring alliance. Wildcat miners, textbook protesters, despairing farmers, opponents of busing: These and others came under our purview.

We sympathized heartily with the pressing concerns of these grassroots activists, and made it an unvarying point of honor to begin by asking each group, "What can *we* do for *you?*"—especially since no one else had dreamed of asking them that. In the back of our minds, however, we maintained perspective. When the time was right, when fearful hearts and minds were at least partially won, we began prodding: "What can *you* do for other groups around the country which share a common neglect? What can the miner do for the farmer? How can the busing foe in South Boston express solidarity with the textbook protesters in West Virginia?"

We posed these questions sincerely because we were always looking for the formula which would unify the disparate protest groups into something lasting and cohesive. We saw The Populist Forum as a vehicle for unity—a catalyst for unifying those we had brought together. Beyond a certain point, people must make things happen for themselves—or you're talking some brand of elitism, not populism.

Besides bolstering morale and functioning as an introduction service among otherwise isolated groups around the country, The Populist Forum arranged extensive media coverage.[16]

Whether or not it was all arranged by Hoy is hard to know, but the media attention paid to Kanawha County was indeed extensive. Through local intervention and publicity work, the Populist Forum in some capacity "helped to transform the controversy from a local dispute over a few textbooks into a debate with national implications about basic questions of power and cultural destiny."[17]

Avis Hill was the Populist Forum's media highlight at one of three populist marches on Washington that "brought together some 15,000 parents from across America and attracted major media attention," according to Hoy.[18] In March 1975, seventy protesters left on chartered buses from Kanawha County and hundreds planned to "drive all night from West Virginia to be on hand."[19] It is unclear who financed the chartered transportation. A press conference at which Hoy and Hill were featured "was given political overtones by the presence of an adviser to Alabama Gov. George C. Wallace and a representative of the National Conference on American Ethnic Groups who said his members never would vote for a presidential candidate who favored school busing."[20] Thus the group spoke under the auspices of ethnicity and with the hope of thwarting racial integration in the schools. Hoy described the larger gathering that followed the press release, doting on Hill: "Speaking before a gathering of 5,000 parents during our third march on Washington, 'little Avis' warned: 'If they can break us in our mountain home, if they can break us in the farm towns of Jefferson County [Kentucky], if they can break us in the streets of South Boston, then they can break us anywhere.'"[21] In addition to getting Hill out of West Virginia to speak to crowds and press conferences in Washington, D.C., Hoy was also intent on fomenting more protest in Kanawha County, even as the textbook controversy was considered by locals to be largely over with.

In the spring of 1975, the textbook controversy had run its course as far as the board of education, including Alice Moore, was concerned. The superintendent, Kenneth Underwood, had resigned under the pressure of being perceived as an outsider, a secular humanist, and/or a socialist. Protesters saw this as a major victory that offset the fact that most of the contested books had been returned to the classrooms and that a federal grand jury had come down hard on those indicted for bombing schools in October. Because of a radical decrease in demonstrations and reports of violence, students, teachers, and school board members experienced a major shift, if not psychological closure. Despite this feeling and general agreement that the battle was over, Avis Hill continued to plan rallies. By the summer of 1975, Hill appeared wearing a coonskin hat at a sparsely attended rally. The look harkened back unmistakably to the frontier icons of Daniel Boone and Davy Crockett and mirrored the mountaineer mascot for sports teams from West Virginia University. It coincided with a new effort to rally protesters as supporters of right-wing populist dissent.

In June and July 1975, "The Populist Forum helped Pastor Hill to record and produce an album which set his people's case to bluegrass music."[22] Robert Hoy says he "wrote six songs" that appear on the album,[23] including one that was denounced in the pages of the *Washington Post* for unfairly attacking "liberals, the National Education Association, communists, and the Supreme Court. Actually," Hoy clarifies, "the point of my song, entitled 'Kanawha County Uprising,' was precisely that these great powers, and a number of others were united against a relative handful of parents in one rural county of America."[24] Hoy thus intended the songs on Avis Hill's record album to narrate the Kanawha County protesters as facing the "united" forces of "great powers."

To narrate the Kanawha County textbook controversy as a matter of right-wing populism, the album, titled *Textbook War*, featured not only Hoy's own populist lyrics but also the acoustic and visual iconography of Appalachia. Acoustically, the recording includes ballads, spirituals, and what might be more accurately described as old-time—rather than bluegrass—rhythms. Visually, the album's cover is a stunning example of selling the iconic images of Appalachia. The album itself is a quintessential artifact of soul on Appalachian ice, of marketable protest and ethnic struggle relying on invocations of nationalism and spirituality and aimed at preventing the future total alienation of white folks.

On the album cover, superimposed on the stone doorway arch of the Kanawha County Jail (which now serves as the Kanawha County Courthouse) is the name Pastor Avis Hill. Below stands the singing group, the Hills of West Virginia, decked out in the patriotic colors that were everywhere that summer of 1975, on the verge of the nation's bicentennial. Three women wear their chin-to-toe dress-flags, the blue field of which displays a configuration of stars to commemorate the thirteen original colonies. This configuration suggests a revolutionary spirit. Two men don bright red vests over white shirts. Centered among them in mountaineer garb is Avis Hill, complete with Bible, shotgun, buckskin fringe, and coonskin cap. This is the cover of the *Textbook War* album, which merged protest, commodity, nationalism, spiritualism, popular culture, technology, and whiteness, all of which came to characterize right-wing campaigns and the discourses of cultural conservatism.

Side A of the album features songs about the protest that shook the Kanawha Valley throughout most of 1974 and the beginning of 1975. If we believe Robert Hoy, he wrote all the songs on side A, because the songs listed on side B are traditional spirituals. But this information clashes with the information on the back of the album. According to the listing, only one song was written by Hoy, and it is titled "Kanawha County Surprise," not "Kanawha County Uprising," as Hoy remembers. It could be that Hoy offered Avis Hill the lyrics for six songs and Hill rejected some. It could be that Hill was not quite as militant as Hoy wished, and opted to replace "uprising" with "surprise," which also could have been the result of a simple transposition and omission of letters during someone's typing. In any case, the populist spirit that Hoy was so eager to promote does come through the music in several songs. The aforementioned "Our Lost Heaven" was the one John Denver's recording company considered a copyright infringement, and "Pipes in the Wind" was a waltz whose lyrics featured the same kind of ethnic pride promoted in George Dietz's *Liberty Bell* magazines.

Like the *Liberty Bell* essay "A Message to All True Sons of Appalachia," the lyrics to "Pipes in the Wind" treaded a fine line between ethnic pride and white racial nationalism. By creating an essentializing link between Appalachians and Scots, the song narrates textbook protesters as populist heroes connected to a time and a place that become less geographical and historical and more about blood and character: "In the land of the mountains [and] the home of brave men / the land from which tyrants all flee / live the sons of the Highlands / the blood of old Scotland and only these brave men are free." Bravery, a character trait, is fused with blood, a biological element here in the lyrics as it is in white racialist fiction such as *The Clansman* and *The Turner Diaries*. Moreover, *only* the brave men, those with Scottish ancestry, are free, according to the lyrics. The song continues: "Freedom, freedom, wild bagpipes are calling / in a place yon memory [holds] dear. / And the blood in the veins of the mountaineer answers, /

every [one] knows of the pipes in the wind." Here again, "blood" is not only an organic substance but a matter of memory as well. Thus the "blood in the veins of the mountaineer" is synonymous with "the blood of old Scotland." Moreover, the "Hills of West Virginia"—meaning the Avis Hill family members, including Tim Hill, Bill Hill, Paula Hill, and Linda Hill, according to the back of the album cover—are one and the same as the state's mountains. As such they are, regardless of their gender, "the sons of the Highlands" as much as they are mountaineers of West Virginia. The equation is complete: to be a warrior in the "textbook war" is to be part of the hills of West Virginia, a true mountaineer whose land-blood-character is proven by answering the call to protest tyranny.

The album cover attributes the song "Pipes in the Wind" to Marjorie Sofranko, but the message of it is not far from Robert Hoy's own sentiments as someone moving between American New Right conservatives and National Front fascists from Great Britain. Given the fact that Hoy helped produce the record album and actually wrote the songs for it but did not play or sing them, it can be said that Hoy was quite literally putting his words in the mouths of Kanawha County protesters. But the situation is far more nuanced than some crude act of ventriloquism. Who wrote the songs is not as important as the fact that the album, whose "main theme is to save our children's souls from hell,"[25] discursively attempts to narrate and reproduce Kanawha County protesters as ethnically identified "populist militants," to use Hoy's phrase, in the "textbook war." This textual and social reproduction of the souls of white folk was far more subtle and enduring than if Hill was only Hoy's ventriloquist doll.

Aside from producing the record album, there was relatively little financial support from the Populist Forum, according to Hill. Hill reported that "we didn't have big monies" despite people "talking about us being mass funded." This is credible testimony if we take into account Hoy's statement that he operated "the Populist Forum as a vehicle for unity—a catalyst for unifying those we had brought together. Beyond a certain point, people must make things happen for themselves—or you're talking some brand of elitism, not populism."[26] Lest Hoy and his network, which extended both to the Washington conservatives of the New Right and the ultraright fascists of the National Front, be considered elitist, the Populist Forum apparently did not extend large sums of money to Hill, who continued to organize even after the language arts curriculum was in use and protests about the books had died down.

"I operated the textbook controversy in the Kanawha Valley out of my office from the '74 period up until '76 or '77," Hill attests. "During all that time, there was about $18,000 came across our books."[27] When Hill attended Washington events, he withstood the glaring inequalities of class stratification in order to meet and mingle with higher-ups in the conservative world:

> We sacrificed. Whenever the Republicans and Democrats were in Washington, D.C., having their national conventions, and for every forum I was there, trying to speak. When they were having their . . . caucuses in their hospitality suites, I was there. And they couldn't understand where I was coming from. But they didn't understand the fact that I'd slept in my van, I had hamburger at McDonald's the night before and went to a service station and washed my face and shaved in a mirror in the service station in order to be there, you see. As long as they could live . . . in the Hilton and have their expense accounts and fly in by jet and get out by jet, why they thought, 'Hey man, you can't do it, don't do it that way.' So they couldn't understand how—the sacrifice we were making.[28]

If it felt strange to hobnob in the hospitality suites at the Hilton, Avis Hill was willing to make the sacrifice because breaking down class barriers was not his stated aim. Maintaining the revolutionary rhetoric of the cover of his album, Hill told his interviewer, "I believe we started a revolution in education. I really do. I believe we fired the shot that was heard around the world. And I believe, maybe not in my lifetime, but somewhere down the road, these old West Virginia hillbillies are going to be looked upon—." The sentence is incomplete, reflecting the same anticlimax of his political career.

Avis Hill became active in politics—local and national—and took up conservative causes because of the Kanawha County textbook controversy. His story epitomizes how working-class people shifted to the Right in the 1970s, and highlights the strong role that the New Right narrative of secular humanism played in his decision to become involved. Despite his Christian upbringing that taught him politics were essentially corrupt and no place for evangelicals, he got involved in right-wing campaigns. Despite the financial "sacrifice" he made—"I lost $54,000 the first year, I lost my business," he said—Hill aligned with conservatives who would for the next twenty-five years establish policies that would economically support those already with hospitality suites at the Hilton. Hill persisted in mobilizing in the populist mode despite the violent threats and acts that he endured locally, possibly from the Klan, which he refused to endorse publicly. Despite having "to rake and scrape to get the filing fee," Hill ran for Congress in 1976, receiving only 10 percent of the vote. "I ran, I ran to speak my point of view," he explained, "to get me a pulpit, really," not necessarily to win.[29] Hill's aspirations were always evangelical. Thus his Christian convictions and Appalachian identity, shaped as they were by New Right narratives and the ideology of "populist militants" such as Hoy, overrode Hill's concerns with material needs and class solidarity. For Hill, for the "Sweet Alices" and other "concerned mothers" that Moore exemplified, and for the millions of other evangelical Christians in the 1970s, political involvement was transformed from dubious dealings in corrupt activity to the heroic salvation of the souls of "our children." Protesting the textbooks in Kanawha County was a key one of the many stories that reproduced evangelicals and Appalachians as political subjects of the Right.

Not Your Great-Grandfather's Miner-Ministers

To read Avis Hill or any of the evangelical ministers as mere dupes of the Right is to repeat the trope of portraying dissenting Appalachians as victims rather than as organized rebels and, in the process, to obscure the powerful history of Appalachians' resistance.[30] It also renders the textbook protesters unaccountable for the political decisions they made. Inspired by the narrative of secular humanism, Hill allied himself with right-wing advocates, as did millions of Christian evangelicals throughout the 1970s.

This phenomenon should be distinguished from the Appalachian "miner-ministers" of the coal wars in the early twentieth century, when miners underwent a remarkable conversion experience to become a formidable organized labor force. Taught to adopt what the company-run churches preached—a "highly *individuated* conception of human salvation"—miner-ministers began preaching a *collective* salvation and organizing unions that led strike after strike.[31] Their symbolism was very similar to what Hill and his cohort used, but there was a big difference, too:

> The working class culture signaled by the Paint Creek strike [in 1912] was a culture that had as its rallying points the symbols of the flag, religion, and the future of its children—and from these symbols drew

lessons not in submissiveness and selfishness, but of entitlement and collective purpose: entitlement to their rights as God-fearing Americans struggling together for a better life for their posterity. Above all the sense of collective purpose must be stressed, because it flew in the face of American slogans of individualism. Middle-class commentators were alarmed by this culture, seeing in it a new form of coercion and enslavement.[32]

In the early part of the twentieth century, therefore, Appalachian working-class protesters emphasized the American values of collectivity and unity before those ideas became completely maligned as communist propaganda. But in 1974, the language arts controversy used some of the same political rhetoric to a different effect: textbook protesters rallied around the flag, religion, and the future of their children in ways that reinforced American ideas of individualism and the conservative politics built around it. Consequently, Alice Moore emerged as an individual hero rejuvenating a decadent civilization.[33] People such as Linda Paul, Avis Hill, Marvin Horan, and the thousands of parents who were protesting were largely depicted as her followers rather than her partners, peers, or comrades. In 1974, a tradition of protest culture turned decidedly right in West Virginia, transforming the focus of such protest from class solidarity to cultural conservatism and right-wing revolution.

Two Narratives of Soul

It may well be true that Kanawha County was an early skirmish in the culture wars of the 1980s and thereafter. But such a formulation needs to be understood as a conservative rendition of how "Appalachia was often called the first battlefield in the war on poverty."[34] Such a formulation reestablishes the ideal of Appalachia as a frontier, and claims that wild revolutionary space for the Right. The impact of the Kanawha County textbook controversy thus lies ultimately in its representation. Each telling of the story is a matter of reinventing Appalachia in relation to America, and of reproducing a sense of ethnicity, of the people involved. So far, telling the story has encompassed two narratives of soul. We can conclude, in the fashion of Bill Best, that the Right "stripped Appalachian soul" in coming to Kanawha County, and thereby retell the captivity narrative of ethnicity as alienated labor. Or we can accept the Right's version and see the Kanawha County textbook controversy as a fight for the souls of "our children" against an ever-oncoming tyranny, and thereby retell the apocalyptic narrative of ethnicity.

In this book I have tried to carve out an intellectual space in between the two classic tales of soul, to muddy the supposed clarity imposed by previous scholars and commentators. My goal has been neither to inflame old sores nor to find a healing compromise to a conflict that caused so many people so much anguish, anger, fear, and resentment. Rather, my aim has been to demonstrate that the Kanawha County textbook controversy represents a discursive pivot point in the history of the national rightward turn since the 1960s. In the process, we have seen how the ideas of soul, Appalachia, and America have been mutually constructed in the latter part of the twentieth century. The legacy of the Kanawha County textbook controversy is at once a recurring *dream* of that soulful Appalachian resistance and a decisive *reality* of political transformation. In this liminal way, "the very existence of Appalachia as a region or culture or people is a consequence rather than a cause of the" textbook controversy, which spurred several renegotiations of American identity that left their mark on contemporary politics.[35]

Protesting textbooks in Kanawha County helped forge an "Aryan" alliance among Klansmen and neo-Nazis, advanced the role of women activists in the New Right, and encouraged evangelicals such as Avis Hill to break the tradition of staying out of politics and align with right-wing campaigns under the auspices of ethnic pride and parental protection. Where once miner-ministers had resisted the coal companies' right-wing line on saving souls, thousands of parents marched with a variety of conservative forces and rationales to fight for "the souls of our children." As an enterprise that became more about the "our" and less about actual children, the textbook controversy in the Kanawha Valley ruptured and realigned the boundaries of community, redefining who was and was not a true son of Appalachia, a concerned mother, and a real American.

EPILOGUE

Writing Appalachia

In the last few weeks of 1974, every kid in Kanawha County, including me, came home from school with a permission slip, which, if signed, allowed access to the new language arts curriculum. Researching and writing this book was a challenge for many reasons, but mostly it was a sweet deal to go back to 1974, a time when I was enrolled in the Kanawha County public school system as a ten year old. This project has been my anchor through the last few years and reconnected me to my childhood home in an important new way. So I am enormously grateful to those who made it possible, first and foremost the woman who signed that permission slip for me, Barbara Mason. Thank you for sharing your early memories of coal camp life, sending clippings from the *Daily Mail*, giving me Grandmother's *McGuffey's Readers*, and breaking long hours of research with fun trips to Milton, Huntington, and Berea. This one is for you, Mom.

As for funding and those who administered it, I thank the Rockefeller Foundation for the Humanities, which sponsored my spring 2002 residency at Marshall University's Center for the Study of Ethnicity and Gender in Appalachia. There in Huntington, Lynda Ann Ewen, Shirley Lumpkin, and Mary Thomas made CSEGA an excellent place to work. Connie Leinen in particular was a tremendous resource with equal parts levity, intellectual verve, and administrative savvy. Susan Henking at Hobart and William Smith Colleges worked her magic to get me to Marshall in the first place, making sure I was not denied things such as health insurance because I was not on the tenure track. Acknowledgment is also due to the Faculty Travel Committee at the University of Nevada, which provided a one-time grant for a research trip. Enormous gratitude goes to my newest colleagues at Oklahoma State University, especially to Carol Moder, Head of the

English Department, and Peter M. A. Sherwood, Dean of the College of Arts and Sciences, for making me feel so welcome and providing a Dean's Incentive Grant that allowed me to finalize the manuscript.

I received excellent research assistance throughout the years. Archivist Richard Fauss at the West Virginia State Archives always went the extra mile for me. Often I felt he was an intellectual partner in thinking through the historical problems of the controversy. With the kind assistance of Ruth Ann Harper at the Kanawha County Board of Education, he arranged for me to listen to all of the recordings of the board's meetings from 1974 and 1975. Likewise, bibliographer Rebecca Schulte from the Spencer Research Library at the University of Kansas, and Cora Teel and Lori Thompson from James E. Morrow Library at Marshall University, were generous with their time and assistance. Also at Marshall, William Paynter sent me a key text. Student assistants, including Heidi Williams, Sharletta Green, Crystal Jackson, Nadia Jimenez, and Sandy Kristine Peterson were enthusiastic about even the most wacky of requests. Sandy endured the added duty of being the first reader of the entire manuscript. In Washington, D.C., Bryan Cornell was a big help at the Library of Congress; Ginger Richards, Heather Kneiss, and Michael Jourdan at People for the American Way pulled out file after file in which I found key items that gave my analysis depth; and Dan Lips was kind enough to meet me at the Heritage Foundation. John White helped me obtain materials from the Southern Historical Collection at Wilson Library at the University of North Carolina, Chapel Hill. I am grateful to UNC for allowing me to quote from the Southern Oral History Program (#4007) interviews B-76, 77, 78, 79, 80. Senior Analyst Chip Berlet at Political Research Associates not only let me loose in the archives in Somerville but also fielded questions about the Christian Crusade, cyberspace neo-Nazis, secular humanism, and the rise of the Right—no one is more knowledgeable than Chip Berlet on such issues.

When it came to learning what actually happened in Kanawha County, I benefited from those people who shared their memories and materials in formal interviews and informal conversations. The Reverend James Lewis generously provided several boxes of primary materials, including the files of the late Harry Stansbury, who served on the board of education at the time of the textbook controversy. In addition to Reverend Lewis's own amazing story, lending me Dr. Stansbury's materials was crucial to this project. No less crucial were insights from Linda Wright, who met with me for several hours on two occasions, taking time to show me the protest headquarters and explain her point of view as a Christian student at the time. Linda Wright inspired me to understand what was at stake for the protesters. Becky Bolte, Robert Hart, Jan Rezek, and Charles W. Loeb Jr. also shared their memories of the textbook controversy. The conflict shaped each of their educational experiences and I thank them for spending time with me. Those who were employed by the school system at the time, including Debra Hayslett, Bill Denman, Roscoe Keeney, the late Emmett Shafer, and especially Nell Wood gave me a sense of the intensity of the conflict. It shook their families and their world; I was fascinated to learn how they had thought through a time of such turmoil in their lives. I also greatly appreciated talking with R. Charles Byers, Ronald English, Ancella Bickley, and a group of former teachers having lunch at the Hallelujah Wings restaurant across the street from the former Garnet High School in Charleston. They gave me the sense that the responses in the African American community were philosophical and strategic. Ronald English, in particular, helped me consider the different kinds of racism present in the Kanawha Valley at the time and the local meanings of such terms as "redneck" and "hillbilly." Curtis Seltzer, who gave me terrific feedback on an early version of chapter 1, and John Taylor provided insights from the point of view of labor relations, and cautioned me about oversimplifying the coal strike and the racial conflict. And, finally, Mike Williams led me to Jerry Dale, Associate Professor of Criminal Justice at Greenbrier College, who for hours and with remarkable humor withstood all of my questions—ranging from the obvious to the absurd—about William Pierce and George Dietz. Without the memories and insights that each of these people shared, this book would be something different—and deficient. I greatly appreciate how much everyone gave of themselves.

I also owe a great debt to readers, audiences, and other intellectual interlocutors of this project from its beginning. I thank my fellow CSEGA-Rockefeller scholars, especially Rachel Jennings and Rosemarie Mincey, and participants in the 2004 National Endowment for the Humanities Summer Teachers' Institute at Ferrum College, especially Sean Chadwell and Danika Brown. Colleagues from the University of Pittsburgh (Carol Stabile, Lisa Brush, Nancy Glazener, and Kathy Blee) and from the University of Nevada, Las Vegas (members of the Huntridge reading group and the faculty research colloquium) advised me on various chapters. Also in Vegas, Matt Wray read and commented on an early version of chapter 4. Another set of thinkers offered insights from their study of Appalachian music and culture, including banjo player and American Studies professor Anna Creadick from Hobart and William Smith Colleges; old–time music historian Kurt Gegenhuber (at celestialmonochord.org); and my fabulous sister, Martha Mason, aka Mace of Acoustic Adventures and the "Listenin' with Mace" radio show in Fairbanks. Academic audiences at annual conventions of the American Studies Association (2002 and 2003), the National Women's Studies Association (2003), the Women of Appalachia conference (2001), and Narrative: An International Conference (2004) provided an excellent sounding board. Editors and anonymous readers for academic journals in which portions of this book have already appeared in some version were also very helpful in shoring up my arguments and keeping my references accurate. Thanks go to Appalachian State University, Sandy Ballard, and *Appalachian Journal*, where a version of chapter 1 appeared in volume 32, number 3, pages 352–78; Carol Stabile and Carrie Rentschler as guest editors for *National Women's Studies Association Journal*, where some insights from the prologue appeared in a different context in volume 17, number 3, pages 39–63; and Allison Bailey and Jacquelyn Zita, special issue editors for *Hypatia*, where a version of chapter 4 appeared in volume 22, number 2, pages 98–121. I also am very grateful to Elizabeth E. Chilton, President of Charleston Newspapers, for granting permission to use various images, and to Laura Belmonte and Brad Manuel for their input.

In the latest phases of the book, Eric Patterson was, as always, a marvelous source of support and suggestions for revision. The anonymous reviewers from Cornell generously commented on the entire manuscript; I am especially indebted to the mysterious Reader B. Sincere thanks also go to Peter Potter, Allison Kalett, John Raymond, Candace Akins, Sara Ferguson, and Michael McGandy, who made the book a reality.

In a remarkable instance of life circling back on itself, an old high school buddy, James Daniel Carter, the grandson of West Virginia labor leader Eugene A. Carter, contacted me as I was formatting the manuscript. He agreed to create the map of Kanawha County. Dan and I had worked together on the yearbook at George Washington High School and it was wonderful to work together again. It is doubtful that he knows how much he saved me during high school or how much I appreciate him returning to my life in time to be part of this book and make me laugh in the midst of finishing it.

Finally, I offer a note on culpability inspired by the reel-to-reel tape recordings of the school board meetings. I was the first person in decades to listen to them. To do so, I sat in a windowless room at the board of education on Elizabeth Street for hours during several days, threading the tapes onto an old machine that made the voices sound sometimes like cartoon chipmunks and sometimes like whales. I took notes and rerecorded the occasionally unintelligible sounds onto cassette tapes. Richard Fauss then worked with those cassette tapes and the reel-to-reels, hunting down and taking parts from several old tape players to reconstruct a machine capable of playing the tapes at an appropriate speed. This process of reconstruction brought the voices of 1974 back to life in a manner reminiscent of Mary Shelley's *Frankenstein* and also of Margaret Atwood's *The Handmaid's Tale*.

When teaching *The Handmaid's Tale*, I sometimes suggest to my students that my generation is like Atwood's main character, Offred, a member of a transitional generation, the last generation that can remember a time before the Christian Right gained so much influence, a pre-1980s America. But now, having written this book, I realize that I am less like Offred and dangerously more like Professor Piexioto, the historian who finds cassette tapes on which Offred has presumably recorded her story of escaping the theocracy that America, in *The Handmaid's Tale*, has become. I have striven methodologically, theoretically, and ethically to avoid the presumptions, pretensions, and pitfalls that Professor Piexioto cannot. As a traditional historian, Piexioto presumes he is merely discovering and uncovering history even as he arranges and manipulates it. Unlike Atwood's character, I realize that the representation of past events is their construction. In writing this book, I have presumed no objectivity or neutrality. But I hope I have been fair, respectful, and accurate. There are many more chapters I could have written, more archives I could have visited, more interviews I could have conducted, and more academic studies and theories I could have consulted. There is no doubt, despite all the help of those who have entrusted me, that I have made mistakes, misrepresenting someone or something along the way. And even though I firmly believe that every representation is also inescapably always a misrepresentation, let me apologize in advance for any undue burden my oversights may cause, especially to those of you from Kanawha County.

Reading Appalachia from Left to Right is not a definitive history of the Kanawha County textbook controversy of 1974, but an invitation to examine its influence. I realize that many may not agree with the perspectives offered herein. This is not a book that presumes to speak for anyone else but me, relaying the way I see things according to my having grown up in Kanawha County at the time of the textbook controversy, and according to the subsequent learning and unlearning involved in obtaining my bachelor's, master's, and doctoral degrees in English language and literatures. Partially because of the kind of education the contested language arts curriculum represented, I value a proliferation of voices and opinions. I hope *Reading Appalachia from Left to Right* helps to lend credence to voices other than my own, especially those that have been dismissed as mere hillbilly babble.

It is fitting, then, to note that as this book was about to go to press, audio documentary maker Trey Kay contacted me and indicated how I might, after several years of looking, find Alice Moore. I sent out a letter. One day the landline sounded its nearly antique ring. Standing in the bedroom, miles away from any thought of work, writing, or West Virginia, I picked up the receiver. It felt heavy.

"Hello?" There was a slight delay and I almost hung up to avoid an automated sales pitch. But something stayed my arm until someone spoke.

"Hello. I am trying to reach Carol Mason." The voice was uncanny.

With telephone etiquette I learned in elementary school, I replied, "This is she."

"This," said the unforgettable voice, "is Alice Moore."

My heart raced and my eyes darted, looking for a pencil. "Mrs. Moore, how good of you to call!"

She laughed the laugh that I had heard countless times on audio tape and proceeded to respond to questions I had sent to another address from which I expected to have the envelope returned to sender. Alice Moore was indeed charming, smart, and very generous. None of her responses was surprising.

By the time that *Reading Appalachia from Left to Right* is no longer what I am writing and has become what you are reading, many people, including Alice Moore, may disagree with my interpretations. But we will all agree that the textbook controversy begun in 1974 was part of a larger, ongoing process of reading ourselves and writing our future. This book is my way of reading that future back to you.

Keywords

Entries for each of the following terms, all of which are contentious and troublesome, are not technical definitions. Instead, they are descriptions intended to indicate basic assumptions behind the use of each term in this book and in relation to the 1974 Kanawha County textbook controversy.

Appalachia   A physical and imaginary space within the United States. As a matter of geography, Appalachia is "a 200,000-square-mile region that follows the spine of the Appalachian Mountains from southern New York to northern Mississippi. It includes all of West Virginia and parts of 12 other states: Alabama, Georgia, Kentucky, Maryland, Mississippi, New York, North Carolina, Ohio, Pennsylvania, South Carolina, Tennessee, and Virginia."[1] As a matter of history and culture, "Appalachia is a creature of the urban imagination. The folk culture, the depressed area, the romantic wilderness, the Appalachia of fiction, journalism, and public policy, have for more than a century been created, forgotten, and rediscovered, primarily by the economic opportunism, political creativity, or passing fancy of urban elites." This is not to say that Appalachia is not real or that residents of Appalachia are figments of anyone's imagination; quite to the contrary, it is to acknowledge that when we call something, even ourselves, Appalachian, we willfully associate it (or ourselves) with particular representations and assumptions—both the bad and the good images—that have come before. "Appalachia" is, inescapably, a frame of reference.[2] Saying "Appalachia" paints a picture.

Christian Right   What resulted from the politicization of evangelicals and fundamentalists in the late 1960s, 1970s, and 1980s. The emergence of the Christian Right was due largely to New Right strategists who mobilized and funded political action committees and organizations led by inspirational religious leaders. Key to the growth of the Christian Right was a revival in millennialist belief at the beginning of the 1970s and the use of television broadcasting and other media.

Conservative   A political and ideological designation with the aim of averting social change and preserving the status quo of American society, including stratifications due to differences in socioeconomic class, gender, sexuality, race, and nationality. A conservative is one whose nationalism embraces the government and works within the electoral system to secure power. During the Kanawha County textbook controversy a conservative was not guaranteed but was likely to be associated with the Republican Party. Conservatism at the time was characterized by "economic libertarianism, social traditionalism, and militant anti-communism."[3]

Cultural conservatism   The name given by New Right strategists who wanted to distinguish their brand of conservatism from that of the Old Right.[4] Key to cultural conservatism is promoting values through policy that defines particular ideas about family, sexuality, gender, reproduction, and work as essential to American life and national survival. Cultural conservatism is proactive rather than reactive, transforming the Old Right's doomsday defeatism into apocalyptic urgency.

Ethnicity   In the context of the Kanawha County textbook controversy, I use this term to refer to the contested senses of belonging and claims to identity that emerged during the conflict. Ethnicity is what developed as people collectively asserted who they were—true Appalachians, for instance, or real Americans—while fighting over the curriculum. Informing my decision to use the term this way are several overlapping academic discussions in addition to those I cite in the prologue. First, ethnicity in Appalachia is presumed to be essentially and purely Scots-Irish, but that romantic depiction of inhabitants has been questioned in terms of demographics and history.[5] Second, ethnicity is generally presumed to be about culture and heritage, something different from race, which is said to refer to biological differences. But this distinction is blurred because categories of race are also now understood to be cultural rather than genetic.[6] Third, historically speaking, the idea of "white ethnics" is pertinent to the textbook controversy because in the early 1970s there was much political activism during which that category gained prominence.[7] In some cases, "white ethnics drew upon a history as victims of discrimination in ways that attenuated their own enjoyment of the privileges of being white, even as it evoked parallels to the historical suffering of nonwhites."[8] All these discussions surrounding ethnicity resonated with the dynamic sense of "us" and "them" during the textbook controversy. Especially with regard to white Appalachian ethnicity, as Emily Satterwhite so well explains in her study of perceptions of the 2003 Smithsonian Folklife Festival, a variety of social and political consequences (intentional or not) results when people rise up against injustice in the name of preserving their Appalachian heritage.

> When white Americans depend upon a vocabulary of ethnicity to explain perceived injustices, however, they also forestall the possibility of articulating and organizing around widely shared socio-economic grievances. If white Americans' interest in "heritage" or in "roots" comes at the expense of learning about the multiplicity of cultural traditions informing U.S. society, it leads to belittling or denying others' oppression and claiming victimhood; if it becomes an exclusive defense of race and nation, then the possibilities for viable democratic pluralism or effective global multilateralism are foreclosed. At the Folklife Festival, a reductive idea of Appalachia as the "Scottish" or "Celtic" foundation for "real" American culture became for some visitors a potent symbol of whites' oppression and white ethnic pride. These visitors' reasons for embracing the "Appalachia: Heritage and Harmony" program should raise concerns about a disquieting willingness to romanticize and identify with a "victimized" Appalachia that shores up an aggressive American nationalism grounded in a nostalgic conception of innocent rural white community.[9]

Evangelical   An umbrella term referring to those Protestants who evangelize by witnessing their faith in an effort to spread the Christian word of God and convert others from a life of sin. Evangelicals "are people for whom only an individual decision to follow Jesus will suffice for salvation. They are concerned not only about their own eternal fate but also about the destiny of those around them. They seek to 'win souls for Christ' by their words and deeds, testifying to the necessity of a life-changing decision to become a Christian. They often speak of that experience as being 'born again.' It is an experience that gives them a sense of personal and intimate communion with Jesus and often shapes their lives and conversations in noticeably pious ways. But even within the evangelical branch there are significant subdivisions."[10]

Fundamentalist   In the context of the Kanawha County textbook controversy, I use this term to refer to those Christians who believe the Bible is the literal word of God. The term is derived from the early twentieth-century publication *The Fundamentals*, which insisted on the infallibility of the Bible as the actual word of God and objected to the European-based textual and historical research on the origins and authority of the Bible, known as the "higher criticism," which was prominent in the late nineteenth century. "During the 1920s fundamentalists actively fought against modernism in their churches and against evolution in their schools. They lost those battles but retreated and reorganized into a network of institutions that has housed much of the conservative wing of American Protestantism ever since."[11]

Left, Left-Wing, Leftist   Broad terms used to designate political action and a philosophy that promotes egalitarianism. "According to historian John Patrick Diggins, generally speaking, the various 'Lefts' of the twentieth century—from the Wobblies, anarchists, and assorted bohemians comprising the Lyrical Left in the early part of the century, to the Communist, progressive, or anti-Stalinist Old Left of the 1930s, to the student radicals comprising the New Left of the 1960s—have 'demanded the liquidation of institutionalized power and interest politics, the elimination of social classes, [and] the replacement of competitive life with one of fraternal participation and cooperative fulfillment.'"[12]

Liberal   A political and ideological designation based on the philosophy of individual rights and freedoms. One whose nationalism embraces the government and works within the electoral system to secure power. Social change for the liberal includes reform of the existing political system, not a radical or revolutionary overturning of it. During the time of the Kanawha County textbook controversy a liberal was not guaranteed to be but was likely to be associated with the Democratic Party. A legacy of New Deal policies of the 1930s aimed at providing relief from the Great Depression, liberalism in 1974 promoted equal rights for women, social welfare, and affirmative action.

National Socialism, Nazi, Neo-Nazi   Political terms associated with German leader Adolf Hitler (1889–1945) and the fascist ideology inspired by him. National Socialism is a particular historical manifestation of ultra-right politics and should not be confused with leftist movements or ideologies. According to Chip Berlet, "Technically, the word NAZI was the acronym for the National Socialist German Worker's Party. It was a fascist movement that had its roots in the European nationalist and socialist movements, and that developed a grotesque biologically-determinant view of so-called 'Aryan' supremacy. (Here we use 'national socialism' to refer to the early Nazi movement before Hitler came to power, sometimes termed the 'Brownshirt' phase, and the term 'Nazi' to refer to the movement after it had consolidated around ideological fascism.)"[13] As chapter 2 explains, the Kanawha County textbook controversy was of interest to two important promoters of National Socialism, Roane County resident George Dietz and William Pierce, who moved to Pocahontas County after the textbook controversy. Dietz, who opposed the books, later declared, "I and my associates live and breathe National Socialism every waking moment (and sometimes sleeping, for that matter) of our lives. We do not doubt ourselves, nor do we wish to hide the fact that we are on the White Man's side. Those who shrink from wearing the Swastika today will next shrink from wearing their White skins."[14] Pierce remained more circumspect, avoiding both the Swastika and the label "Nazi" while in West Virginia. "Nonetheless, while it was right to declare that [Pierce's National Alliance] was not 'Nazi,' potential members were those who could distinguish between the 'eternal truths' of National Socialism, 'the truths on which our own creed is based,' and 'the mythical image created by the Jews.' In discussions with those it sought to recruit, the Alliance stressed that discretion with regard to knowing when and how to explain its view of National Socialism was vital."[15] I use these terms to indicate Pierce's and Dietz's unwavering allegiance to Hitler's ideas, regardless of how and when they openly embraced the labels themselves.

New Right   Those particular strategists who, after the defeat of Barry Goldwater in the 1964 presidential election, became determined to shift the country away from the policies and beliefs that emerged with the social movements (including civil rights, feminist, and antiwar efforts) of the 1960s. What was "new" about the New Right was their use of technology and media and their focus on cultural values rather than economics. The New Right was ideologically synonymous with cultural conservatism.

Old Right   The kind of conservatism that considered free-market capitalism the foundation of national vitality, and the economic collectivism of socialism or communism, as well as the policies of New Deal liberalism, anathema to it. Faced with defeats that crushed conservative hopes to retain racial segregation, to flush out supposed communists in government, and to perpetuate military imperialism, the Old Right assumed a reactionary stance of opposing social change.

Right, Right-Wing, Rightist   Umbrella terms I use to designate those in the United States whose politics do not equate the constitutional claim that "all men are created equal" with the drive toward social or economic egalitarianism.[16] "To be right-wing means to support the state in its capacity as enforcer of order and to oppose the state as distributor of wealth and power downward and more equitably in society."[17] This definition suffices in most cases, but not all. "Some rightist movements, such as Father Coughlin's Social Justice movement in the 1930s and George Wallace's American Independent Party in the 1960s, have advocated downward redistribution of wealth and power—not to everyone, but to certain groups below the elite. And some right-wing movements, such as the Ku Klux Klan of the late 1860s or various Patriot/militant groups in the 1990s, have rejected the state altogether and have sought to overthrow it, in the process rejecting and disrupting the state's order-enforcement role."[18]

Ultraright   A term designating those politically motivated individuals and groups whose aims are revolutionary and whose tactics are extralegal. The ultraright militantly opposes the government for various reasons and takes measures to foment dissent against it. I use this term instead of "far right."

White, Whiteness   In the context of the Kanawha County textbook controversy, these terms refer to how and why those involved claimed, rejected, or ignored identification as members of the dominant population of the area. The larger question that inspires use of these terms in this study is, Why do working white Americans choose the psychological "wages of whiteness"—those social rewards for claiming to be white by creating distance from those deemed nonwhite—over the prosperity they might gain by joining with people of color and collaboratively opposing exploitative economic arrangements? Or, as one recent popular book title put it, "what's the matter with Kansas" and other white communities that consistently support conservative politicians and policies that economically hold them back?[19] With the publication of *The Wages of Whiteness* in the 1990s, historian David Roediger helped launch the historical and critical study of whiteness as both a "category, into which immigrants were or were not put, and as a consciousness, which immigrants embraced and rejected in specific circumstances."[20] Since then, academics have used "whiteness" as an analytical term helpful for determining the social conditions and historical changes in how we determine who in society is white.[21]

White Supremacist   An ideological designation for those who believe in the biological, cultural, and/or spiritual purity of white people and take measures to promote the view of a white-dominated society as the natural order.

Notes

Prologue

1. Ann L. Page and Donald A. Clelland, "The Kanawha County Textbook Controversy: A Study of the Politics of Life Style Concern," *Social Forces* 57, no. 1 (September 1978): 268.
2. Ibid., 282.
3. Ben A. Franklin, "West Virginia," *New York Times*, January 5, 1975.
4. John Alexander Williams, *West Virginia: A History* (Morgantown: West Virginia University Press, 2001), 188.
5. Ibid., 196.
6. James Moffett, *Storm in the Mountains: A Case Study of Censorship, Conflict, and Consciousness* (Carbondale: Southern Illinois University Press, 1988), 13.
7. Sources for the following description of protest: Page and Clelland, "Kanawha County Textbook Controversy," 269–70; "Textbook Timeline," *Charleston Daily Mail*, September 7, 1999, http://www.dailymail.com/static/specialsections/lookingback/lb09073.htm; "Text Controversy—Beginning to Present," *Charleston Gazette*, November 1, 1974.
8. Page and Clelland, "Kanawha County Textbook Controversy," 269.
9. "Proposed County," *Charleston Daily Mail*, January 15, 1975.
10. Etienne Balibar and Emmanuel Wallerstein, *Race, Nation, Class: Ambiguous Identities* (New York: Verso, 1991), 98.
11. Rey Chow, *The Protestant Ethnic and the Spirit of Capitalism* (New York: Columbia University Press, 2002), chapter 1.
12. I use the term "white" here and elsewhere in accordance with scholarship that recognizes its historical construction as a racial and social category. For discussion of this construction in Appalachia specifically, see Patricia D. Beaver and Helen M. Lewis, "Uncovering the Trail of Ethnic Denial:

Ethnicity in Appalachia," in *Cultural Diversity in the U.S. South: Anthropological Contributions to a Region in Transition,* ed. Carole Hill and Patricia D. Beaver (Athens: University of Georgia Press, 1998).

13. Matt Wray, *Not Quite White* (Durham, N.C.; Duke University Press, 2006).

14. The relationship between ethnicity and race is a messy one. Historical accounts reveal how white privileges become immigrants' reward for assimilation into U.S. society, how biological designations competed with cultural ones throughout the twentieth century, and how discussions of ethnicity supplant concerns with racism. See David Roediger, *Working toward Whiteness: How America's Immigrants Became White* (New York: Basic Books, 2005), 3–35; Henry Yu, "Ethnicity," in *Keywords for American Cultural Studies,* ed. Bruce Burgett and Glenn Hendler (New York: New York University Press, 2007), 103–8; E. San Juan Jr., "The Cult of Ethnicity and the Fetish of Pluralism: A Counterhegemonic Critique," *Cultural Critique* (1991): 215–29.

15. Ronald Lora, "Education: Schools as Crucible in Cold War America," in *Reshaping America: Society and Institutions, 1945–1960,* ed. Robert H. Bremner and Gary W. Reichard (Columbus: Ohio State University Press, 1982), 223–60.

16. Ibid.

17. Jonathan Zimmerman, *Whose America? Culture Wars in the Public Schools* (Cambridge: Harvard University Press, 2002).

18. Joseph Moreau, *School Book Nation: Conflicts over American History Textbooks from the Civil War to the Present* (Ann Arbor: University of Michigan Press, 2003).

19. "KKK Imperial Wizard Urges West Virginians to Reject Textbooks," *Herald Advertiser,* January 19, 1975.

20. Anthony Harkins, *Hillbilly: A Cultural History of an American Icon* (New York: Oxford University Press, 2004), 15.

21. Ibid.

22. Carroll Smith-Rosenberg, *Disorderly Conduct: Visions of Gender in Victorian America* (New York: Knopf, 1985), 104.

23. Ibid., 93.

24. Harkins, *Hillbilly,* 49.

25. Smith-Rosenberg, *Disorderly Conduct,* 98.

26. Ibid., 107.

27. For more on Appalachia and the War on Poverty, see Allen W. Batteau, *The Invention of Appalachia* (Tucson: University of Arizona Press, 1990), chapter 8, and John Alexander Williams, *Appalachia: A History* (Chapel Hill: University of North Carolina Press, 2002), 348–50.

28. For a discussion on the distinctions between these terms, see Harkins, *Hillbilly,* 95–112.

29. Annalee Newitz and Matt Wray, eds., *White Trash: Race and Class in America* (New York: Routledge, 1997), 169.

30. Ibid., 171.

31. Harkins, *Hillbilly*, 7.

32. J.W. Williamson, *Hillbillyland: What the Movies Did to the Mountains and What the Mountains Did to the Movies* (Durham: University of North Carolina Press, 1995), 225–63.

33. Carol Mason, "The Hillbilly Defense: Culturally Mediating U.S. Terror at Home and Abroad," *National Women's Studies Association Journal* 17, no. 3 (2005): 39–63.

34. Harkins, *Hillbilly*, 7.

Introduction

1. Kanawha County Board of Education meetings, March 28–December 12, 1974 (twenty-six audiocassette tapes recorded by author from reel-to-reel tape recordings with permission of the board of education; rerecorded and reengineered by Richard Fauss, West Virginia State Archives). Voices featured in this chapter are from June 27, 1974.

2. Eldridge Cleaver, *Soul on Ice* (New York: Delta Books, 1968).

3. For examples of Appalachian protest culture, see John Gaventa, *Power and Powerlessness: Quiescence and Rebellion in an Appalachian Valley* (Urbana: University of Illinois Press, 1982); Stephen Fisher, *Fighting Back in Appalachia* (Philadelphia, Temple University Press, 1993); Chad Montrie, *To Save the Land and the People: A History of Opposition to Surface Coal Mining in Appalachia* (Chapel Hill: University of North Carolina Press, 2003).

4. David A. Peyton, "'Community Spirit' One Explanation for Current Protest over Books," *Herald Advertiser*, November 11, 1974.

5. Ibid.

6. Chow, *Protestant Ethnic*, chapter 1.

7. Robert C. Small Jr., "Textbook Protestors as People," *English Journal* 65, no. 3 (March 1976): 19.

8. James C. Hefly, *Textbooks on Trial* (Wheaton, Ill.: Victor Books, 1976); Connaught Coyne Marshner, *Blackboard Tyranny* (New Rochelle, N.Y.: Arlington House Publishers, 1978); William Martin, *With God on Our Side: The Rise of the Religious Right in America* (New York: Broadway Books, 1996); Dwight Billings and Robert Goldman, "Comment on 'The Kanawha County Textbook Controversy,'" *Social Forces* 57, no. 4 (June 1979): 1393–98; Lisa McGirr, "A History of the Conservative Movement from the Bottom Up," *Journal of Policy History* 14, no. 3 (2002): 331–39.

Chapter 1. A Modern American Conflict

 1. Harkins, *Hillbilly*, 7.
 2. Peter Strafford, "Class Warfare over Text Books," *London Times*, October 12, 1974. Rpt. as Peter Strafford, "Class Warfare over U.S. Textbooks," *South China Morning Post*, October 19, 1974.
 3. Linda Wright, interview by author, tape recording and handwritten notes, May 28, 2002, Huntington, West Virginia.
 4. Ibid.
 5. Curtis Seltzer, "West Virginia Book War: A Confusion of Goals," *The Nation* 219, no. 14 (November 2, 1974): 432.
 6. Richard Bauman, "Snake Handling—Should It Be Banned?" *Liberty: A Magazine of Religious Freedom* 70, no. 3 (May–June 1975): 2–5.
 7. John Egerton, "The Battle of the Books," *Progressive* 39, no. 6 (June 1975): 17.
 8. F. David Wilkin, "The Kanawha County, West Virginia, Textbook Issue: Social Policy in Dispute" (term paper, Graduate School of Education, Harvard University, 1975), 43.
 9. Before taking up the textbook cause, Fike was a vocal advocate of un-regulated capitalist enterprise, was active in Republican Party politics, and served as West Virginia state coordinator of the Conservative Caucus. Fike employed about sixty people at the time of the textbook controversy. In the 1980s and 1990s, he became notorious as an embittered opponent of the Environmental Protection Agency, which condemned his chemical company grounds in Nitro, about fifteen miles from Charleston, because of unlabeled, deteriorating industrial vats that were seeping unidentified chemicals into the ground. Sometimes citizens from nearby homes had been evacuated as a result. See Elmer Fike, *Textbook Controversy in Perspective and Other Related Essays* (Nitro, West Virginia). See also "Glitch in the System: Elmer Fike," West Virginia Public Broadcasting, Different Drummer series, Morgantown, West Virginia (n.d.), video-recording.
10. James A. Deeter, "The Kanawha County Textbook Controversy: A Review and Analysis from a Ten Year Perspective" (master's thesis, Marshall University, 1985), 74–75.
11. Billings and Goldman, "Comment," 1394.
12. Linda Wright, interview, tour and conversation with author, November 9, 2003, tape recording, Kanawha City and Campbells Creek, West Virginia. Andrew Gallagher, "Horan in Campbells Creek," *Charleston Gazette*, November 21, 1974.
13. Peyton, "Community Spirit."
14. Billings and Goldman, "Comment," 1395.

15. Donald A. Clelland and Ann L. Page, "Kanawha County Revisited: Reply to Billings and Goldman," *Social Forces* 59, no. 1 (September 1980): 283–84.

16. Wilkin, "The Kanawha County, West Virginia, Textbook Issue," 31.

17. Calvin Trillin, "U.S. Journal: Kanawha County, West Virginia," *New Yorker* (September 30, 1974), 121–22.

18. Trillin, "U.S. Journal," 122.

19. Seltzer, "West Virginia Book War," 433.

20. As with Seltzer's analysis, Parker asserts that "the mine shutdown until October 11 had more to do with a United Mine Worker contract due in November than with textbooks. Depleted coal stocks would result in better contract terms for miners. Also, the miners were heady with recent victory. They had just organized the Brookside mine in eastern Kentucky. During the Arab oil boycott they made Gov. Arch A. Moore, Jr., back down on limiting gasoline, saying that they needed gas to drive to work in the mines." Franklin Parker, *Battle of the Books: Kanawha County* (Bloomington, Ind.: Phi Delta Kappa Educational Foundation, 1975), 11.

21. Two books in particular develop and perpetuate this idea of Appalachians as stuck in the past. See Jack Weller, *Yesterday's People: Life in Contemporary Appalachia* (Lexington: University of Kentucky Press, 1965) and Rodger Cunningham, *Apples on the Flood: The Southern Mountain Experience* (Knoxville: University of Tennessee Press, 1987).

22. Trillin, "U.S. Journal," 126.

23. Hefley, *Textbooks on Trial*, 158.

24. Sara Diamond, *Roads to Dominion: Right-Wing Movements and Political Power in the United States* (New York: Guilford Press, 1995), 13.

25. Emmett Shafer, interview by author, May 7, 2002, tape recording and handwritten notes, Charleston, West Virginia.

26. James Lewis, Alice Moore, Robert Dornan, and Hilarion Cann, debate on cassette audiotape, West Virginia State Archives.

27. Wilkin, "The Kanawha County, West Virginia, Textbook Issue," 38.

28. "Lies Inspired by Birchers," *Charleston Gazette*, April 2, 1970.

29. James Lewis, "Christian Century," Lewis Papers.

30. The local John Birch Society bookstore owner was George Dietz, a notable white supremacist.

31. Charles Secrest letter to Kenneth Spencer, February 28, 1975, Wilcox Collection of Contemporary Political Movements, Spencer Research Library, University of Kansas.

32. Charles Secrest, "Reality Therapy Sessions," *Christian Crusade Weekly*, April 6, 1975.

33. Franklin Parker's report on the selection procedure supports the recordings of school board meetings on this point: "The textbook committee finished its work on 28 Feb. 1974, and sent its recommendations and rationale to

the school board's March 12 meeting. (Board member Alice Moore, who later led the assault on the texts, missed this meeting.) The 325 recommended texts and supplementary books were placed in the public library and in the school board's reading room for public review. Few people went to see the books" between February 28 and April 11, when Moore launched her first objection. Parker, *Battle of the Books*, 8.

34. Alice Moore, interview by Bill Longan, August 23, 1975 (B-79), in the Southern Oral History Program Collection (#4007), Southern Historical Collection, Wilson Library, University of North Carolina at Chapel Hill, 1.

35. Kanawha County Board of Education meeting, recorded December 12, 1974.

36. For more on Buffalo Creek, see Gerald M. Stern, *The Buffalo Creek Disaster: How the Survivors of One of the Worst Disasters in Coal-mining History Brought Suit against the Coal Company—and Won* (New York: Vintage, 1976), and Dennis Deitz and Carlene Mowery, *Buffalo Creek: Valley of Death* (South Charleston, W. Va.: Mountain Memory Books, 1992).

37. Russell W. Gibbons, "Textbooks in the Hollows," *Commonweal* 101, no. 9 (December 6, 1974): 231.

38. Ben A. Franklin, "The Appalachian Creekers: Literally, A World Apart," *New York Times*, October 27, 1974.

39. William N. Denman, "'Them Dirty, Filthy Books': The Textbook War in West Virginia," *Free Speech Yearbook* 15 (1976): 39.

40. Moffett, *Storm in the Mountains*, 226.

41. Ibid., 187.

42. Ibid., 236.

43. George Hillocks Jr., "Books and Bombs: Ideological Conflict and the Schools—A Case Study of the Kanawha County Book Protest," *School Review* 86, no. 4 (August 1978): 651.

44. Hillocks, "Books and Bombs," 640.

45. James Lewis, interview by author, May 7, 2002, tape recording and handwritten notes, Charleston, West Virginia.

46. George W. Shannon, "Pro-Integration Textbooks Opposed," *The Citizen* (February 1975): 10.

47. Roscoe Keeney, interview by author, November 8, 2003, tape recording and handwritten notes, Charleston, West Virginia. Keeney is the uncle of Delbert Rose. See also Scott Widmeyer, "TV, Radio Tower Blast Plan Told," *Charleston Daily Mail*, January 1975.

48. Kanawha County Board of Education meeting, recorded April 11, 1974. See also statements by Dr. Kenneth Young, refuting the accusation that "what the textbook people do is to wine and dine the teachers who were on the textbook committee." Ken M. Young interview by James Deeter, March 12, 1985, Oral History of Appalachia Collection No. OH 64–237, Special Collections, Marshall University.

49. Wilkin, "The Kanawha County, West Virginia, Textbook Issue," 40.   .

50. Nelle Teaford Wood interview by James Deeter, March 12, 1985, Oral History of Appalachia Collection No. OH 64–239, Special Collections, Marshall University.

51. Sophia Nelson was speaking during the public hearings. Kanawha County Board of Education meeting, recorded June 27, 1974.

52. Moore interview, 6.

53. Resolution adopted at the thirtieth annual meeting of the West Virginia State Conference of Branches of the National Association of the Advancement of Colored People on September 14, 1974, in Williamson, West Virginia. Stansbury Papers.

54. Mildred Ruth Holt and India W. Harris, letter to board of education, September 18, 1974. Stansbury Papers.

55. Louise P. Anderson, letter to board of education, September 18, 1974. Stansbury Papers.

56. Kay Michael, "Honorary Klan Member Active in Book Protest," *Charleston Gazette*, January 11, 1975.

57. Moore interview, 30.

58. Wilkin, "The Kanawha County, West Virginia, Textbook Issue," 20. See also Kay Michael, "Racial Overtones Claimed in Dispute," *Charleston Daily Mail*, November 7, 1974.

59. Ronald English, interview by James Deeter, March 12, 1985, Oral History of Appalachia Collection No. OH 64–238, Special Collections, Marshall University.

60. Doris Colomb, interview by Bill Longan, August 22, 1975 (B-76), in the Southern Oral History Program Collection (#4007), Southern Historical Collection, Wilson Library, University of North Carolina at Chapel Hill.

61. Moffett, *Storm in the Mountains*, 97.

62. Wood interview, March 15, 1985.

63. Information from Wright interview, May 28, 2002, is corroborated by Parker, *Battle of the Books*, 29.

64. Joe William Trotter Jr., *Coal, Class, and Color: Blacks in Southern West Virginia*, 1915–32 (Urbana: University of Illinois Press, 1990), 126.

65. "'Vigilantes' Urge Book Action," *Charleston Gazette*, September 20, 1974.

66. Moore interview, 12; Parker, *Battle of the Books*, 29.

67. Jerry Wellman, letter to board of education, June 13, 1974. Stansbury Papers.

68. Ibid.

69. Shannon, "Pro-Integration Textbooks Opposed," 4.

70. David R. Roediger, *Colored White: Transcending the Racial Past* (Berkeley: University of California Press, 2002), 24.

71. Harkins, *Hillbilly*, 5.

72. Ronald Lewis, *Transforming the Appalachian Countryside: Railroads,*

Deforestation, and Social Change in West Virginia, 1880–1920 (Chapel
Hill: University of North Carolina Press, 1998); Dwight Billings and
Kathleen Blee, *The Road to Poverty: The Making of Wealth and Hardship
in Appalachia* (Cambridge: Cambridge University Press, 2000); for
the "internal colony" theory, see Helen Lewis, "Fatalism or the Coal
Industry?" *Mountain Life & Work* 46, no. 11 (December 1970): 4–15.

Chapter 2. True Sons of Appalachia

1. Moreau, *School Book Nation*; Zimmerman, *Whose America?*
2. According to John E. Stealey III, "in trans-Allegheny Virginia, Kanawha
   County had the highest slave population in 1850." "Slavery in the Kanawha
   Salt Industry," in *Appalachians and Race: The Mountain South from
   Slavery to Segregation,* ed. John C. Inscoe (Lexington: University Press of
   Kentucky, 2001), 55.
3. Dwight B. Billings, "Religion as Opposition: A Gramscian Analysis,"
   American Journal of Sociology 96, no. 1 (July 1990): 23.
4. Ibid. See also Ronald Lewis, *Black Coal Miners in America* (Lexington:
   University of Kentucky Press, 1987).
5. Trotter, *Coal, Class, and Color,* 102.
6. For racial stratification of community life as well as in the labor force in
   southern West Virginia at the beginning of the twentieth century, see
   Trotter, *Coal, Class, and Color,* 125–44.
7. Curtis Seltzer, phone conversation and correspondence with author, 2005.
8. The Ku Klux Klan influenced Nazism in the first half of the twentieth
   century, but Klan members did not necessarily embrace Nazism. "The
   KKK's terrorism and violence in the South, often with cooperation of the
   state apparatus, provided the model for Hitler's 'revolt of the poor whites.'
   The rules for Hitler's Slave State relied heavily on black codes of the
   [American] South." Debby Dobratz and Stephanie Shanks, "The Contemporary KKK and the American Nazi Party: A Comparison to American
   Populism at the Turn of the Century," *Humanity and Society* 12, no. 1
   (1988): 20–50. See also John Drabble, "From White Supremacy to White
   Power: The FBI, COINTELPRO-WHITE HATE and the Nazification of
   the Klan." *American Studies* 48, no. 3 (Fall 2007).
9. "Genealogy of Textbook Controversy," *Charleston Daily Mail,* November
   20, 1974.
10. Michael, "Honorary Klan Member Active in Book Protest."
11. Patsy Sims, *The Klan* (Lexington: University Press of Kentucky, 1996), 8, 18.
12. Michael, "Honorary Klan Member Active in Book Protest."
13. "Klan Organizes Area Legal Office," *Charleston Gazette,* February 9, 1975.
14. Patsy Sims, *The Klan* (Lexington: University Press of Kentucky, 1996), 9.

15. Ibid., 10.

16. Ibid., 94.

17. Associated Press, "Wizard Hits Rival KKK Organization," *Charleston Gazette*, April 9, 1975.

18. "Five United Klans Members Protest Books," *Charleston Gazette*, September 17, 1975; "Board of Education Scene of Cross Burning," *Charleston Daily Mail*, September 16, 1975.

19. "State Klan Head Files Book Charge," *Sunday Gazette-Mail*, December 14, 1975.

20. Ed Miller, "Rev. Horan Praised," letter to the editor, *Charleston Gazette*, January 14, 1976.

21. Sims, *The Klan*, 25.

22. Chip Berlet and Matthew Lyons, *Right-Wing Populism in America* (New York: Guilford Press, 2000), 107.

23. Sims, *The Klan*, 103.

24. James Ridgeway, *Blood in the Face* (New York: Thunder's Mouth Press, 1990), 69–70.

25. Sims, *The Klan*, 102.

26. Ibid., 92.

27. Ibid., 92.

28. Ibid., 252.

29. Diamond, *Roads to Dominion*, 152.

30. Martin Lee, *The Beast Reawakens* (Boston: Little, Brown, 1997), 335. See also Drabble, "From White Supremacy to White Power."

31. Robert Miles, "Klan Changing," letter to the editor, *Charleston Gazette*, April 17, 1975. For a discussion of Miles's 1983 publication that articulated the five eras of Klan history, see Mattias Gardell, *Gods of the Blood: The Pagan Revival and White Separatism* (Durham, N.C.: Duke University Press, 2003), 81.

32. Ridgeway, *Blood in the Face*, 85.

33. Robert Miles, "Klan Changing," letter to the editor.

34. Don Stillman, "UMWA to Battle Ku Klux Klan," *United Mine Workers Journal* (September 15, 1975): 23. Stillman reports that the "Ku Klux Klan's fascist program led it to discuss merger with the Nazi Bund in the late 1930's."

35. "George P. Dietz, 79," *The Hur Herald*, May 1, 2007; http://www.hurherald.com/obits.php?=23225. George P. Dietz, "The Americans Are Coming!" *Liberty Bell* (April 1975): 13.

36. *White Power Report* (July 1978): 61.

37. "The Kanawha Fight Is About More Than Textbooks," *World Magazine* (February 22, 1975), reprinted as "Red Joke of the Month!" *Liberty Bell* 2, no. 8 (April 1975): 17–19. See also National Education Association, Teacher

Rights Division, *Inquiry Report: Kanawha County, West Virginia: A Textbook Study in Cultural Conflict* (Washington, D.C., 1975), 48.

38. Dr. Joseph Sheppe, "Textbook Protest in W.VA," *Liberty Bell* (December 1974): 5.

39. Abraham H. Kalish, "Out with Learning," *Liberty Bell* (June 1975): 10.

40. *Liberty Bell* (December 1974): 21.

41. Ibid., 4.

42. Abraham H. Kalish, "Quality Education—USA," *Liberty Bell* (June 1975): 9.

43. Ibid.

44. According to Alan Stang, "The destructive 'look-say' method, in which children are taught to 'read' not by learning the alphabet, but by memorizing the shapes of words—as if the English language were Chinese." Alan Stang, "The N.E.A. Dictatorship of the Educariat," *American Opinion* (March 1972): 4.

45. *McGuffey's First Eclectic Reader, Revised Edition* (New York: American Book Company, 1879), ii.

46. Glenn C. Roberts, "A Message to All True Sons of Appalachia," *Liberty Bell* (December 1974): 6.

47. Roberts, "A Message," 6.

48. Ibid., 7. See also Jeff Biggers, *The United States of Appalachia* (Emeryville, Cal.: Shoemaker and Hoard, 2006), for an alternative telling of the King's Mountain story.

49. Roberts, "A Message," 7.

50. Ibid., 7.

51. Ibid., 8.

52. Berlet and Lyons, *Right-Wing Populism*, 183.

53. Roberts, "A Message," 8.

54. "Reverberations of a Belch by Robert Welch," *Liberty Bell* (November 1976): 17–18.

55. Dietz reproduced the correspondence with the John Birch Society, *Liberty Bell* (November 1976): 20–21.

56. *White Power Report* (December 1976): 34. All *White Power Report* issues were obtained from the Wilcox Collection of Contemporary Political Movements, Spencer Research Library, University of Kansas.

57. *White Power Report* (January 1977): 36.

58. *White Power Report* (January 1977): 51.

59. Marcia Kramer, "Two Groups Accused of Funding Nazis," *Daily News*, May 15, 1977. Reprinted in *White Power Report* (July 1977). Evidence of Dietz's desire to defend those under suspicion of Nazi war crimes by the Office of Special Investigation of the Justice Department is contained in the following: "The O.S.I. Witch Hunt" seeks "contributions for the legal defense of Dr. Rudolph," a man accused of Nazi crimes, "and others

already similarly harassed by OSI may be mailed to: OLDTIMER'S DEFENSE FUND, Inc., P.O. Box 1000, Huntsville, AL 35801." Supplement to *Liberty Bell* (October 1986).

60. Ibid.

61. *White Power Report* (July 1978): 54.

62. George Dietz letter to Joseph Dilys, August 10, 1983, Wilcox Collection of Contemporary Political Movements, Spencer Research Library, University of Kansas.

63. Ibid.

64. Wesley McCune, "Extremists Are Linked by a Computer Network," *Group Research Report* 25, no. 3 (March 1986): 10. People for the American Way Library.

65. There is some debate as to whether it was 1983 or 1984 when the first bulletin board system went online. See Berlet, "Early Racist and Anti-Semitic Bulletin Board Systems (BBS)," Political Research Associates, available at http://www.publiceye.org/hate/earlybbs.html, and "When Hate Went Online," paper presented at the annual meeting of the Northeast Sociological Association, Fairfield, Connecticut, April 2001.

66. Chip Berlet located and posted the first responses to the BBS.

67. *National Socialist Vanguard Report* 10, no. 4 (October–December 1992): 3. People for the American Way Library.

68. Ann Burlein, *Lift High the Cross: Where White Supremacy and the Christian Right Merge* (Durham, N.C.: Duke University Press, 2002), 91.

69. *National Socialist Vanguard Report* 10, no. 4 (October–December 1992): 3. People for the American Way Library.

70. Berlet, "When Hate Went Online."

71. By May 1982, *Attack!* became *National Vanguard*.

72. "Education for Death," *Attack!* 34 (1975), reprinted in *The Best of Attack! And National Vanguard Tabloid 1970–1982*, ed. Kevin A. Strom (Arlington, Va.: National Vanguard Books, 1984).

73. "Gov't Pushes Porn in Sex-Ed Classes," *Attack!* 33 (1975), reprinted in Strom, *Best of Attack! and National Vanguard Tabloid*.

74. Ibid.

75. E. P. Thornton, "A Conservative Speaks Out," *Liberty Bell* 2, no. 8 (April 1975): 2.

76. "Tests Show Students Learning Less," *Attack!* 40 (1975), reprinted in Strom, *The Best of Attack! and National Vanguard Tabloid*.

77. "Education for Death," *Attack!* 34 (1975), reprinted in Strom, *The Best of Attack! And National Vanguard Tabloid*.

78. Martin Durham, "From Imperium to Internet: The National Alliance and the American Extreme Right," *Patterns of Prejudice* 36, no. 3 (2002): 57.

79. Ibid., 51. Durham is quoting Mark Potok of the Southern Poverty Law Center.

80. Ibid., 57–58, for more on the issue of violence.

81. Anti-Defamation League, *Explosion of Hate: The Growing Danger of the National Alliance*; http://www.adl.org/explosion_of_hate/print.html. Records from the Pocahontas County Courthouse confirm this sale.

82. Nicholas Goodrick-Clarke, *Black Sun: Aryan Cults, Esoteric Nazism, and the Politics of Identity* (New York: New York University Press, 2002), 21. Jerry Dale, interview by author, May 22, 2002, tape recording and handwritten notes, Lewisburg, West Virginia.

83. Robert S. Conte, *History of the Greenbrier, America's Resort* (Charleston, W. Va.: Pictorial Histories Publishing, 1998), 194–218.

84. Dale interview.

85. The following is derived from Batteau, *Invention of Appalachia*, 186.

86. This analysis is derived from Batteau, *Invention of Appalachia*, 13.

87. "Dr. No." West Virginia Public Broadcasting System, Different Drummer series, Morgantown, West Virginia (n.d.), videorecording.

88. W. J. Guillaume, "The Importance of Conan," *Attack!* 52 (1977), reprinted in Strom, *The Best of Attack! And National Vanguard Tabloid.*

89. National Alliance, "Why National Vanguard Books?" visited in 2002, www.natall.com.

90. Brad Whitsel, "Aryan Visions for the Future in the West Virginia Mountains," *Terrorism and Political Violence* 7, no. 4 (Winter 1995): 117.

91. Goodrick-Clarke, *Black Sun*, 21.

92. Andrew Macdonald [William Pierce], *Turner Diaries* (New York: Barricade Books, 1978), 203. R. S. Griffin, *The Fame of a Dead Man's Deeds: An Up-Close Portrait of White Nationalist William Pierce* (Bloomington, Ind.: 1st Books, 2001), 30.

93. Michael Barkun, *Religion and the Racist Right: The Origins of the Christian Identity Movement* (Durham: University of North Carolina Press, 1994), 226–27.

94. Whitsel, "Aryan Visions," 117.

95. In arguing that Pierce's Cosmotheistic Church is more than a means at tax evasion, Whitsel does not dig far enough into Pierce's past. According to Jerry Dale, a clear pattern of attempted tax evasion was established during the 1970s when he filed for exemption based on the National Alliance being an "educational" organization. It did not work, so Pierce created the Cosmotheistic Church, which held no worship services of any kind. As for taking seriously Pierce's non-Christian spiritualism (as distinguished from the Cosmotheistic Church itself), Whitsel is smart to suggest that it should not be reductively viewed as only providing a religious "front" for the National Alliance.

96. Southern Poverty Law Center, *The Rise of National Alliance*; http://www. splcenter.org/intellicenceproject/alliance.html.

97. Tim Miller, "The Electronic Fringe," *Washington Post Magazine*, July 14, 1985. Uncatalogued ephemera, Liberty Bell Publications. Wilcox Collection of Contemporary Political Movements, Spencer Research Library, University of Kansas.

98. Commentary following Tim Miller, "The Electronic Fringe," *Liberty Bell* (1985). Wilcox Collection of Contemporary Political Movements, Spencer Research Library, University of Kansas.

99. *White Power Report* 1, no. 11 (August 1977): 52.

100. William P. Hoar, "Parents Revolt: When Textbooks Are Propaganda," *American Opinion* (November 1974): 8.

101. See Stephen Cornell, "That's the Story of Our Life," in *We Are a People: Narrative and Multiplicity in Constructing Ethnic Identity*, ed. Paul Spickard and W. Jeffrey Burroughs (Philadelphia: Temple University Press, 2000), 41–53.

102. For sociological analyses on the role of the Internet in white supremacist organizing, see Robert Futrell and Pete Simi, "White Power Cyberculture: Building a Movement," *Public Eye* 20, no. 2 (Summer 2006): 1, 7–11, and Josh Adams and Vincent J. Roscigno, "White Supremacists, Oppositional Culture, and the World Wide Web," *Social Forces* 84, no. 2 (December 2005): 759–78.

103. Beyond the scope of this chapter is William Pierce's 1999 acquisition of Resistance Records, an attempt to recruit young people. See Devin Burghardt, ed., *Soundtracks to the White Revolution: White Supremacist Assaults on Youth Music Subculture* (Chicago: Center for a New Community, 1999).

Chapter 3. Sweet Alice and Secular Humanism

1. *Charleston Gazette* reporter Mike Snyder first coined the name "Sweet Alice" Moore, according to editor Don Marsh. Perhaps Snyder recalled Thomas Dunn English's late nineteenth-century poem, "Ben Bolt," the first line of which is "Don't you remember sweet Alice, Ben Bolt." The verse was written in West Virginia, according to Harrison Salisbury, who referenced it in an influential article about the role of the mountaineer state in the 1960 presidential election, which entailed a visit to West Virginia by John F. Kennedy Jr. The first stanza of the poem reveals that Alice, "whose hair was so brown," is dead, which in the poem functions as a memento mori sentimentalizing the passage of youth and the fleeting nature of young love. In the context of the textbook controversy, the allusion could have been meant as a reminder that this, too, shall pass, or as a mean-spirited desire to see

Moore dead, politically or otherwise. However, the name circulated widely, among Moore's allies as well as her enemies, and there is little evidence that suggests its popularity relied on, or was recognized as, an allusion to English's poem. For more on Salisbury's reference to Sweet Alice, see Batteau, *Invention of Appalachia*, 150. See also Don Marsh, "Coinage," *Charleston Gazette*, November 11, 1974.

2. Biographical information on Alice Moore is somewhat contradictory. Compare these two statements. "Alice Moore is the product of a rural, southern background. She came from Amory, Mississippi, where she had married at the age of 16 and graduated from Amory High School." Paul J. Kaufman, "Alice's Wonderland; or, School Books Are for Banning," *Appalachian Journal* 2, no. 3 (1975): 164. "The daughter of a dispatcher for TVA, Moore was raised in Acton, Tennessee, a small town in the southern part of the state about six miles from Corinth, Mississippi. . . . She asserted her independence at the age of seventeen by choosing to marry Darrell Moore, a young minister in the area. Choosing motherhood over a college education, Moore read avidly and kept abreast of the world through her own initiative." Joe Kincheloe, "Alice Moore and the Kanawha County Textbook Controversy," *Journal of Thought* 15, no. 1 (Spring 1980): 23.

3. Michael Lind, *Up from Conservatism: Why the Right Is Wrong for America* (New York: Free Press, 1996).

4. Berlet and Lyons, *Right-Wing Populism*, 204.

5. Lind, *Up from Conservatism*, 123.

6. Moore interview.

7. Alice Moore was interviewed by WSAZ on January 19, April 6, and April 9, 1973. Supplemental Tape Sequence, Kanawha County Textbook Controversy, West Virginia State Archives, videorecording.

8. Wood interview, March 15, 1985.

9. "Text Selection Explained," *Charleston Gazette*, September 27, 1974: 6B.

10. Alison Cross, *West Virginia Textbook War: The Rev. James Lewis Story*, April 20, 1994, teleplay for Plautus II Productions. Lewis Papers.

11. "Just Too Busy for Rollers," *Charleston Gazette*, September 24, 1974.

12. L. T. Anderson, "The Amusing Coincidences," *Charleston Gazette*, September 12, 1974.

13. Rev. Ron Sanger, letter to Harry Stansbury, November 9, 1974. Stansbury Papers.

14. Moffett, *Storm in the Mountains*, 92. Hill was issued a warning from John Denver's recording label to remove the albums from sale and to respect the song's copyright.

15. Moffett, *Storm in the Mountains*, 48.

16. See, for example, photos published in the *Charleston Gazette*, September 19, 1974.

17. Kincheloe, "Alice Moore," 24.

18. Moore interview, 28.

19. "Alice Moore Explains Citizens' Rights on Bad Textbooks," October 1974. Stansbury Papers.

20. For a discussion of Old Right divisions between isolationists and interventionists, see Jerome L. Himmelstein, *To the Right: The Transformation of American Conservatism* (Berkeley: University of California Press, 1990), 28–62.

21. Glen Jeansonne, *Women of the Far Right: The Mothers' Movement and World War II* (Chicago: University of Chicago Press, 1996), 63.

22. Jeansonne, *Women of the Far Right*, 178.

23. Linda Kintz, "Clarity, Mothers, and Mass-Mediated Soul: A Defense of Ambiguity," in *Media, Culture and the Religious Right*, ed. Linda Kintz and Julia Lesage (Minneapolis: University of Minnesota Press, 1998), 124.

24. Ibid., 126.

25. Himmelstein, *To the Right*; Diamond, *Roads to Dominion*.

26. Michelle Nickerson, "Education or Indoctrination: The Politics of Education and Mental Health in Cold War Los Angeles," paper presented at the annual convention of the American Studies Association, Houston, Texas, November 2002. See also Michelle Nickerson, "Women, Domesticity, and Postwar Conservatism," *OAH Magazine of History* 17, no. 2 (January 2003): 17–21.

27. Wilkin, "The Kanawha County, West Virginia, Textbook Issue," 40.

28. Zimmerman, *Whose America?*, 105.

29. Moore was not absolutely against sex education; she wanted students to learn about reproduction through biology. But she was adamantly opposed to exploring human sexuality as a part of learning about sexual reproduction. Here is how she explained the difference to F. David Wilkin: "I did not vote for sex education. We have had sex education here since we've been teaching Biology. I never did oppose that. What I opposed was teaching that premarital sex wasn't necessarily wrong, that there wasn't any authority outside yourself to determine these things. The purpose of the (proposed) sex education program was to influence the way students think, feel and act about sex. I always have been opposed to that type of sex education. What I voted for was the biology-type of sex education." Wilkin, "The Kanawha County, West Virginia, Textbook Issue," 38.

30. "Parents vs. Educators: Split Widens over Schools," *U.S. News and World Report* (January 27, 1975): 32.

31. Janice Irvine, *Talk about Sex: The Battles over Sex Education in the United States* (Berkeley: University of California Press, 2002), 47.

32. Moffett, *Storm in the Mountains*, 107–9.

33. Irvine, *Talk about Sex*, 59.

34. Jean Hardisty, *Mobilizing Resentment: Conservative Resurgence from the John Birch Society to the Promise Keepers* (Boston: Beacon Press, 1999); Lisa McGirr, *Suburban Warriors* (Princeton: Princeton University Press, 2002); Nickerson, "Women, Domesticity, and Postwar Conservatism." See also Rebecca Klatch, "Coalition and Conflict among Women of the New Right," *Signs* 13, no. 4 (1988): 671–94; and Marjorie J. Spruill, "Gender and America's Right Turn," in *Rightward Bound: Making America Conservative in the 1970s*, ed. Bruce J. Schulman and Julian E. Zelizer (Cambridge: Harvard University Press, 2008).

35. Nickerson, "Education or Indoctrination."

36. Nickerson, "Education or Indoctrination." Also pertinent is the discussion of how cold war anxieties centered on children. See Julia L. Mickenberg, *Learning from the Left: Children's Literature, the Cold War, and Radical Politics in the United States* (New York: Oxford University Press, 2006), 132–44.

37. Frances FitzGerald, "A Disciplined, Charging Army," *New Yorker* (May 18, 1981), http://www.newyorker.com/archive/1981/05/18/1981_05_18_053_TNY_CARDS_000336703.

38. Zimmerman, *Whose America?*, 209.

39. Ibid.

40. This is true in Berlet and Lyons, *Right-Wing Populism*; Diamond, *Roads to Dominion*; Zimmerman, *Whose America?*; and Joan DelFattore, *What Johnny Shouldn't Read: Textbook Censorship in America* (New Haven: Yale University Press, 1992).

41. Even more so than the conspiracist narrative of secular humanism, a conspiracist narrative of antiabortion politics was enormously important to the New Right's influence. Essentially an apocalyptic narrative that positioned Christian "warriors" as soldiers in a holy war, the "pro-life" idea that abortion signaled the End Times of humanity and America was deployed by many New Right organizations and far-right opponents of abortion. See Carol Mason, *Killing for Life: The Apocalyptic Narrative of Pro-life Politics* (Ithaca: Cornell University Press, 2002).

42. Kaufman, "Alice's Wonderland," 165.

43. Gary K. Clabaugh, *Thunder on the Right: The Protestant Fundamentalists* (Chicago: Nelson-Hall Company, 1974), 35.

44. Berlet and Lyons, *Right-Wing Populism*, 209.

45. Martin E. Marty, "Secular Humanism, the Religion of," *University of Chicago Magazine* (Summer 1987): 2–5, 12.

46. Susan Jacoby, "In Praise of Secularism," *The Nation* (April 19, 2004): 17.

47. Robert T. Rhode, "Is Secular Humanism the Religion of Public Schools?" in *Dealing with Censorship*, ed. James E. Davis (Urbana, Ill: National Council of Teachers of English, 1979), 121.

48. DelFattore, *What Johnny Can't Read*, 59.

49. Marty, "Secular Humanism," 12.

50. Wilkin, "The Kanawha County, West Virginia, Textbook Issue," 40.

51. Irvine, *Talk about Sex*, 51.

52. Clayton L. McNearney, "The Kanawha County Textbook Controversy," *Religious Education* 70, no. 5 (September–October 1975): 532–33.

53. "Once the John Birch Society joined the anti-sex education campaign, a proliferation of groups sprung up, including TACT, Truth About Civil Turmoil; MOMS, Mothers for Moral Stability; POSE, Parents Opposed to Sex Education; COST, Citizens Opposing Sex Training; PROMISE, Parents Reserve the Option of Morality in Sex Education; POISE, Persons Opposed to Institutional Sex Education; TASTE, Truth About Sex Training in Education; and OOPS, the Oshkosh Organization of Parents." Many of these organizations were either completely or partially connected to right-wing parent organizations, according to Clabaugh; this is no doubt true of MOTOREDE, TACT, POSE, and MOMS chapters, which all "had ties with either the John Birch Society or the Christian Crusade." Clabaugh, *Thunder on the Right*, 54–55.

54. Clabaugh argues persuasively that literature from both the Christian Crusade and the John Birch Society was sold in American Opinion bookstores. *Thunder on the Right*, 50.

55. Clabaugh, *Thunder on the Right*, 62–63.

56. Ibid., 63.

57. "Max Rafferty Observes 'New' Start in Education," *Christian Crusade Weekly* 15, no. 4 (January 5, 1975).

58. *Christian Crusade Weekly* 15, no. 16 (March 30, 1975).

59. Ibid.

60. According to Berlet and Lyons, "Catholics in the 1950s first began to criticize the influence of secular humanism on U. S. society." But the secular humanist conspiracy theory did not take shape until the 1970s and was a major aspect of moving "from Old Right to New Right." Berlet and Lyons, *Right-Wing Populism*, 209.

61. Tim LaHaye's *Battle for the Mind* (Old Tappan, N.J.: Fleming Revell, 1980) is also considered a definitive explanation of the secular humanism conspiracy from the conservative point of view. Francis A. Schaeffer's *A Christian Manifesto* (Westchester, Ill.: Crossway Books, 1981) was the theological elaboration on his widespread denouncement of humanism offered in his collaboration with C. Everett Koop, *Whatever Happened to the Human Race?* (Old Tappan, N.J.: Fleming Revell, 1979), which was published simultaneously with the production of the film by that name. Both LaHaye and Schaeffer were profound influences on the New Right.

62. Lee Edwards, *Power of Ideas: The Heritage Foundation at 25 Years* (Ottawa, Ill.: Jameson Books, 1997), 9.

63. Onalee McGraw, *Secular Humanism and the Schools: The Issue Whose Time Has Come* (Washington, D.C.: Heritage Foundation, 1976), 20.

64. Ibid., 9.

65. Marty, "Secular Humanism," 5.

66. Lind, *Up from Conservatism*, 165–66.

67. Ibid.

68. Sue Mullin, "Marshner: Irish Fire on the Right," *Washington Times*, July 27, 1982.

69. Ibid.

70. Connaught Coyne Marshner, *Blackboard Tyranny* (New Rochelle, N.Y.: Arlington House Publishers, 1978), 186–87.

71. Berlet and Lyons, *Right-Wing Populism*, 209. "Text Hearing Crowd Light," *Charleston Daily Mail*, January 20, 1975.

72. *With God on Our Side: The Rise of the Religious Right in America*, episode 3: "We Are Family." Lumiere Productions, PBS Home Video, a department of the Public Broadcasting Service. 1996.

73. Mullin, "Marshner."

74. "Connie Marshner: Pro-Family Dynamo," *Conservative Digest* (May–June 1980).

75. Martin, *With God on Our Side*, 176.

76. Leo P. Ribuffo, "Family Policy Past as Prologue: Jimmy Carter, the White House Conference on Families, and the Mobilization of the New Christian Right," *Review of Policy Research* 23, no. 2 (2006): 326. Martin, *With God*, 176.

77. Martin, *With God*, 176.

78. The following quotations are from Martin, *With God*, 184, 188, 187.

79. Ribuffo, "Family Policy," 334.

80. "Stacking the Panel Backfired," *Charleston Gazette*, September 27, 1974.

81. Marshner, "Dear Friend" letter delivered from 721 Second Street, N.E., Washington, D.C., invitation to attend Family Forum II of 1982. People for the American Way Library.

82. Ibid.

83. Sara Diamond, *Spiritual Warfare: The Politics of the Christian Right* (Boston: South End Press, 1989), 84.

84. Marshner, *Blackboard Tyranny*, 17–18.

85. Ibid., 25.

86. Ibid., 161.

87. Ibid., 37–38.

88. Frederick Clarkson, "Theocratic Dominionism Gains Influence, Part I, Overview and Roots," *Public Eye Magazine* 3, nos. 1 and 2 (March–June 1994).

89. Ibid.

90. Marshner, "Dear Friend" letter.

91. Frank Schaeffer, *Crazy for God* (Cambridge, Mass.: Avalon Publishers, 2007), 333.

92. Clarkson, "Theocratic Dominionism Gains Influence." See also Schaeffer, *Crazy for God*, 334: "The Theonomists, Reconstructionists, and Dominionists were the theocratic/authoritarian-party-in-waiting of American Christendom. And we Schaeffers were helping them expand their national base."

93. Robert Walker, "You in the Political Scene," *Christian Life* (July 1985): 52.

94. Mullin, "Marshner."

95. Ibid.

96. Marshner, *Blackboard Tyranny*, 231.

97. Connaught Coyne Marshner, "Humanism vs. Secular Humanism," *Conservative Digest* (April 1985): 24.

98. Marshner, *Blackboard Tyranny*, 231.

99. F. David Wilkin, "Kanawha County," 17. Wood interview, May 2002.

100. Moore interview.

101. Marshner, *Blackboard Tyranny*, 231.

102. Lynn Withrow, "Ruthlawn Principal Opposed: Parents, Faculty to Ask Board to Remove Her," *Charleston Daily Mail*, May 1, 1974.

103. "Silent Majority Underestimated," letter to the editor from "a parent," *Charleston Daily Mail*, September 25, 1974.

104. Marshner, *Blackboard Tyranny*, 232, 78.

105. Ibid., 73.

106. Ibid., 233.

107. Ibid., 212.

108. Ibid., 236.

109. Michael Omi and Howard Winant, *Racial Formation in the United States: From the 1960s to the 1990s* (New York: Routledge, 1994), 127–28.

110. Marshner, *Blackboard Tyranny*, 236–37.

111. Mullin, "Marshner."

112. Ibid.

113. Judith F. Krug, "Kanawha County," *Rise of the Right: Human and Civil Rights in Jeopardy*, Report of the 17th Annual Conference on Human and Civil Rights in Education, 7–8.

114. Marshner, *Blackboard Tyranny*, 180, 182, 199, 242.

115. Ibid., 180, 181, 243.

116. Ibid., 259.

117. Ibid., 34.

118. Lind, *Up from Conservatism*, 150.

119. Marshner, *Blackboard Tyranny*, 264.

Chapter 4. Reproducing the Souls of White Folk

1. Roediger, *Colored White*, 146.

2. Ibid., 147.

3. Walter Benn Michaels, "The Souls of White Folk," in *Literature and the Body: Essays on Populations and Persons*, ed. Elaine Scarry (Baltimore: Johns Hopkins University Press, 1988), 192.

4. Ibid.

5. As one of "the most brilliant close readers at work in the academy," Michaels is generally admired for producing "dazzling, close readings of the nativist-modernist texts." Although few have argued against his individual readings of those texts, many have disagreed with the larger criticisms of identity politics, multiculturalism, and poststructuralist theory that Michaels has derived from his textual analyses. See Michael Millner, "Post Post-Identity," a pithy review essay of Michaels's work, including *Our America: Nativism, Modernism, and Pluralism* (Durham, N.C.: Duke University Press, 1995) and *The Shape of the Signifier: 1967 to the End of History* (Princeton: Princeton University Press, 2004), and criticism of it in *American Quarterly* 57, no. 2 (June 2005): 541–54. In quoting from this earlier essay that only later was included in his larger arguments, I am interested less in endorsing wholesale Michaels's grandiose critiques and more in utilizing the historical contextualization of *The Clansman* and *The Turner Diaries* within the racialist discourses of the early twentieth century and the late 1970s that Michaels very credibly constructs. Especially because Pierce is overtly indebted to Teutonic racial theories first articulated at the turn of the century, Michaels's comparison of these two books is valid, even if elsewhere he may be more "circuitous" or "ahistorical" than scholars—especially sociologists—would like.

6. Michaels, "Souls of White Folk," 190.

7. Ibid.

8. Two aspects of theories of whiteness are pertinent here: its invisibility and its function as property. For a key discussion of whiteness as legal property, see Cheryl Harris, "Whiteness as Property," *Harvard Law Review* 106 (June 1993): 1710–91. For a discussion of whiteness as invisibility even in visual representation, see Richard Dyer, *White* (New York: Routledge, 1997).

9. Thomas A. Knight, "Last Protester in Jail Freed by Judge Goad," *Charleston Gazette*, October 19, 1974.

10. Hill interview.

11. For more discussion of the New Warrior, see James William Gibson, *Warrior Dreams* (New York: Hill and Wang, 1994).

12. Michaels, "Souls of White Folk," 193.

13. Amy Elizabeth Ansell, *New Right, New Racism: Race and Reaction in the United States and Britain* (New York: New York University Press, 1997), 20.

14. Michaels, "Souls of White Folk," 192.

15. Ibid., 199.

16. Ibid., 206.

17. One of the most compelling analyses in this vein is Toni Morrison, *Playing in the Dark* (New York: Vintage, 1993).

18. Elmer Fike, "Textbook Controversy in Perspective," Wilcox Collection of Contemporary Political Movements, Spencer Research Library, University of Kansas.

19. Elmer Fike, "Hope, November 28, 1974," *Textbook Controversy in Perspective and Other Related Essays* (Nitro, W. Va.).

20. George Lipsitz, "The Possessive Investment in Whiteness," in *White Privilege: Essential Readings on the Other Side of Racism*, ed. Paula S. Rothenberg (New York: Worth Publishers, 2005), 76.

21. Ibid.

22. Fike, "Hope."

23. Elmer Fike, "Promoting Racism, January 30, 1975," *Textbook Controversy in Perspective and Other Related Essays* (Nitro, W. Va.).

24. Fike, "Textbook Controversy in Perspective."

25. Ibid.

26. Ibid.

27. "Study Solution to Books Issue," *Christian Crusade Weekly* 15, no. 11 (February 23, 1975): 5.

28. Fike, "Textbook Controversy in Perspective."

29. Carol Mason, "Reproducing the Souls of White Folk," *Hypatia* 22, no. 2 (2007): 98–121.

30. Susan Metzger, review of *The Protestant Ethnic and the Spirit of Capitalism*, by Rey Chow; http://mclc.osu.edu/rc/pubs/reviews/metzger.htm.

31. Rey Chow, *The Protestant Ethnic and the Spirit of Capitalism* (New York: Columbia University Press, 2002), 180.

32. Ibid.

33. Ibid., 179.

34. Ibid., 46.

35. For explanation of this double temporality as *kairos*, an antidote to chronological time, see Carol Mason, *Killing for Life* (Ithaca: Cornell University Press, 2002), 146–48.

36. Chow, *Protestant Ethnic*, 179.

37. Ibid., 154.

38. Ibid., 179.

39. Ibid., 180.

40. Linda Paul, "Legally Adopted Sin in the West Virginia Schools," *Christian Crusade Weekly* 15, no. 9 (February 9, 1975): 1.

41. Chow, *Protestant Ethnic*, 49.

42. Ibid., 49.

43. Pauline Tucker, *Charleston Daily Mail*, September 27, 1974.

44. Kanawha County Board of Education meeting, recorded December 12, 1974.

45. Kanawha County Board of Education meeting, recorded October 10, 1974.

46. "Parents [*sic*] Anger Justifiable in Textbook Controversy," *Christian Crusade Weekly* 14, no. 45 (November 3, 1974): 5.

47. Omi and Winant, *Racial Formation*, 127–28.

48. For an extended discussion, see Monique Guillory and Richard C. Green, eds., *Soul: Black Power, Politics, and Pleasure* (New York University Press, 1998).

49. Cleaver, *Soul on Ice*, 202.

50. Ibid., 210.

51. Kathleen Rout, *Eldridge Cleaver* (Boston: Twayne Publishers, 1991), 22–37.

52. Cleaver, *Soul on Ice*, 203.

53. Williams, *West Virginia: A History*, 191.

54. Joe William Trotter Jr. "Memphis Tennessee Garrison and West Virginia's African American Experience: Historical Afterword," in *Memphis Tennessee Garrison: The Remarkable Story of a Black Appalachian Woman*, ed. Ancella R. Bickley and Lynda Ann Ewen (Athens: Ohio University Press, 2001), 224–25.

55. Ibid. Trotter is quoting R. Charles Byers, professor of education at West Virginia State College.

56. Gary Peller, "Race-consciousness," in *Critical Race Theory: The Key Writings That Formed the Movement*, ed. Kimberle Crenshaw, Neil Gotanda, Gary Peller, and Kendall Thomas (New York: New Press, 1995), 150.

57. Ibid., 133.

58. Marshner, *Blackboard Tyranny*, 170.

59. Beyond the scope of this book is the genealogy of deploying "the children" in political discourses and protest movements. Important to take into account in such an inquiry would be how conservative cold war anxieties centered around children, how newborns and birthing scenes function in leftist literature and film, and how such discussions shifted from worrying about children's futures to presenting the child as a national, racial, feminist, and/or class symbol of the future.

60. Lee Edelman, *No Future: Queer Theory and the Death Drive* (Durham, N.C.: Duke University Press, 2004), 3.

61. Burlein, *Lift High the Cross*, 8.

62. For a more sociological view of this phenomenon, see Chip Berlet, "When Alienation Turns Right: Populist Conspiracism, the Apocalyptic Style

and Neo-fascist Movements," in *Trauma, Promise, and the Millennium: The Evolution of Alienation*, ed. Lauren Lagnman and Devorah Kalekin-Fishman (Lanham, Md.: Rowman and Littlefield, 2005).

Chapter 5. The Right Soul

1. Bill Best, "Stripping Appalachian Soul: The New Left's Ace in the Hole," *Mountain Review* 4, no. 3 (1979): 15.
2. Batteau, *Invention of Appalachia*, 189.
3. Best, "Stripping," 16.
4. Ibid.
5. Ibid.
6. Ibid.
7. Batteau, *Invention of Appalachia*, 108.
8. Hill interview.
9. Ibid.
10. Ibid.
11. Ibid.
12. Robert J. Hoy, "Lid on a Boiling Pot," in *The New Right Papers*, ed. Robert W. Whitaker (New York: St. Martin's Press, 1982), 100.
13. Russ Bellant, *The Coors Connection: How Coors Family Philanthropy Undermines Democratic Pluralism* (Boston: South End Press, 1991), 71.
14. Hoy, "Lid on a Boiling Pot," 100.
15. Ibid., 84.
16. Ibid., 88.
17. Ibid., 90.
18. Ibid.
19. "70 Protesters Head for Rally," *Charleston Gazette*, March 19, 1975.
20. Ibid.
21. Hoy, "Lid on a Boiling Pot," 90–91.
22. Ibid.
23. Ibid., 93.
24. Ibid., 91.
25. Avis Hill and The Hills of West Virginia, *Textbook War*, 33 $\frac{1}{3}$ rpm 12-inch sound disc (LP), Library of Congress, Motion Picture, Broadcasting and Recorded Sound Division.
26. Hoy, "Lid on a Boiling Pot," 88.
27. Hill interview.
28. Ibid.
29. Ibid.
30. Batteau, *Invention of Appalachia*, 198.
31. Billings, "Religion as Opposition," 19.

32. Batteau, *Invention of Appalachia*, 108–9.

33. Ibid., 196.

34. Ibid., 7.

35. Ibid., 17.

Appendix

1. Appalachia Regional Commission, "The Appalachian Region," available at http://www.arc.gov/index.do?nodeId=2.

2. Batteau, *Invention of Appalachia*, 1, 200.

3. Himmelstein, *To the Right*, 14.

4. William Marshner and William S. Lind, *Cultural Conservatism: Towards a New National Agenda* (Washington, D.C.: University Press of America, 1987).

5. Emily Satterwhite, "'That's What They're All Singing About': Appalachian Heritage, Celtic Pride, and American Nationalism at the 2003 Smithsonian Folklife Festival." *Appalachian Journal* 32, no. 3 (Spring 2005), 302–38. See pages 319–23 for a review of misconceptions regarding the claim of Appalachia as essentially Celtic and Scots-Irish. See also Patricia D. Beaver and Helen M. Lewis, "Uncovering the Trail of Ethnic Denial: Ethnicity in Appalachia," in *Cultural Diversity in the U.S. South: Anthropological Contributions to a Region in Transition*, ed. Carole Hill and Patricia D. Beaver (Athens: University of Georgia Press, 1998).

6. A major study that has had great influence in many disciplines regarding the category of race and its cultural construction is Michael Omi's and Howard Winant's 1986 book *Racial Formation in the United States: From the 1960s to the 1980s* (New York: Routledge). For an extended discussion of its impact among the humanities, see the dossier of essays on the book and its 1994 edition, "Reflections on the Volume *Racial Formation in the United States*," *PMLA* 123, no. 5 (October 2008): 1540–73.

7. Matthew Frye Jacobson, *Whiteness of a Different Color: European Immigrants and the Alchemy of Race* (Cambridge: Harvard University Press, 1998).

8. Henry Yu, "Ethnicity," in *Keywords for American Cultural Studies*, ed. Bruce Burgett and Glenn Hendler (New York University Press, 2007), 107.

9. Satterwhite, "'That's What They're All Singing About'," 329.

10. Nancy T. Ammerman, "North American Protestant Fundamentalism," in *Fundamentalisms Observed*, ed. Martin E. Marty and R. Scott Appleby (Chicago: University of Chicago Press, 1994), 2–3.

11. Ibid., 2.

12. Mickenberg, *Learning from the Left*, 9.

13. Chip Berlet, "Fascism," http://www.publiceye.org/fascist/berlet_fascism. html.

14. George P. Dietz, *White Power Report* (December 1976): 34.

15. Martin Durham, "From Imperium to Internet: The National Alliance and the American Extreme Right," *Patterns of Prejudice* 36, no. 3 (2002): 56.

16. Barry Goldwater [L. Brent Bozell], *Conscience of a Conservative* (Shepherdsville, Ky.: Victor Publishing, 1960): 62.

17. Diamond, *Roads to Dominion*, 9.

18. Berlet and Lyons, *Right-Wing Populism*, 6.

19. Thomas Frank, *What's the Matter with Kansas? How Conservatives Won the Heart of America* (New York: Metropolitan Books, 2004). The problem with Frank's book is that it does not take into account the impact of religion in the turn to conservatism, as Paul Boyer notes in his essay, "The Evangelical Resurgence in 1970s American Protestantism," in *Rightward Bound: Making America Conservative in the 1970s*, ed. Bruce J. Schulman and Julian E. Zelizer (Cambridge: Harvard University Press, 2008).

20. Roediger, *Wages of Whiteness*, and *Colored White*, 22.

21. For critical accounts of theorizing whiteness, see also Robyn Wiegman, "Whiteness Studies and the Paradox of Particularity," *Boundary* 2 26, no. 3 (1999): 115–50; Margaret Anderson, "Whitewashing Race: A Critical Perspective on Whiteness," in *White Out: The Continuing Significance of Racism*, ed. Ashley W. Doane and Eduardo Bonilla-Silva (New York: Routledge, 2003); Mike Hill, *After Whiteness: Unmaking an American Majority* (New York: New York University Press, 2004): 173–84; Matt Wray, *Not Quite White: White Trash and the Boundaries of Whiteness* (Durham, N.C.: Duke University Press, 2006); and Joel Olson, *The Abolition of White Democracy* (Minneapolis: University of Minnesota Press, 2004).

Sources and Selected Bibliography

Manuscript Collections and Archives

Charleston, West Virginia
James Lewis Papers (private collection)
Harry Stansbury Papers (private collection)
West Virginia State Archives

Huntington, West Virginia
James E. Morrow Library, Special Collections, Marshall University, William Denman Papers, MS 103

Lawrence, Kansas
Spencer Research Library, University of Kansas, Wilcox Collection of Contemporary Political Movements

Somerville, Massachusetts
Political Research Associates Archives

Washington, D.C.
Library of Congress
People for the American Way Library

Interviews and Oral Histories

Byers, R. Charles. Interview by author. Tape recording and handwritten notes. Institute, West Virginia. November 10, 2003.
Colomb, Doris. Interview by Bill Longan. Transcript. Southern Oral History Program Collection (#4007), Southern Historical Collection, Wilson Library, University of North Carolina at Chapel Hill. August 22, 1975.

Dale, Jerry. Interview by author. Tape recording and handwritten notes. Lewisburg, West Virginia. May 22, 2002.

Denman, William. Conversation with author. Huntington, West Virginia. May 10, 2002.

English, Ronald. Interview by James Deeter. Transcript. Oral History of Appalachia Collection No. OH 64–238, Special Collections, Marshall University. March 12, 1985.

English, Ronald. Interview by author. Tape recording and handwritten notes. Charleston, West Virginia. June 16, 2004.

Hayslett, Deborah. Conversation with author. Charleston, West Virginia. April 17, 2002.

Hill, Rev. Avis L. Interview by James Deeter. Transcript. Oral History of Appalachia Collection No. OH 64–236, Special Collections, Marshall University. March 12, 1985.

Horan, Marvin. Interview by Bill Longan. Transcript. Southern Oral History Program Collection (#4007), Southern Historical Collection, Wilson Library, University of North Carolina at Chapel Hill. August 21, 1975.

Keeney, Roscoe. Interview by author. Tape recording and handwritten notes. Charleston, West Virginia. November 8, 2003.

Kinsolving, Mathew. Interview by Bill Longan. Transcript. Southern Oral History Program Collection (#4007), Southern Historical Collection, Wilson Library, University of North Carolina at Chapel Hill. August 23, 1975.

Lewis, James. Interview by author. Tape recording and handwritten notes. Charleston, West Virginia. May 7, 2002.

Loeb, Charles W., Jr. Interview by author. Tape recording and handwritten notes. Charleston, West Virginia. November 10, 2003.

Moore, Alice. Interview by Bill Longan. Transcript. Southern Oral History Program Collection (#4007), Southern Historical Collection, Wilson Library, University of North Carolina at Chapel Hill. August 23, 1975.

Moore, Alice. Phone conversation with author. December 5, 2008.

Seltzer, Curtis. Phone conversation and correspondence with author. Summer 2005.

Shafer, Emmett. Interview by author. Tape recording and handwritten notes. Charleston, West Virginia. May 7, 2002.

Stump, Doug. Interview by Bill Longan. Transcript. Southern Oral History Program Collection (#4007), Southern Historical Collection, Wilson Library, University of North Carolina at Chapel Hill. August 21, 1975.

Wood, Nelle [sic] Teaford. Interview by James Deeter. Transcript. Oral History of Appalachia Collection No. OH 64–239, Special Collections, Marshall University. March 12, 1985.

Wood, Nell. Interview by author. Tape recording and handwritten notes. Russell, Kentucky. May 9, 2002.

Wright, Linda. Interview by author. Tape recording and handwritten notes. Huntington, West Virginia. May 28, 2002.

———. Interview, tour, and conversation with author. Tape recording. Kanawha City and Campbells Creek, West Virginia. November 9, 2003.

Young, Ken M. Interview by James Deeter. Transcript. Oral History of Appalachia Collection No. OH 64–237, Special Collections, Marshall University. March 12, 1985.

Newspapers, Periodicals, Tabloids

American Opinion (Belmont, Massachusetts)

Attack! Revolutionary Voice of the National Alliance (Arlington, Virginia)

Charleston Gazette (West Virginia)

Charleston Daily Mail (West Virginia)

Sunday Gazette-Mail (Charleston, West Virginia)

Christian Crusade Weekly (Tulsa, Oklahoma)

Elmer's Tune (Nitro, West Virginia)

Liberty Bell (Reedy, West Virginia)

National Vanguard (Arlington, Virginia)

White Power Report (Reedy, West Virginia)

Audio and Visual Recordings

Kanawha County Board of Education meetings, March 28–December 12, 1974. Twenty-six audio cassette tapes recorded by author from various reel-to-reel tape recordings with permission of the board of education; rerecorded and reengineered by Richard Fauss, West Virginia State Archives.

With God on Our Side: The Rise of the Religious Right in America. Episode 3: "We Are Family." Lumiere Productions. Distributed by PBS Home Video, a department of the Public Broadcasting Service, 1996. Videocassette.

Hill, Avis, and the Hills of West Virginia. *Textbook War.* 33 1/3 rpm 12-inch sound disc (LP). Library of Congress. Motion Picture, Broadcasting and Recorded Sound Division. Call number: Avis Hill 31443. Library of Congress control number: 94752345.

Supplemental Tape Sequence, Kanawha County Textbook Controversy. VHS tape developed by Richard Fauss, West Virginia State Archives, including news footage from Charleston, West Virginia, television stations: WCHS, January 5, 1971; WSAZ, January 19, 1973; WSAZ, April 6, 1973; WCHS, April 9, 1973; WCHS, circa December 12, 1974.

"Dr. No." West Virginia Public Broadcasting, Different Drummer series, Morgantown, West Virginia, no date. Documentary of William Pierce. Videocassette. Cabell County Public Library. Call number: 921 PIERCE D.

"Glitch in the System: Elmer Fike." West Virginia Public Broadcasting, Different Drummer series, Morgantown, West Virginia, no date. Videocassette. Cabell County Public Library. Call number: 921 FIKE G.

Reports, Theses, and Papers

Candor, Catherine A. "A History of the Kanawha County Textbook Controversy." PhD diss., Virginia Polytechnic Institute, 1976.

Damewood, Elizabeth Rhodes. "Kanawha County's 'Great Textbook Controversy': Regional Heritage, National History, and Public Education, 1974–1975." A paper submitted to the Kelley Honors Seminar, Department of History, Davidson College, North Carolina, 1990.

Deeter, James A. "The Kanawha County Textbook Controversy: A Review and Analysis from a Ten-Year Perspective." Master's thesis, Marshall University, 1985.

Goode, Don J. "A Study of Values and Attitudes in a Textbook Controversy in Kanawha County, West Virginia: An Overt Act of Opposition to Schools." PhD diss., Michigan State University, 1984.

National Education Association, Teacher Rights Division. *Inquiry Report: Kanawha County, West Virginia, a Textbook Study in Cultural Conflict.* Washington, D.C.: 1975.

Wilkin, F. David. "The Kanawha County, West Virginia, Textbook Issue: Social Policy in Dispute." Term paper, Graduate School of Education, Harvard University, 1975. Stansbury Papers.

Sources Cited

Ammerman, Nancy T. "North American Protestant Fundamentalism." In *Fundamentalisms Observed*, edited by Martin E. Marty and R. Scott Appleby. Chicago: University of Chicago Press, 1994.

Anderson, Margaret. "Whitewashing Race: A Critical Perspective on Whiteness." In *White Out: The Continuing Significance of Racism*, edited by Ashley W. Doane and Eduardo Bonilla-Silva. New York: Routledge, 2003.

Ansell, Amy Elizabeth. *New Right, New Racism: Race and Reaction in the United States and Britain.* New York: New York University Press, 1997.

Anti-Defamation League. *Explosion of Hate: The Growing Danger of the National Alliance.* Available at http://www.adl.org/explosion_of_hate/print.html (accessed January 23, 2002).

Appalachia Regional Commission. "The Appalachian Region." Available at http://www.arc.gov/index.do?nodeId=2 (accessed June 12, 2008).

Balibar, Etienne, and Emmanuel Wallerstein. *Race, Nation, Class: Ambiguous Identities.* London: Verso, 1991.

Barkun, Michael. *Religion and the Racist Right: The Origins of the Christian Identity Movement.* Durham, N.C.: University of North Carolina Press, 1994.

Batteau, Allen W. *The Invention of Appalachia.* Tucson: University of Arizona Press, 1990.

Bauman, Richard. "Snake Handling—Should It Be Banned?" *Liberty: A Magazine of Religious Freedom* 70, no. 3 (May–June 1975): 2–5.

Bellant, Russ. *The Coors Connection: How Coors Family Philanthropy Undermines Democratic Pluralism.* Boston: South End Press, 1991.

Berlet, Chip. "Christian Identity: The Apocalyptic Style, Political Religion, Palingenesis, and Neo-Fascism." *Totalitarian Movements and Political Religions* 5, no. 3 (Winter 2004): 269–306.

——. "Early Racist and Antisemitic Bulletin Board Systems (BBS)." Political Research Associates. Available at http://www.publiceye.org/hate/earlybbs. html.

——. "Fascism." Political Research Associates. Available at http://www.publiceye. org/fascist/berlet_fascism.html.

——. "When Alienation Turns Right: Populist Conspiracism, the Apocalyptic Style, and Neo-fascist Movements." In *Trauma, Promise, and the Millennium: The Evolution of Alienation*, edited by Lauren Lagnman and Devorah Kalekin-Fishman. Lanham, Md.: Rowman and Littlefield, 2005.

——. "When Hate Went Online." Paper presented at the annual meeting of the Northeast Sociological Association, Fairfield, Connecticut, April 2001.

Berlet, Chip, and Matthew Lyons. *Right-Wing Populism in America: Too Close for Comfort.* New York: Guilford Press, 2000.

Best, Bill. "Stripping Appalachian Soul: The New Left's Ace in the Hole." *Mountain Review* 4, no. 3 (1979): 14–16.

Biggers, Jeff. *The United States of Appalachia.* Emeryville, Cal.: Shoemaker and Hoard, 2006.

Billings, Dwight B. "Religion as Opposition: A Gramscian Analysis." *American Journal of Sociology* 96, no. 1 (July 1990): 1–31.

Billings, Dwight, and Kathleen Blee. *The Road to Poverty: The Making of Wealth and Hardship in Appalachia.* Cambridge: Cambridge University Press, 2000.

Billings, Dwight, and Robert Goldman. "Comment on 'The Kanawha County Textbook Controversy.'" *Social Forces* 57, no. 4 (June 1979): 1393–98.

Bonilla-Silva, Eduardo. *White Supremacy and Racism in the Post-Civil Rights Era.* Boulder, Colo.: Lynne Rienner, 2001.

Boyer, Paul. "The Evangelical Resurgence in 1970s American Protestantism." In *Rightward Bound: Making America Conservative in the 1970s*, edited by Bruce J. Schulman and Julian E. Zelizer. Cambridge: Harvard University Press, 2008.

Brown, Michael K., Martin Carnoy, Elliott Currie, Troy Duster, David B. Oppenheimer, Marjorie M. Shultz, and David Wellman. *Whitewashing Race: The Myth of a Color-Blind Society.* Berkeley: University of California Press, 2003.

Burlein, Ann. *Lift High the Cross: Where White Supremacy and the Christian Right Merge*. Durham, N.C.: Duke University Press, 2002.

Chow, Rey. *The Protestant Ethnic and the Spirit of Capitalism*. New York: Columbia University Press, 2002.

Clabaugh, Gary K. *Thunder on the Right: The Protestant Fundamentalists*. Chicago: Nelson-Hall Company, 1974.

Clarkson, Frederick. "Theocratic Dominionism Gains Influence." *Public Eye* 8, nos. 1 and 2 (March–June 1994). Available at http://www.publiceye.org/magazine/v08n1/chrisrec.html.

Cleaver, Eldridge. *Soul on Ice*. New York: Delta Books, 1968.

Clelland, Donald A., and Ann L. Page. "Kanawha County Revisited: Reply to Billings and Goldman." *Social Forces* 59, no. 1 (September 1980): 281–84.

Conte, Robert S. *The History of the Greenbrier, America's Resort*. Charleston, W. Va.: Pictorial Histories Publishing, 1998.

Cornell, Stephen. "That's the Story of Our Life." In *We Are a People: Narrative and Multiplicity in Constructing Ethnic Identity*, edited by Paul Spickard and W. Jeffrey Burroughs. Philadelphia: Temple University Press, 2000.

Cunningham, Rodger. *Apples on the Flood: The Southern Mountain Experience*. Knoxville: University of Tennessee Press, 1987.

Davis, James E., ed. *Dealing with Censorship*. Urbana, Ill.: National Council of Teachers of English, 1979.

Deitz, Dennis, and Carlene Mowery. *Buffalo Creek: Valley of Death*. South Charleston, W. Va.: Mountain Memory Books, 1992.

DelFattore, Joan. *What Johnny Shouldn't Read: Textbook Censorship in America*. New Haven: Yale University Press, 1992.

Denman, William N. "'Them Dirty, Filthy Books': The Textbook War in West Virginia." *Free Speech Yearbook* 15 (1976): 37–45.

Diamond, Sara. *Roads to Dominion: Right-Wing Movements and Political Power in the United States*. New York: Guilford Press, 1995.

———. *Spiritual Warfare: The Politics of the Christian Right*. Boston: South End Press, 1989.

Dixon, Thomas, Jr. *The Clansman: An Historical Romance of the Ku Klux Klan*. Lexington: University of Kentucky Press, 1970.

Dobratz, Debby, and Stephanie Shanks. "The Contemporary KKK and the American Nazi Party: A Comparison to American Populism at the Turn of the Century." *Humanity and Society* 12, no. 1 (1988): 20–50.

Drabble, John. "From White Supremacy to White Power: The FBI, COINTELPRO-WHITE HATE and the Nazification of the Klan." *American Studies* 48, no. 3 (Fall 2007).

Durham, Martin. "From Imperium to Internet: The National Alliance and the American Extreme Right." *Patterns of Prejudice* 36, no. 3 (2002): 50–61.

Dyer, Richard. *White*. New York: Routledge, 1997.

Edelman, Lee. *No Future: Queer Theory and the Death Drive*. Durham, N.C.: Duke University Press, 2004.

Edwards, Lee. *The Power of Ideas: The Heritage Foundation at 25 Years*. Ottawa, Ill.: Jameson Books, 1997.

Egerton, John. "The Battle of the Books." *Progressive* 39, no. 6 (June 1975): 13–17.

Fike, Elmer. *Textbook Controversy in Perspective and Other Related Essays*. Nitro, W. Va.: n.p., 1974.

Fisher, Stephen. *Fighting Back in Appalachia*. Philadelphia: Temple University Press, 1993.

FitzGerald, Frances. "A Disciplined, Charging Army." *New Yorker* (May 18, 1981), http://www.newyorker.com/archive/1981/05/18/1981_05_18_053_TNY_CARDS_000336703.

Frank, Thomas. *What's the Matter with Kansas? How Conservatives Won the Heart of America*. New York: Metropolitan Books, 2004.

Franklin, Ben A. "The Appalachian Creekers: Literally, a World Apart." *New York Times*, October 27, 1974.

———. "West Virginia." *New York Times*, January 5, 1975.

Futrell, Robert, and Pete Simi. "White Power Cyberculture: Building a Movement." *Public Eye* 20, no. 2 (Summer 2006): 1, 7–11.

Gardell, Mattias. *Gods of the Blood: The Pagan Revival and White Separatism*. Durham, N.C.: Duke University Press, 2003.

Gaventa, John. *Power and Powerlessness: Quiescence and Rebellion in an Appalachian Valley*. Urbana: University of Illinois Press, 1982.

Gibbons, Russell W. "Textbooks in the Hollows." *Commonweal* 101, no. 9 (December 6, 1974): 231–34.

Goldwater, Barry [L. Brent Bozell]. *Conscience of a Conservative*. Shepherdsville, Ky.: Victor Publishing, 1960.

Goodrick-Clarke, Nicholas. *Black Sun: Aryan Cults, Esoteric Nazism, and the Politics of Identity*. New York: New York University Press, 2002.

Griffin, Robert S. *The Fame of a Dead Man's Deeds: An Up-Close Portrait of White Nationalist William Pierce*. Bloomington, Ind.: 1st Books, 2001.

Guillory, Monique, and Richard C. Green, eds. *Soul: Black Power, Politics, and Pleasure*. New York: New York University Press, 1998.

Hardisty, Jean. *Mobilizing Resentment: Conservative Resurgence from the John Birch Society to the Promise Keepers*. Boston: Beacon Press, 1999.

Harkins, Anthony. *Hillbilly: A Cultural History of an American Icon*. New York: Oxford University Press, 2004.

Harris, Cheryl. "Whiteness as Property." *Harvard Law Review* 106 (June 1993): 1710–91.

Hefley, James C. *Textbooks on Trial*. Wheaton, Ill.: Victor Books, 1976.

Hill, Carole, and Patricia D. Beaver, eds. *Cultural Diversity in the U.S. South: Anthropological Contributions to a Region in Transition.* Athens: University of Georgia Press, 1998.

Hill, Mike. *After Whiteness: Unmaking an American Majority.* New York: New York University Press, 2004.

Hillocks, George, Jr. "Books and Bombs: Ideological Conflict and the Schools— A Case Study of the Kanawha County Book Protest." *School Review* 86, no. 4 (August 1978): 632–54.

Himmelstein, Jerome L. *To the Right: The Transformation of American Conservatism.* Berkeley: University of California Press, 1990.

Hoy, Robert J. "Lid on a Boiling Pot." In *The New Right Papers,* edited by Robert W. Whitaker. New York: St. Martin's Press, 1982.

Inscoe, John C. *Appalachians and Race: The Mountain South from Slavery to Segregation.* Lexington: University Press of Kentucky, 2001.

Irvine, Janice. *Talk about Sex: The Battles over Sex Education in the United States.* Berkeley: University of California Press, 2002.

Jacobson, Matthew Frye. *Whiteness of a Different Color: European Immigrants and the Alchemy of Race.* Cambridge: Harvard University Press, 1998.

Jacoby, Susan. "In Praise of Secularism." *The Nation* (April 19, 2004): 17.

Jeansonne, Glen. *Women of the Far Right: The Mothers' Movement and World War II.* Chicago: University of Chicago Press, 1996.

Kaufman, Paul J. "Alice's Wonderland; or, School Books Are for Banning." *Appalachian Journal* 2, no. 3 (1975): 164.

Kincheloe, Joe. "Alice Moore and the Kanawha County Textbook Controversy." *Journal of Thought* 15, no. 1 (Spring 1980): 21–34.

Kintz, Linda. "Clarity, Mothers, and Mass-Mediated Soul: A Defense of Ambiguity." In *Media, Culture, and the Religious Right,* edited by Linda Kintz and Julia Lesage. Minneapolis: University of Minnesota Press, 1998.

Klatch, Rebecca. "Coalition and Conflict among Women of the New Right." *Signs* 13, no. 4 (1988): 671–94.

LaHaye, Tim. *Battle for the Mind.* Old Tappan, N.J.: Fleming Revell, 1980.

Lee, Martin. *The Beast Reawakens.* Boston: Little, Brown, 1997.

Lewis, Helen. "Fatalism or the Coal Industry? Contrasting Views of Appalachian Problems." *Mountain Life & Work* 46, no. 11 (December 1970): 4–15.

Lewis, Ronald. *Black Coal Miners in America.* Lexington: University of Kentucky Press, 1987.

——. *Transforming the Appalachian Countryside: Railroads, Deforestation, and Social Change in West Virginia, 1880–1920.* Chapel Hill: University of North Carolina Press, 1998.

Lind, Michael. *Up from Conservatism: Why the Right Is Wrong for America.* New York: Free Press, 1996.

Lipsitz, George. "The Possessive Investment in Whiteness." In *White Privilege: Essential Readings on the Other Side of Racism*, edited by Paula S. Rothenberg. New York: Worth Publishers, 2005.

Lora, Ronald. "Education: Schools as Crucible in Cold War America." In *Reshaping America: Society and Institutions, 1945–1960*, edited by Robert H. Bremner and Gary W. Reichard. Columbus: Ohio State University Press, 1982.

Macdonald, Andrew [William Pierce]. *The Turner Diaries.* New York: Barricade Books, 1978.

Marshner, Connaught Coyne. *Blackboard Tyranny.* New Rochelle, N.Y.: Arlington House Publishers, 1978.

Marshner, William, and William S. Lind. *Cultural Conservatism: Towards a New National Agenda.* Washington, D.C.: University Press of America, 1987.

Martin, William. *With God on Our Side: The Rise of the Religious Right in America.* New York: Broadway Books, 1996.

Marty, Martin E. "Secular Humanism, the Religion of." *University of Chicago Magazine* (Summer 1987): 2–5, 12.

Mason, Carol. "The Hillbilly Defense: Culturally Mediating U.S. Terror at Home and Abroad." *National Women's Studies Association Journal* 17, no. 3 (2005): 39–63.

——. *Killing for Life: The Apocalyptic Narrative of Pro-life Politics.* Ithaca: Cornell University Press, 2002.

——. "Reproducing the Souls of White Folk." *Hypatia* 22, no. 2 (Spring 2007): 98–121.

McCune, Wesley. "Extremists Are Linked by a Computer Network." *Group Research Report* 25, no. 3 (March 1986): 10.

McGirr, Lisa. "A History of the Conservative Movement from the Bottom Up." *Journal of Policy History* 14, no. 3 (2002): 331–39.

——. *Suburban Warriors.* Princeton: Princeton University Press, 2002.

McGraw, Onalee. *Secular Humanism and the Schools: The Issue Whose Time Has Come.* Washington, D.C.: Heritage Foundation, 1976.

McGuffey's First Eclectic Reader, Revised Edition. New York: American Book Company, 1879.

McNearney, Clayton L. "The Kanawha County Textbook Controversy." *Religious Education* 70, no. 5 (September–October 1975): 532–33.

Michaels, Walter Benn. *Our America: Nativism, Modernism, and Pluralism.* Durham, N.C.: Duke University Press, 1995.

——. *The Shape of the Signifier: 1967 to the End of History.* Princeton: Princeton University Press, 2004.

——. "The Souls of White Folk." In *Literature and the Body: Essays on Populations and Persons*, edited by Elaine Scarry. Baltimore: Johns Hopkins University Press, 1988.

Mickenberg, Julia L. *Learning from the Left: Children's Literature, the Cold War, and Radical Politics in the United States*. New York: Oxford University Press, 2006.

Millner, Michael. "Post Post-Identity." *American Quarterly* 57, no. 2 (June 2005): 541–54.

Moffett, James. *Storm in the Mountains: A Case Study of Censorship, Conflict, and Consciousness*. Carbondale: Southern Illinois University Press, 1988.

Montrie, Chad. *To Save the Land and People: A History of Opposition to Surface Coal Mining in Appalachia*. Chapel Hill: University of North Carolina Press, 2003.

Moreau, Joseph. *School Book Nation: Conflicts over American History Textbooks from the Civil War to the Present*. Ann Arbor: University of Michigan Press, 2003.

Morrison, Toni. *Playing in the Dark*. New York: Vintage, 1993.

Mullen, Sue. "Marshner: Irish Fire on the Right." *Washington Times*, July 27, 1982.

Newitz, Annalee, and Matt Wray, eds. *White Trash: Race and Class in America*. New York: Routledge, 1997.

Nickerson, Michelle. "Education or Indoctrination: The Politics of Education and Mental Health in Cold War Los Angeles." Paper presented at the annual convention of the American Studies Association, Houston, Texas, November 2002.

——. "Women, Domesticity, and Postwar Conservatism." *OAH Magazine of History* 17, no. 2 (January 2003): 17–21.

Olson, Joel. *Abolition of White Democracy*. Minneapolis: University of Minnesota Press, 2004.

Omi, Michael, and Howard Winant. *Racial Formation in the United States: From the 1960s to the 1990s*. New York: Routledge, 1994.

Page, Ann L., and Donald A. Clelland. "The Kanawha County Textbook Controversy: A Study of the Politics of Life Style Concern." *Social Forces* 57, no. 1 (September 1978): 265–81.

"Parents vs. Educators: Split Widens over Schools." *U.S. News and World Report* (January 27, 1975).

Parker, Franklin. *The Battle of the Books: Kanawha County*. Bloomington, Ind.: Phi Delta Kappa Educational Foundation, 1975.

Peller, Gary. "Race-consciousness." In *Critical Race Theory: The Key Writings That Formed the Movement*, edited by Kimberle Crenshaw, Neil Gotanda, Gary Peller, and Kendall Thomas. New York: New Press, 1995.

Peyton, David A. "'Community Spirit' One Explanation for Current Protest over Books." *Herald Advertiser* (Huntington, W. Va.), November 11, 1974.

Ribuffo, Leo P. "Family Policy Past as Prologue: Jimmy Carter, the White House

Conference on Families, and the Mobilization of the New Christian Right." *Review of Policy Research* 23, no. 2 (2006): 311–37.

Ridgeway, James. *Blood in the Face.* New York: Thunder's Mouth Press, 1990.

Roediger, David R. *Colored White: Transcending the Racial Past.* Berkeley: University of California Press, 2002.

———. *The Wages of Whiteness: Race and the Making of the American Working Class.* New York: Verso, 1991.

———. *Working toward Whiteness: How America's Immigrants Became White.* New York: Basic Books, 2005.

Rout, Kathleen. *Eldridge Cleaver.* Boston: Twayne Publishers, 1991.

San Juan, E., Jr. "The Cult of Ethnicity and the Fetish of Pluralism: A Counterhegemonic Critique." *Cultural Critique* (1991): 215–29.

Satterwhite, Emily. "'That's What They're All Singing About': Appalachian Heritage, Celtic Pride, and American Nationalism at the 2003 Smithsonian Folklife Festival." *Appalachian Journal* 32, no. 3 (Spring 2005): 302–338.

Schaeffer, Francis A. *A Christian Manifesto.* Westchester, Ill.: Crossway Books, 1981.

Schaeffer, Frank. *Crazy for God.* Cambridge, Mass.: Avalon Publishers, 2007.

Seltzer, Curtis. "West Virginia Book War: A Confusion of Goals." *The Nation* 219, no. 14 (November 2, 1974): 430–34.

Shannon, George W. "Pro-Integration Textbooks Opposed." *The Citizen* (February 1975): 4, 10.

Sims, Patsy. *The Klan.* Lexington: University Press of Kentucky, 1996.

Small, Robert C., Jr. "Textbook Protestors as People." *English Journal* 65, no. 3 (March 1976): 18–19.

Smith-Rosenberg, Carroll. *Disorderly Conduct: Visions of Gender in Victorian America.* New York: Knopf, 1985.

Southern Poverty Law Center. "The Rise of the National Alliance." Available at http://www.splcenter.org/intellicenceproject/alliance.html (accessed January 23, 2002).

Spruill, Marjorie J. "Gender and America's Right Turn." In *Rightward Bound: Making America Conservative in the 1970s,* edited by Bruce J. Schulman and Julian E. Zelizer. Cambridge: Harvard University Press, 2008.

Stern, Gerald M. *The Buffalo Creek Disaster: How the Survivors of One of the Worst Disasters in Coal-Mining History Brought Suit against the Coal Company—and Won.* New York: Vintage, 1976.

Stillman, Don. "UMWA to Battle Ku Klux Klan." *United Mine Workers Journal* (September 15, 1975): 23.

Strafford, Peter. "Class Warfare over Text Books." *London Times* (October 12, 1974), 12a. Rpt. as Peter Strafford, "Class Warfare over U.S. Textbooks," *South China Morning Post* (October 19, 1974).

Strom, Kevin A., ed. *The Best of Attack! And National Vanguard Tabloid 1970–1982*. Arlington, Va.: National Vanguard Books, 1984.

Trillin, Calvin. "U.S. Journal: Kanawha County, West Virginia." *New Yorker* (September 30, 1974), 119–27.

Trotter, Joe William, Jr., *Coal, Class, and Color: Blacks in Southern West Virginia, 1915–32*. Urbana: University of Illinois Press, 1990.

———. "Memphis Tennessee Garrison and West Virginia's African American Experience: Historical Afterword." In *Memphis Tennessee Garrison: The Remarkable Story of a Black Appalachian Woman*, edited by Ancella R. Bickley and Lynda Ann Ewen. Athens: Ohio University Press, 2001.

Walker, Robert. "You in the Political Scene." *Christian Life* (July 1985): 50–53.

Weller, Jack. *Yesterday's People: Life in Contemporary Appalachia*. Lexington: University of Kentucky Press, 1965.

Whitsel, Brad. "Aryan Visions for the Future in the West Virginia Mountains." *Terrorism and Political Violence* 7, no. 4 (Winter 1995): 117–39.

Wiegman, Robyn. "Whiteness Studies and the Paradox of Particularity." *Boundary 2* 26, no. 3 (1999): 115–50.

Williams, John Alexander. *Appalachia: A History*. Chapel Hill: University of North Carolina Press, 2002.

———. *West Virginia: A History*. Morgantown: West Virginia University Press, 2001.

Williamson, J. W. *Hillbillyland: What the Movies Did to the Mountains and What the Mountains Did to the Movies*. Durham: University of North Carolina Press, 1995.

Wray, Matt. *Not Quite White: White Trash and the Boundaries of Whiteness*. Durham, N.C.: Duke University Press, 2006.

Yu, Henry. "Ethnicity." In *Keywords for American Cultural Studies*, edited by Bruce Burgett and Glenn Hendler. New York: New York University Press, 2007.

Zimmerman, Jonathan. *Whose America? Culture Wars in the Public Schools*. Cambridge: Harvard University Press, 2002.

Index